WHY ARE SO MANY AMERICANS IN PRISON?

WHY ARE SO MANY AMERICANS IN PRISON?

Steven Raphael and Michael A. Stoll

Russell Sage Foundation • New York

The Russell Sage Foundation

Library of Congress Cataloging-in-Publication Data

Raphael, Steven, 1968–
  Why are so many Americans in prison? / Steven Raphael and Michael A. Stoll.
    pages cm.
  Includes bibliographical references and index.
  ISBN 978-0-87154-712-5 (pbk. : alk. paper) — ISBN 978-1-61044-801-7 (ebook)
    1. Prisons—United States.   2. Corrections—United States.   3. Criminal justice, Administration of—United States.   I. Stoll, Michael A.   II. Russell Sage Foundation.
III. Title.
    HV9471.R37 2013
    365'.973—dc23   2013005776

The paper used in this publication meets the minimum requirements of American National Standard for Information Sciences-Permanence of Paper for Printed Library Materials. ANSI Z39.48-1992.

Text design by Genna Patacsil.

RUSSELL SAGE FOUNDATION
112 East 64th Street, New York, New York 10065
10 9 8 7 6 5 4 3 2 1

*In memory of John Quigley, our dear colleague,
mentor, and friend*

CONTENTS

TABLES AND FIGURES

ABOUT THE AUTHORS

Steven Raphael is professor of public policy at the Goldman School of Public Policy at the University of California, Berkeley.

Michael A. Stoll is professor and chair of public policy at the University of California, Los Angeles Luskin School of Public Affairs.

ACKNOWLEDGMENTS

The findings in this book rest on our research over the past decade on various aspects of incarceration and corrections policy. Along the way we have received valuable feedback, encouragement, and support from countless colleagues, friends, and family. We are especially thankful for the feedback over the years from Shawn Bushway, Phil Cook, Sheldon Danziger, John Ellwood, Harry Holzer, Jens Ludwig, Rob MacCoun, Justin McCrary, Daniel Nagin, Derek Neil, Emily Owens, Peter Reuter, Jill Weader, David Weiman, and Bruce Western. We are also grateful to our coauthors from several research projects discussed in this book: Paolo Buonanno, Aaron Chalfin, Candace Hamilton, Rucker Johnson, Elizabeth Kneebone, Chris Meyer, Sarah Tahamont, and Rudolf Winter-Ebmer. We are especially grateful to Eugene Smolensky for encouraging us to write a book in the first place and for expecting us to finish it eventually. We would also like to thank Eric Wanner and Suzanne Nichols of the Russell Sage Foundation for their generous support for our research over the years and for their patience with our highly nonlinear pace of progress in completing the manuscript for this book.

Our families have always been a constant source of inspiration and support for all that we do. Steven Raphael wishes to especially thank Kelly Raphael, Antonio Raphael, and Ariana Raphael for their unwavering love and support and for the many ideas that they have contributed over the years to this and many other projects. Michael Stoll wishes to thank Kenya, for her unconditional love and open mind in debating and discussing the many ideas that came up during this project and others, even while she faced pressure to achieve tenure, and daughters Emera, Samina, and Myla, for helping keep life rich with joy and meaning.

CHAPTER 1

The Emergence of Mass Incarceration

Between 1970 and the present, a form of American exceptionalism has emerged that stands in stark contrast to the conventional sense of this phrase. Alexis de Tocqueville described an American exceptionalism based on the egalitarian nature of the American political system and the public institutions that ensure political competition and that balance and check the powers of each branch of government, whereas the exceptionalism that is the subject of this book lies in the large and unprecedented expansion of the police power of the state. This exceptionalism suppresses the liberty of literally millions of adult Americans, mostly minority men, in exchange for enhanced public safety and the satisfaction of public demands for just deserts. This new exceptionalism has been driven largely by reactive policy changes induced in large part by political competition rather than deliberate and measured policy-making regarding crime control and corrections. This exceptionalism has a disproportionate impact on the poorest segments of society, in terms of both costs and benefits.

The United States currently incarcerates people in the nation's state and federal prisons and local jails at a rate higher than any other country in the world. This incarcerated population is relatively fluid, with hundreds of thousands being released each year as similar numbers are admitted, though the stock of inmates serving very long sentences has increased steadily. Since nearly all people who are admitted to prison are eventually released, the high

U.S. incarceration rate has left in its wake a large population of former prisoners residing among the non-institutionalized population.

The large increases in the U.S. incarceration rate have certainly had a great impact on the social welfare of many U.S. residents along multiple dimensions. On the positive side, today's crime rates are appreciably lower than in the past, owing in some part to the higher incarceration rate. Crime rates have declined for all serious felony crimes, with pronounced decreases in the most serious violent offenses. Moreover, victimization rates have declined the most among low-income households and in the poorest neighborhoods of the nation's cities. To the extent that the prison boom of recent decades is responsible for these crime trends, one can argue that the increasing prison and jail populations have generated a tangible and progressively distributed benefit.

However, incarcerating so many people also generates a number of direct as well as indirect social costs. Perhaps the most visible costs are direct corrections expenditures. Surely there are many competing priorities (for example, public education or tax relief) that are to some degree displaced by corrections expenditures. Moreover, in light of the severe contraction in state and local government revenues caused by the Great Recession of 2007 to 2009, state governments across the country are keenly aware of the fiscal impacts of corrections spending and are exploring alternatives to incarceration in an attempt to save money while not compromising public safety.

Less obvious are the collateral consequences of incarceration for former inmates, their families, and the communities from which they come. A sizable fraction of men have prior prison time on their increasingly publicly available criminal history records, a fact that is likely to harm their employment prospects (Western 2002; Holzer, Raphael, and Stoll 2006; Raphael 2011). Additional consequences suggested by recent research include an erosion of family stability among high-offending demographic groups (Wildeman 2009; Johnson 2009; Wakefield and Wildeman 2012), the legal disenfranchisement of current and former inmates in a number of states (Uggen et al. 2006), and the acceleration of the transmission of communicable diseases such as AIDS among inmates and their non-incarcerated intimates (Johnson and Raphael 2009). Moreover, each of these collateral consequences of incarceration has a disproportionate impact on minority communities, perpetuating and most likely exacerbating racial inequality in the United States. The racially disparate nature of the rise in U.S. incarceration rates has led to what the legal scholar Michelle Alexander (2010) characterizes as a new, redesigned racial caste system akin to the pre–civil rights era Jim Crow laws that governed all manner of interracial interactions and that subjugated African Americans in the U.S. South.

Less well studied are the effects of the extreme geographic concentration of former prison inmates in communities that disproportionately send people to prison. We might hypothesize that the children in such communities have distorted expectations about their own futures and change their behavior accordingly. For example, the perceived benefits from joining a gang may be enhanced by the expectation that one will eventually do time. Similarly, the perceived benefits from formal education may be diminished by such an expectation. Moreover, the connections between criminal gangs on the street and prison gangs may be strengthened by the large inflows and outflows between specific sending communities and state prisons. Again, such factors have a disproportionate impact on minority, and in particular African American, communities given the racial composition of the U.S. prison population and the persistent racial residential segregation of U.S. metropolitan areas.

Why are so many Americans in prison? What do we gain from incarcerating millions of people? What are the fiscal and social costs of incarceration, and how are they distributed among different segments of the American public? Answering these questions is the central aim of this book.

HOW MANY, WHO, AND HOW MUCH DOES IT COST?

U.S. corrections policy is best characterized as fifty largely independent state correctional systems and a system of federal prisons. Each state has its own criminal code, violations of which are adjudicated in county and state courts. Those individuals awaiting trial who are denied or cannot make bail are held in local jails, as are those who have been arrested and are awaiting arraignment. Those found guilty and sentenced to serve time are sent to either local county jails (usually for misdemeanor and felony sentences of less than one year) or state prison (for felony offenders sentenced to a year or more). The federal prison system houses those who have violated federal law and been tried, convicted, and sentenced to prison in federal court.

Once an individual enters a state prison system, the nature of the actual institution where the inmate will be housed can vary considerably. Those with relatively short sentences and little history of violence or escape may be housed in unfenced work camps where inmates have a fairly high degree of liberty. Inmates facing long sentences or those deemed at high risk for escape or misconduct are housed in more secure facilities, often enclosed by electrified fences and monitored by armed correctional officers. Housing conditions in these more secure facilities vary from dorm housing with frequent and regular access to common prison yards to celled housing with very little time outside one's cell.

The size of a state's prison population is governed largely by sentencing policy and state crime rates. With fifty state criminal codes, differential levels of discretion afforded to local and state judges in sentencing criminal offenders, cross-state variation in parole policies, and cross-state differences in underlying crime rates, it is difficult to describe a uniform U.S. system of corrections. Nonetheless, trends in sentencing and parole reforms have been similar in all states to varying degrees in the last few decades, and all states have consequently experienced great increases in their state incarceration rates. These state changes in incarceration rates have combined with changes to federal sentencing to increase the nation's overall incarceration rate.

How Large Is the Incarcerated Population?

At year-end 2009, approximately 2.3 million people were incarcerated in U.S. prisons and jails. Roughly 1.52 million of these individuals were held in either the federal prison system or one of the state prison systems, while 760,000 were held in local jails. The population under the jurisdiction of either a state or the federal prison system was somewhat larger (1.61 million). The 90,000 inmates under state or federal jurisdiction who were not in prison were often being held in local jails, sometimes for court proceedings or in transit between institutions, but often owing to overcrowding in state prisons.

For purposes of comparison over time or across states or nations, the raw number of prison and jail inmates is not particularly informative, since more populous regions will have larger prison populations as a result of size alone. For example, at year-end 2009 the California prison population (171,275) was nearly five times that for Alabama (31,874), despite the fact that the proportion of residents incarcerated in Alabama was nearly one and a half times that for California. Hence, throughout this book, in characterizing the size of incarcerated populations, we present either incarceration rates expressed as the number of inmates per 100,000 residents or the proportion of specific populations that are incarcerated at a given point in time. This effectively adjusts for population growth in overtime comparisons and for differences in population size for cross-area comparisons.

Figure 1.1   State and Federal Prison Inmates per 100,000 U.S. Residents, 1925 to 2009

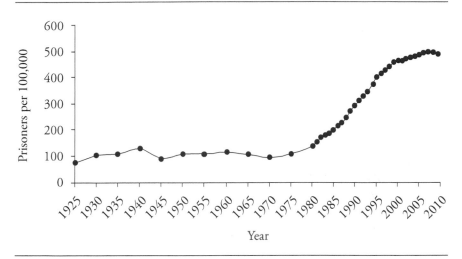

Source: Authors' compilation based on Bureau of Justice Statistics, *National Prisoner Statistics* (various years).

Figures 1.1 to 1.3 display long-term trends in U.S. prison and jail incarceration rates.[1] For prison incarceration rates, we are fortunate to have data covering the relatively long period from 1925 through 2009. The prison incarceration rate exhibited remarkable stability for the first fifty or so years (figure 1.1). Between 1925 and 1940, we observe the tail end of an earlier incarceration boom, associated largely with Prohibition and a greater propensity to police and punish public-order crimes, such as drug abuse and prostitution.[2] From 1940 through 1975, however, the nation's prison incarceration rate stabilized between 100 and 110 per 100,000 residents. After 1975, the prison incarceration rate increased nearly fivefold, peaking at 503 per 100,000 in 2007 and then declining slightly to a rate of 497 by 2009. In 2009 federal prisons contributed about 67 inmates per 100,000 U.S. residents, while the state prisons contributed the remainder.

Given the independence of state criminal justice systems, we would expect the incarceration trends for individual states to vary greatly, and indeed they do. Figure 1.2 presents the change in prison incarceration rates between 1977 and 2009 by state. The figure ranks states in descending order by the change in the state rate, with Southern states shaded in black, Western states shaded in white, and Midwestern and Northeastern states shaded in gray. The average

Figure 1.2   Change in Prison Populations per 100,000 U.S. Residents from 1977 to 2009, by State

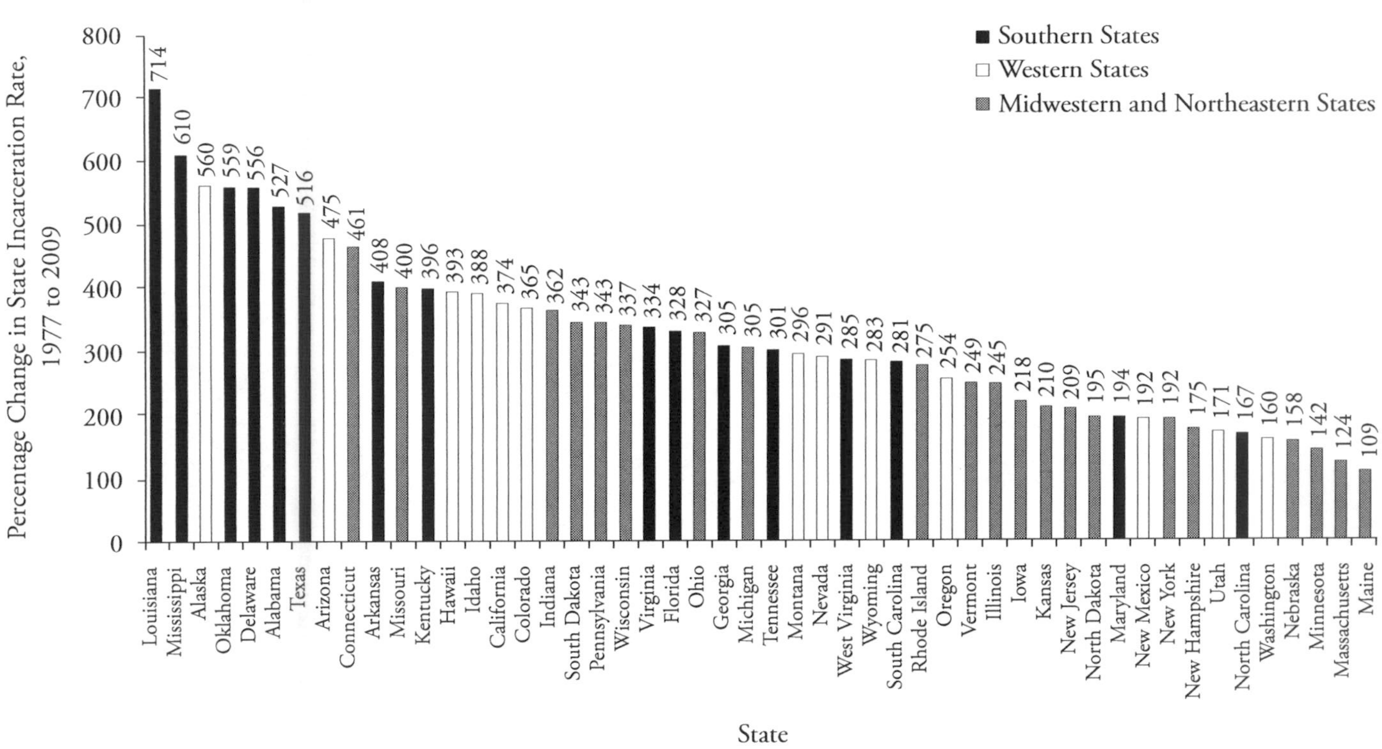

Legend:
- ■ Southern States
- □ Western States
- ▨ Midwestern and Northeastern States

Percentage Change in State Incarceration Rate, 1977 to 2009 (y-axis): 0, 100, 200, 300, 400, 500, 600, 700, 800

State	Value
Louisiana	714
Mississippi	610
Alaska	560
Oklahoma	559
Delaware	556
Alabama	527
Texas	516
Arizona	475
Connecticut	461
Arkansas	408
Missouri	400
Kentucky	396
Hawaii	393
Idaho	388
California	374
Colorado	365
Indiana	362
South Dakota	343
Pennsylvania	343
Wisconsin	337
Virginia	334
Florida	328
Ohio	327
Georgia	305
Michigan	305
Tennessee	301
Montana	296
Nevada	291
West Virginia	285
Wyoming	283
South Carolina	281
Rhode Island	275
Oregon	254
Vermont	249
Illinois	245
Iowa	218
Kansas	210
New Jersey	209
North Dakota	195
Maryland	194
New Mexico	192
New York	192
New Hampshire	175
Utah	171
North Carolina	167
Washington	160
Nebraska	158
Minnesota	142
Massachusetts	124
Maine	109

State (x-axis label)

Source: Authors' compilation based on Bureau of Justice Statistics, *National Prisoner Statistics* (various years).

Figure 1.3   Inmates in County Jails per 100,000 U.S. Residents, 1980 to 2009

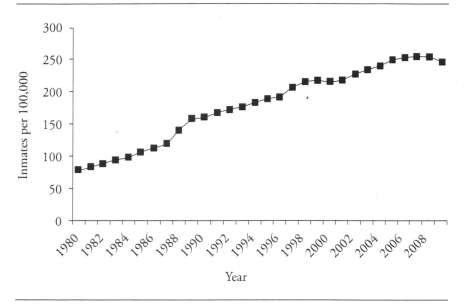

Source: Authors' compilation based on Bureau of Justice Statistics, *Annual Survey of Jails* (various years).

increase across all states over this twenty-two-year period is 316 inmates per 100,000 U.S. residents. However, there is great variation around this average. In general, Southern states and states in the Southwest experienced the largest increases in prison growth, while states in the Northeast and the Midwest experienced the smallest increases. Nonetheless, all states registered marked increases in the relative sizes of their prison populations. In the federal prison system, there were approximately 15 federal prisoners per 100,000 U.S. residents in 1977. By 2009, this figure had increased by four and a half times over, to 68 per 100,000 residents.

Figure 1.3 presents comparable information for incarceration in the nation's jails. For the total jail population, we have data only for the post-1980 period. Not surprisingly, the increase in the nation's prison incarceration rate corresponds to a threefold increase in the nation's jail incarceration rate (from 80 per 100,000 in 1980 to 247 per 100,000 in 2009). This reflects in part an increase in the number of individuals held in local jails while their cases were being adjudicated as well as an increase in the number of convicted individuals serving their sentences in jail.

With the number of prison and jail inmates combined, the United States currently incarcerates 743 individuals per 100,000 residents. How does this compare to other nations? Fortunately, the International Centre for Prison Studies at the University of Essex regularly collects and disseminates international incarceration statistics, permitting us to compare the United States to the rest of the world. Table 1.1 displays total incarceration rates (prisons plus jails) for various groups of countries. The United States is first among the five countries with the highest incarceration rates in the world, followed by the central African nation of Rwanda, Russia, the Republic of Georgia, and the Virgin Islands. The U.S. incarceration rate is several times larger than those of our North American neighbors (6.4 times that of Canada and 3.7 times that of Mexico). Incarceration rates among the fifteen original members of the European Union range from 59 to 159 per 100,000; these rates are roughly comparable to U.S. incarceration rates prior to 1980. The bottom of the table presents selected percentiles of the distribution of incarceration rates for all nations of the world. The figures indicate that half of all nations have an incarceration rate of 133 per 100,000 or less; that 75 percent of nations have incarceration rates of 225 per 100,000 or less; and that 90 percent of all nations have incarceration rates of 343 per 100,000 or less. The U.S. incarceration rate is more than double the incarceration rate for the nation at the ninetieth percentile of the global distribution of incarceration rates.

Thus, the U.S. incarceration rate is exceptionally high. The nation's incarceration rate is many times what it was in years past, especially when compared to levels in the pre-1980 period. Moreover, the nation's incarceration rate is high relative to other nations of the world, especially when compared with high-income countries in Western Europe and elsewhere.

Who Does Time in the United States?

Those who serve time are far from a representative cross-section of the U.S. adult public. In general, the majority of prison and jail inmates are men, racial and ethnic minorities, and those with very low levels of educational attainment. Consequently, the probability of doing time as well as the probability of having served a prison term varies considerably across demographic subgroups. We can employ data from the U.S. census as well as data from surveys of jail and prison inmates to characterize the incarcerated population and assess the scope of incarceration among specific subpopulations.

Table 1.2 presents our tabulations from the nationally representative Sur-

Table 1.1   International Comparison of Incarceration Rates Inclusive of Pretrial Detentions and Jail, 2008 to 2011

	Total Incarceration Rate (per 100,000)	Year
Top five countries		
United States	743	2009
Rwanda	595	2010
Russian Federation	568	2011
Republic of Georgia	547	2011
Virgin Islands	539	2011
Other North American		
Canada	117	2008
Mexico	200	2010
Original fifteen members of the European Union		
Austria	104	2011
Belgium	97	2010
Denmark	74	2011
Finland	59	2011
France	102	2011
Germany	85	2010
Greece	101	2010
Ireland	99	2011
Italy	111	2011
Luxembourg	139	2010
Netherlands	94	2010
Portugal	116	2011
Spain	159	2011
Sweden	78	2010
United Kingdom	152	2011
Percentiles of distribution across all countries		
Twenty-fifth	77	—
Fiftieth	133	—
Seventy-fifth	225	—
Ninetieth	343	—
Ninety-fifth	423	—

Source: Authors' compilation based on International Centre for Prison Studies (n.d.)

vey of Inmates in State and Federal Corrections Facilities (SISFCF) for 2004 (the most recent year from this survey series). The table presents average characteristics for state and federal prison inmates for basic demographic and educational attainment outcomes, criminal history, and health and mental health characteristics, as well as characteristics of the conviction offense resulting in their admission to prison. Although the majority of inmates are in one of the fifty state prison systems (90.4 percent), the federal prison system is quite large: in 2008 the number of federal prisoners (roughly 208,000) exceeded the prison populations of the largest states.

The table reveals several stark patterns. First, the prison population in 2004 was overwhelmingly male (93 percent of inmates in both the state and federal systems were male), a pattern that describes U.S. prison populations throughout most of the twentieth century. Educational attainment prior to prison admission was quite low. Among state prison inmates, fully two-thirds had less than a high school education prior to admission on the current prison term. Among federal inmates, 56 percent had less than a high school degree. By comparison, 19 percent of the adult resident population of the United States had less than a high school degree.[3]

Racial and ethnic minorities are heavily overrepresented among the incarcerated. In 2004 approximately one-fifth of state prison inmates were Hispanic, as were one-quarter of federal prisoners. Slightly less than half of both state and federal prisoners were African American. By comparison, blacks and Hispanics constituted 11 and 13 percent of the general adult population.

Prison inmates tend to be older than one might expect given the age trajectory of criminal offending. In particular, numerous researchers have demonstrated a sharp drop-off in offending after eighteen years of age, with greater proportions of those who are criminally active as youth desisting as their cohort ages through its twenties (Grogger 1998; Sampson and Laub 2003). Table 1.2 reveals that the inmate at the median of the age distribution is in his midthirties, suggesting that for many prison is the lasting result of crime committed in their earlier years. However, the median prisoner age is certainly younger than the median U.S. adult age (forty-four). These survey data reveal relatively early criminal initiation among those serving time. The median age at first arrest is seventeen, while the comparable median age for federal prison inmates is eighteen. Moreover, when asked when they started engaging in various criminal activities, median inmates indicate that they were fourteen years of age. Fully 75 percent indicate that they were criminally active by age sixteen.

The SISFCF also permits characterization of the physical and mental health of prison inmates. In particular, inmates were asked whether they had ever been diagnosed with a series of physical and mental health conditions. It is difficult to assess whether prison inmates are more likely to suffer from the health conditions listed in the table, since the survey asks whether they have ever been diagnosed but does not measure the annual incidence or prevalence of the condition in question. Moreover, we would want to age-adjust in drawing comparisons to the general population. Nonetheless, there are some conditions for which the lifetime cumulative risk for inmates appears to be particularly high. For example, 9.5 percent of state inmates indicated in 2004 that they had been diagnosed with hepatitis at some point in time. The combined annual incidence of hepatitis A, B, and C in 2006 among the U.S. population was approximately 3.1 per 100,000 (Wassley, Grytdal, and Gallagher 2008). Thus, the lifetime risk for state inmates is over three thousand times the annual incidence of the disease. For other conditions, such as diabetes, in which having ever been diagnosed is likely to be quite close to the prevalence rate, the proportion of inmates indicating that they were diabetic does not appear to be particularly high (4.7 percent of state inmates and 6.1 percent of federal inmates, compared with 11.2 for all U.S. men age twenty or older).

It is perhaps easier to compare the prevalence of chronic mental health conditions to those of the general adult population. For example, the inmate survey reveals that 9.7 percent of state inmates reported in 2004 that they had been diagnosed with manic depression, bipolar disorder. The comparable figure for all U.S. adults is roughly 2.6 percent. While 4.6 percent of state prison inmates and 1.9 percent of federal prison inmates indicated that they had been diagnosed with schizophrenia, the comparable figure for U.S. adults is 1.1 percent.[4] Prison inmates certainly have high rates of current and prior substance abuse issues. Over 60 percent of both state and federal prison inmates indicated that they had participated in an alcohol or drug treatment program while incarcerated.

A key difference between state and federal inmate populations lies in the offenses for which inmates are incarcerated. Roughly half of state prisoners are incarcerated for violent offenses, while one-fifth of state inmates are in for

Table 1.2   Characteristics of State and Federal Prisoners, 2004

	State Prisoners	Federal Prisoners
Proportion of prison population	0.904	0.096
Proportion male	0.932	0.929
Education attainment prior to admissions		
Elementary school	0.029	0.040
Middle school	0.165	0.143
Some high school, no degree	0.472	0.374
High school graduate	0.195	0.214
More than high school	0.139	0.227
Proportion Hispanic	0.182	0.251
Race		
White	0.487	0.433
Black	0.430	0.460
Other	0.083	0.107
Age distribution		
Twenty-fifth percentile	27	29
Fiftieth percentile	34	35
Seventy-fifth percentile	42	44
Age at first arrest		
Twenty-fifth percentile	15	16
Fiftieth percentile	17	18
Seventy-fifth percentile	21	23
Age first engaged in criminal activity		
Twenty-fifth percentile	12	12
Fiftieth percentile	14	14
Seventy-fifth percentile	16	16
Health conditions		
Diabetes	0.047	0.061
Heart problems	0.093	0.086
Kidney problems	0.061	0.057
Asthma	0.144	0.115
Hepatitis	0.095	0.076
Indicators of mental health issues or substance abuse		
Participated in alcohol/drug treatment program	0.605	0.649
Manic depression, bipolar	0.097	0.041

Table 1.2   (Continued)

	State Prisoners	Federal Prisoners
Schizophrenia	0.046	0.019
Post-traumatic stress disorder	0.057	0.031
Anxiety disorder	0.071	0.046
Personality disorder	0.059	0.032
Other mental health problem	0.019	0.008
Any diagnosed mental health problem	0.248	0.144
Ever attempted suicide	0.129	0.059
Have a definite date of release	0.660	0.842
Year of expected release		
2003 or 2004	0.459	0.266
2005	0.159	0.147
2006	0.091	0.111
2007	0.061	0.084
2008 or later	0.190	0.323
Expect to eventually be released conditional on not having a definite release date	0.872	0.863
Offense		
Murder, homicide, or manslaughter	0.139	0.029
Sexual assault	0.107	0.009
Robbery	0.127	0.085
Assault	0.086	0.017
Other violent crime	0.020	0.006
Burglary	0.082	0.005
Fraud or larceny	0.078	0.034
Auto theft	0.012	0.001
Other property crime	0.010	0.001
Drugs	0.213	0.552
Weapons	0.025	0.110
Other	0.101	0.150

Source: Authors' tabulations based on the Bureau of Justice Statistics (2004b).

drug offenses. As we will see in subsequent chapters, the proportion incarcerated for drug offenses has increased considerably and represents an important contribution to growth in state incarceration rates. For federal inmates, over half (55.2 percent) are incarcerated for drug law violations, while fewer than 15 percent are in for a violent offense.

Figure 1.4   Point-in-Time Estimates of the Proportion of Adults Age Eighteen to Sixty-Five Incarcerated in 2007, by Gender: Total and by Type of Correctional Facility

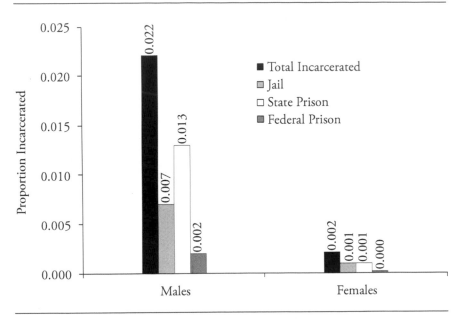

Source: Authors' tabulations from various surveys (see note 5).

The overrepresentation of certain demographic groups among the incarcerated (men, African Americans, those with low educational attainment) necessarily translates into a higher proportion being incarcerated on any given day among these groups. To estimate such proportions, we combine survey data from the U.S. Census Bureau, survey data for prison and jail inmates, and estimates of incarceration totals from the U.S. Bureau of Justice Statistics (BJS).[5] Figure 1.4 presents our estimates of the proportion of adult men and women, eighteen to sixty-five years of age, who were incarcerated in 2007 in any institution, who were incarcerated in a federal prison, who were incarcerated in a state prison, and who were incarcerated in a local jail. Overall, 2.2 percent of men were incarcerated on any given day, with most incarcerated in a state or federal prison. The percentage of women who were incarcerated was much lower, at 0.2 percent.

Figure 1.5 delves deeper into the incarceration proportion for men, providing separate estimates for four mutually exclusive race-ethnicity categories:

Figure 1.5   Point-in-Time Estimates of the Proportion of Men Age
Eighteen to Sixty-Five Incarcerated in 2007, by Race-
Ethnicity: Total and by Type of Correctional Facility

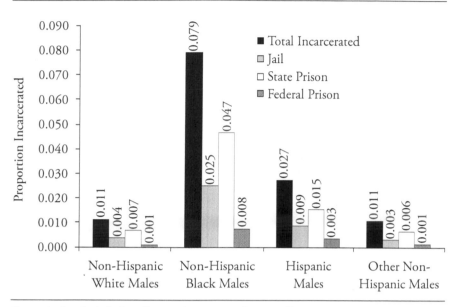

Source: Authors' tabulations from various surveys (see note 5).

non-Hispanic whites, non-Hispanic blacks, Hispanics, and other non-Hispanics. The figure reveals enormous racial and ethnic disparities in incarceration rates. On any given day in 2007, nearly 8 percent of African American men were incarcerated in prison or jail, with 70 percent of black incarcerated men being held in a state or federal prison. In contrast, only 1.1 percent of non-Hispanic white men were incarcerated on any given day. Hispanic men occupied a spot between blacks and whites: overall 2.7 percent were incarcerated, with 2.4 percent incarcerated in a federal or state prison.

Our characterization of state and federal prisoners reveals that the less-educated are heavily overrepresented among prison and jail inmates. We have also seen, both in the characterization of prison inmates and in the gender- and race-specific incarceration rates, that minority men are heavily overrepresented among those doing time. To assess the interactions of these three dimensions (education, gender, and race), table 1.3 presents estimates of the proportion of men with less than a high school degree who were incarcerated in 2007, as well as men who were high school graduates or held GEDs, by race-ethnicity and broad age ranges. The table reveals several salient patterns. First, a comparison of the figures in table 1.3 with those in figure 1.5 reveals the much higher incidence of incarceration among the relatively less educated. Second, within racial-ethnic groups and educational attainment categories, the proportion incarcerated was highest among those age thirty-one to forty. Third, incarceration rates were considerably higher among those without a high school degree relative to those with a high school degree or GED within all race-age groupings.[6]

Perhaps the starkest pattern to emerge from this table is the very large racial and ethnic disparity in incarceration rates among the least-educated males. Roughly 26 percent of non-Hispanic black men between ages eighteen and thirty with less than a high school degree are in prison or jail on any given day, with the majority of these men in prison. Among black male high school dropouts who are thirty-one to forty years old, fully 34 percent are incarcerated on any given day. The comparable two figures for whites in these age and education categories are 5.5 and 6.9 percent, respectively, while the comparable figures for Hispanics are 6.1 and 4.2 percent, respectively. In chapter 6, we will show that the high proportions of the least-educated black men who are incarcerated are comparable in magnitude, and sometimes exceed, the proportion of these men who are not institutionalized and are gainfully employed.

The incarceration proportions for high school graduates reveal more muted yet still sizable racial disparities. While 12 percent of black men in their thirties with a high school degree or GED are incarcerated on any given day, the comparable figure for white and Hispanic men are 2.9 and 3.1 percent, respectively. Notably, the percentage of black high school graduates who are incarcerated actually exceeds the comparable figures for white and Hispanic high school dropouts.

An alternative characterization of who serves time focuses on the cumulative or lifetime risk of going to prison. Because the U.S. prison population tends to turn over relatively quickly (annual prison admissions and releases are consistently equal to half the prison population), the drastic increases in incarceration rates over the last three decades have left in their wake a large and growing population of former inmates. The distribution of former prisoners across demographic subgroups of the non-institutionalized population is an important determinant of social inequality, since former inmates tend to be scarred and stigmatized by their experience and face substantial hurdles in the labor market. Moreover, given the racial and socioeconomic concentra-

Table 1.3   Point-in-Time Estimates of the Proportion of Prime-Age, Less-Educated Men Incarcerated in 2007, by Race-Ethnicity and Type of Correctional Facility

	Total Incarceration	In Jail	In State Prison	In Federal Prison
Less than a high school degree				
Non-Hispanic white				
Eighteen to thirty	0.055	0.029	0.025	0.001
Thirty-one to forty	0.069	0.029	0.037	0.002
Forty-one to fifty	0.033	0.010	0.021	0.001
Non-Hispanic black				
Eighteen to thirty	0.263	0.111	0.138	0.014
Thirty-one to forty	0.339	0.094	0.209	0.035
Forty-one to fifty	0.183	0.051	0.119	0.013
Hispanic				
Eighteen to thirty	0.061	0.025	0.032	0.004
Thirty-one to forty	0.042	0.013	0.025	0.004
Forty-one to fifty	0.028	0.009	0.016	0.003
Non-Hispanic other				
Eighteen to thirty	0.064	0.026	0.033	0.004
Thirty-one to forty	0.055	0.017	0.032	0.007
Forty-one to fifty	0.025	0.009	0.014	0.002
High school graduate/GED				
Non-Hispanic white				
Eighteen to thirty	0.019	0.007	0.012	0.001
Thirty-one to forty	0.029	0.008	0.019	0.002
Forty-one to fifty	0.015	0.004	0.010	0.001
Non-Hispanic black				
Eighteen to thirty	0.083	0.028	0.047	0.008
Thirty-one to forty	0.121	0.031	0.074	0.016
Forty-one to fifty	0.063	0.015	0.043	0.005
Hispanic				
Eighteen to thirty	0.026	0.009	0.015	0.002
Thirty-one to forty	0.031	0.008	0.018	0.005
Forty-one to fifty	0.024	0.006	0.013	0.005
Non-Hispanic other				
Eighteen to thirty	0.020	0.006	0.012	0.002
Thirty-one to forty	0.024	0.006	0.016	0.003
Forty-one to fifty	0.013	0.002	0.009	0.002

Source: Authors' tabulations based on Bureau of Justice Statistics (2002, 2004b), U.S. Census Bureau (2007a), and Bureau of Justice Statistics, *National Prisoner Statistics* (various years). See note 5 for a description of the estimation methodology.

tion of former inmates among certain groups, prior incarceration is a factor that probably contributes to racial inequality in the United States above and beyond such factors as educational attainment, family background, and racial labor market discrimination.

Two metrics are commonly employed to measure the cumulative risk of incarceration: the proportion of adults who have ever served time, and the projected lifetime likelihood of serving time for a person born in a specific year (that is, a given birth cohort). When incarceration rates are increasing, the projected lifetime risk tends to be greater than the proportion who have ever served time, since a child born during a high-incarceration-rate era faces a different set of risks when passing through the high-risk age ranges than did adults born during periods with lower incarceration rates.

Table 1.4 presents tabulations produced by the Bureau of Justice Statistics for both measures for the years 1974 and 2001 (corresponding to the period of greatest increase in the nation's incarceration rate) (Bonczar 2003). The proportions of U.S. adults who have ever been incarcerated basically double over this time period, with the largest absolute increase for black males. As of 2001, roughly 5 percent of all adult men had served time in a state or federal prison, while the figure for black men stood at 16.6 percent. The Bureau of Justice Statistics does not present such estimates for educational subgroups within these race-gender categories. However, several academic researchers have generated independent estimates that reveal an extraordinarily high prevalence of prior prison experience among the least-educated minority men. In an analysis of administrative records from the California Department of Corrections, Steven Raphael (2005) estimates that at the close of the 1990s over 90 percent of the state's black male high school dropouts and 10 to 15 percent of black male high school graduates had served time in prison.[7] Becky Pettit and Bruce Western (2004) estimate that for all African American men born between 1965 and 1969, the proportion who had been to prison by 1999 was 20.5 percent for all black men, 30.2 percent for black men without a college degree, and 58.9 percent for black men without a high school degree.

The final two columns of table 1.4 show the BJS estimate of the lifetime risk of incarceration for children born in 1974 and 2001. Not surprisingly, the figures show pronounced increases in the lifetime risk for all groups. Note that the increases in lifetime risk are considerably larger than the increases in the proportion with prior prison time. However, with sufficient time and

Table 1.4   Proportion of U.S. Adults Who Had Ever Served Time and the Predicted Lifetime Risk of Serving Prison Time by Year of Birth, 1974 and 2001

	Proportion of Adults Ever Serving Time in a State or Federal Prison		Lifetime Risk of Serving Time in a State or Federal Prison for a Child Born in . . .	
	1974	2001	1974	2001
Total	0.013	0.027	0.019	0.066
Males	0.023	0.049	0.036	0.113
White	0.014	0.026	0.022	0.059
Black	0.087	0.166	0.134	0.322
Hispanic	0.023	0.077	0.040	0.172
Females	0.002	0.005	0.003	0.018
White	0.001	0.003	0.002	0.009
Black	0.006	0.017	0.011	0.056
Hispanic	0.002	0.007	0.004	0.022

Source: Authors' compilation based on data from Bonczar (2003).

stable incarceration rates at the new higher levels, these two sets of figures will eventually converge.[8] The lifetime risk of serving prison time for a child born in 2001 stood at 6.6 percent for all children and 11.3 percent for males. For black males born in 2001, the BJS estimates a lifetime risk at the startlingly high level of 32.2 percent, implying that one of every three black male children born in 2001 will do time.

How Much Do We Spend?

A full accounting of the social costs of incarceration would include both the direct fiscal outlays for correctional services and the value of the indirect social consequences of incarceration, including impacts on the future earnings of a former inmate, effects on family and children, the public health impacts, and so on. In a cost-benefit framework, such direct and indirect costs would be measured against the benefits of incarceration derived from crime reduction and the satisfaction of the public's demand for punishment for those who transgress. We will postpone a more complete discussion of costs and benefits until the final chapter of this book. To start this conversation here, however, we provide an overview of the fiscal impact of correctional expenditures.[9]

Figure 1.6   Total Direct Expenditures (in Millions of Dollars) on
Corrections in 2007, by Level of Government

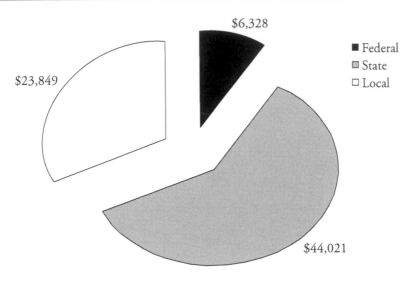

$6,328

■ Federal
▨ State
□ Local

$23,849

$44,021

Total corrections expenditures for 2007 = $74,198 million

Source: Authors' compilation based on Bureau of Justice Statistics, *Justice Expenditures and Employment Extracts* (various years).

Figure 1.6 provides a breakdown of correctional expenditures in fiscal year 2007 according to the level of government where the direct cash outlay occurred.[10] The United States spent $74 billion in 2007 on corrections, approximately $250 per resident. The lion's share of correctional expenditures occurs at the state level (roughly 60 percent), while approximately one-third of correctional expenditures are made by local governments throughout the country. As we would expect, the sharp increase in incarceration has resulted in pronounced increases in correctional expenditures. Figure 1.7 displays total correctional expenditures adjusted for inflation to 2007 dollars as well as per-capita annual expenditures for the period from 1980 to 2007. Total correctional expenditures increased 4.3 times over this period, from $17.3 billion to $74.1 billion. To be sure, some of this increase reflects the fact that the U.S. resident population increased by roughly 33 percent over this period; with a larger population, we would expect more prison inmates. However, per-capita expenditure also increased, slightly more than tripling between 1980 and 2007.

Figure 1.7   Total Corrections Expenditures and Per-Capita
              Corrections Expenditures (in 2007 Dollars) in All Levels
              of Government Combined for 1980 to 2007 (Adjusted
              for Inflation)

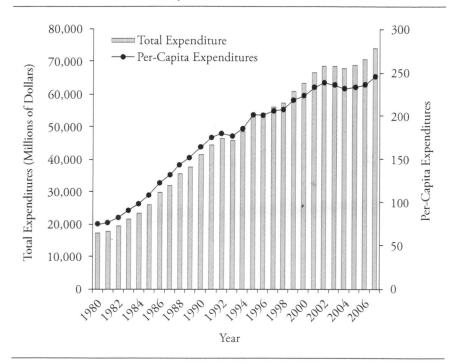

Source: Authors' compilation based on Bureau of Justice Statistics, *Justice Expenditures and Employment Extracts* (various years).

In recent years, a relatively small percentage of correctional expenditures has been devoted to new prison construction, with over 95 percent of correctional expenditures attributable to operating costs. However, during the late 1980s and early 1990s, substantial proportions of correctional allocations were devoted to the construction of new facilities. Figure 1.8 presents current and historical data on annual capital expenditures made by the states in the corrections category. Since the data source for this series permits a longer analysis, we present total state capital expenditures for the period from 1970 to 2008, adjusted for inflation to 2008 dollars.[11] The figure reveals relatively high capital expenditures in the late 1980s and through the 1990s, with annual capital expenditures peaking in 1991 at $4.3 billion. In more recent

Figure 1.8   Total State Capital Expenditures in Corrections, 1970 to 2008 (in Millions of 2008 Dollars)

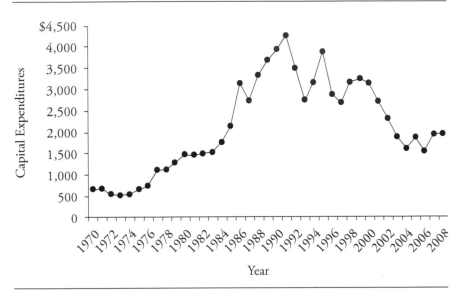

Source: Authors' compilation based on U.S. Census Bureau (2009).

years, states have scaled back prison construction, and several have actually begun to close existing facilities.

Annual expenditures per inmate vary greatly across states. Table 1.5 presents estimates of annual expenditures per inmate from 2005 to 2011 culled from searches of the fifty state correctional department websites.[12] Expenditures per inmate vary considerably, from the low of approximately $15,000 per year in Alabama and Texas to over $45,000 per year in Alaska, California, Massachusetts, and Rhode Island. Averaging across all states yields an estimate of roughly $30,000 per year.

Although few states provide detailed breakdowns of these annual cost estimates, the numbers for the states that do suggest that labor and medical expenditures account for the largest component of correctional operating costs. For example, the California Legislative Analyst's Office estimates that of the $47,102 spent per inmate per year in fiscal year 2008–2009, $19,663 was attributable to security expenditures (largely correctional officer salaries), facility operations cost $7,124 per inmate, and $12,442 was devoted to inmate health care. Only $2,562 was spent on food, inmate activities, and clothing,

Table 1.5   Annual Expenditures per Prison Inmate, by State, 2005 to 2011

State	Average Annual Expenditures	Estimate Year
Alabama	$15,118	2009
Alaska	49,800	2011
Arizona	22,535	2007
Arkansas	21,969	2009
California	48,843	2008
Colorado	32,334	2009
Connecticut	32,733	2009
Delaware	30,000	2010
Florida	19,469	2009
Georgia	16,950	2010
Hawaii	—	—
Idaho	19,060	2010
Illinois	24,899	2009
Indiana	19,203	2010
Iowa	31,383	2009
Kansas	24,953	2010
Kentucky	26,178	2010
Louisiana	20,385	2010
Maine	43,363	2010
Maryland	31,200	2008
Massachusetts	45,917	2010
Michigan	35,285	2010
Minnesota	32,573	2009
Mississippi	17,827	2010
Missouri	17,984	2010
Montana	34,310	2010
Nebraska	33,410	2010
Nevada	—	—
New Hampshire	32,492	2010
New Jersey	34,600	2010
New Mexico	39,000	2010
New York	45,000	2009
North Carolina	27,134	2010
North Dakota	—	—
Ohio	21,659	2005
Oklahoma	19,827	2010
Oregon	30,828	2010
Pennsylvania	32,986	2010

Table 1.5   (Continued)

State	Average Annual Expenditures	Estimate Year
Rhode Island	45,309	2010
South Carolina	16,312	2009
South Dakota	15,330	2009
Tennessee	23,145	2010
Texas	15,527	2008
Utah	—	—
Vermont	54,383	2010
Virginia	24,024	2010
Washington	34,617	2010
West Virginia	24,266	2010
Wisconsin	32,080	2010
Wyoming	—	—

Source: Authors' searches of state department of correction websites or legislation documented from the states that offer annual cost estimates. Exact sources for each state are available from the authors upon request.

while $1,612 per inmate was attributable to rehabilitation activities.[13] Hence, security expenditures, facilities operations, and medical expenditures account for roughly 83 percent of per-inmate costs in the state, while basic inmate support and rehabilitation accounts for a relatively small share of costs. Mississippi spends considerably less per inmate than California ($17,827 per year), yet has a relatively similar cost structure. Food, education, and training account for only 9 percent of per-inmate expenditures. The remaining 91 percent goes to salaries, inmate medical expenditures, allocated administrative expenditures, and annual debt service for prior capital investments.[14]

With the recent economic downturn and the contraction in state revenue sources, states throughout the country have been scouring their budgets looking for areas of potential savings. Given the increases in correctional expenditures documented here and the fact that in recent decades growth in corrections spending has outpaced growth in state spending overall, it is not surprising that states are scrutinizing their corrections and sentencing practices with an eye to saving money while not compromising public safety.[15] In general, corrections expenditures consume a relatively small yet increasing share of state general fund expenditures. For example, in fiscal year 2009 corrections accounted for 7.2 percent of state general fund expenditures. By contrast, state expenditures on the Medicaid program accounted for 15.7 percent of state general fund expenditures, higher education expenditures were 11.5 percent, and spending on elementary and secondary education accounted for 35.8 percent.[16] These descriptive statistics for the nation as a whole mask considerable variation across states. The slice of general funds allocated to corrections ranges from 2.7 percent of general funds in Minnesota to 22.8 percent in Michigan. In the two states with the largest prison systems (California and Texas), general fund expenditures on corrections are somewhat above the national average (10.2 percent in California and 7.5 percent in Texas).

There is relatively little research on the question of what types of spending are being displaced by increasing correctional expenditures. The scant research suggests that there has been little displacement effect on higher education spending (Gunter, Orszag, and Kane 2002) and K-12 spending (Ellwood and Guetzkow 2009). However, at least one research team has found that states that devote increasing shares of the general fund to corrections contemporaneously reduce antipoverty expenditures (Ellwood and Guetzkow 2009). This is particularly ironic, as prison inmates are drawn disproportionately from the ranks of the poor, who are the primary recipients of income and in-kind support from the states.

OUTLINE OF THE BOOK

The increase in incarceration rates over the past three decades puts the United States in a league of its own. We are incarcerating more people today than we ever have, and we stand out as the nation that most frequently and intensely uses incarceration to punish those who break the law. We are increasingly locking up larger and larger proportions of young minority men and generating a very large pool of former prison inmates who face considerable difficulties in attempting to establish productive and law-abiding roles for themselves among the non-incarcerated. These correctional practices are expensive, and although they tend to consume a small proportion of state budgets, it is likely that they are displacing discretionary spending in other budgetary domains.

How did we get here? What are the social consequences, positive or negative, of this enormous policy experiment? Are there alternative crime control strategies that would rely less heavily on incarceration yet not compromise public safety? This book is devoted to answering these questions.

We devote the next three chapters to explaining why the incarceration rate grew so much over a relatively short period of time. We begin in chapter 2 by providing a simple framework for thinking about the forces that determine the size of a dynamic population among whom entrances and exits lead to constant churning in who is incarcerated on any given day. In particular, we highlight the role of the prison admissions rate and the fact that higher admissions translate directly into higher incarceration rates. Moreover, we dissect the determinants of prison admissions rates into a behavioral component (the crime rate) and a policy component (clearances by arrest, convictions, and likelihood of being sentenced to prison conditional on arrest and conviction). We document trends in each of these factors for state and federal prison systems and for specific felony offenses. This analysis reveals very large increases in prison admissions rates driven entirely by changes in the propensity to send convicted offenders to prison.

Chapter 2 also lays out the connection between the amount of time an inmate sentenced to prison can expect to serve and the prison population on any given day. Put simply, longer sentences generate larger prison populations. We document substantial increases in the amount of time that those sentenced to prison can expect to serve today relative to years past in both the state and federal prison systems. Because prison time for specific offenses has increased, these empirical facts are indicative of policy changes over the last few decades that have generally enhanced the severity of punishment for certain crimes.

In chapter 3, we seek to answer five questions. First, to what extent does tougher sentencing explain the growth in U.S. incarceration rates since the early 1980s? Second, how important are changes in criminal behavior in explaining these trends? Third, can we identify specific changes in sentencing practices that have been principal drivers of incarceration growth? For example, to what extent are longer sentences to blame as opposed to higher admissions rates? Fourth, are there specific offenses for which we have cracked down particularly hard that bear a disproportionate share of the blame for incarceration growth? Finally, how do the answers to these questions differ for the state and federal prison incarceration rates?

To address these questions we build and calibrate a simple model of incarceration rates. The model takes empirical estimates of prison admissions rates and expected time served and calculates the incarceration rate that will eventually be reached given stable values for these factors and enough time. A particularly useful feature of this model is that by adjusting the admissions rates and time served to, say, values from 1984, we can simulate what the incarceration rate would be if we were to roll back all sentencing practices or select sentencing practices to those of years past.

Our simulation results yield several findings. First, there is very little evidence supporting the hypothesis that changes in criminal activity have driven up the nation's incarceration rate. Crime rates are currently at all-time lows, and the hypothetically higher crime rates that we might have observed had there been no increase in incarceration since the early 1980s are far from sufficient to have caused the increases in incarceration in recent years.

In contrast, there is overwhelming evidence that the elevated rates of prison admissions per crime and expected time served are the principal drivers of incarceration growth. There are some key differences between the federal and state prison systems. For example, among the states, tougher drug sentences account for one-fifth of incarceration growth over the two-decade period we study, while tougher sentences for violent crime account for half. By contrast, growth in the federal prison system is driven primarily by tougher sentences for drug offenders and other public-order crimes. Nonetheless, in both systems legislatively driven policy changes have driven incarceration growth. In other words, so many Americans are in prison because we are choosing through our public policies to put them there.

This finding, of course, begs the question of what policy choices are driving the harsher sentencing policies. This is the subject matter of chapter 4. Corrections and sentencing policy at the state level has changed considerably. Many states have moved away from indeterminate sentencing regimes, whereby a judge would issue a minimum as well as a maximum sentence and parole boards exercised great discretion in determining the ultimate length of time served. In its place, most states now employ determinate sentencing: a single sentence is handed down, and the amount of time served is determined by the original sentence with time off for good behavior according to administrative formulae. Determinate sentencing has greatly reduced the influence and authority of parole boards. In addition, many states have passed truth-in-sentencing laws that require inmates to serve a specified minimum percentage of their original sentence. Aside from these broader reforms, numerous state laws have enhanced sentences for specific offenses, and many states have passed repeat-offenders statutes—such as California's "three-strikes" law—that greatly enhance the prison terms of newly convicted offenders with prior violent felony convictions. Collectively, these policy changes have driven the enormous increase in state incarceration rates since the mid-1970s. The increase in the federal prison incarceration rates can be traced largely to the incarceration of drug offenders and the minimum sentences mandated in federal sentencing guidelines. Chapter 4 provides a detailed discussion of each of these developments.

Having identified the root causes of the increase in incarceration rates, we devote the following two chapters to a discussion of the factors that are commonly offered as explanations for increasing incarceration rates yet upon closer inspection do not appear to be the principal driving forces. Chapter 5 explores the contribution of the deinstitutionalization of the mentally ill. At its peak during the 1950s, the number of mental hospital patients per 100,000 U.S. residents stood at roughly 330 (a population over 600,000). By the end of the twentieth century, through a series of policy reforms and changes in legal precedent, the inpatient mental hospital population shrank to trivially small numbers (below 20 per 100,000 by 2000). In conjunction with the very high incidence of severe mental illness among prison inmates as well as research documenting a connection between certain mental illnesses and criminal activity, we can certainly make a circumstantial case that the drastic changes in mental health policy driving deinstitutionalization are in part responsible for increasing incarceration growth.

A careful analysis of U.S. census data from 1950 through 2000 reveals, however, several problems with this hypothesis. First, the composition of the mental hospital population of the 1950s differed greatly from the composition of the prison population, with the elderly heavily overrepresented, women constituting nearly half of the mental hospital population, and racial minorities not overrepresented among mental hospital inpatients. Many of the groups with high institutionalization rates in 1950 did not experience subsequent increases in incarceration. A simple compositional analysis reveals that, at most, deinstitutionalization can explain only a small share of the increase in prison populations. Moreover, direct estimates of the rate at which those individuals most likely to be hospitalized at midcentury have been "transinstitutionalized" from mental hospitals to prisons suggest relatively modest effects for most groups, though the transinstitutionalization rate appears substantial for white men during the 1980s and 1990s. Although deinstitutionalization is not responsible for a large proportion of the overall increase in incarceration, we do find that up to one-quarter of the nearly

300,000 severely mentally ill inmates currently incarcerated would probably have been in mental hospitals in years past.

Chapter 6 explores the potential contribution to incarceration growth of three other factors: the changing demographic composition of the United States, the diminished labor market opportunities for low-skilled men, and the crack epidemic of the 1980s. There have been several demographic changes since 1980 that in isolation should have led to lower crime rates and, by extension, lower incarceration rates. First, the nation has aged. Second, the foreign-born proportion of the population has increased. Finally, the average levels of educational attainment have increased. Since older people, immigrants, and the more educated tend to be less likely to commit crime, demographic forces alone should have reduced crime and incarceration, yet incarceration rates have increased dramatically.

It is indeed the case that the earnings and employment opportunities for low-skilled men—and perhaps for low-skilled minority men in particular—have eroded since the mid-1970s. Although these diminished opportunities may in part reflect the increasing numbers of former prison inmates among low-skilled men, broader forces in the economy that have greatly increased the economic returns to education, increased earnings inequality, and led to absolute declines in the real value of the wages earned by the least skilled may have driven more men into crime and into the criminal justice system. It is difficult to assess directly the impact of diminished legitimate job opportunities on incarceration rates, but there are several findings from existing empirical research that can be used to calculate ballpark estimates. In particular, several economists have analyzed the sensitivity of criminal offending to changes in earnings potential, and there are various sources that can be employed to estimate the likelihood of being incarcerated for committing a crime. Combining this information with data from the U.S. Census Bureau, we estimate the likely effect of earnings trends on crime and incarceration and conclude that this may have had a modest positive effect on incarceration growth, equal in magnitude yet somewhat smaller than the effects of changing demographics, and of opposite sign. In other words, our research suggests that broad demographic changes and declining labor market prospects for less-skilled men have probably had individual impacts on incarceration that largely cancel one another out.

The appearance of crack cocaine in the mid-1980s greatly increased cocaine use in relatively poor minority neighborhoods and is commonly cited as a key determinant of the spike in violent crime between the mid-1980s and the early 1990s. The timing of the crack epidemic, along with the particular connections between the market for crack and violence, suggests that this particular behavioral shock may have been an important behavioral contributor to the growth in incarceration. Our analysis suggests that the direct role of crack cocaine in explaining prison growth is greatly exaggerated. To start, our earlier analysis of the broad determinants of incarceration growth finds little room for behavior in explaining this increase: nearly all prison growth is explained by policy choices. Hence, the possible contribution of crack cocaine to prison growth operating through behavior is bounded from above by this prior analysis. Second, the crack cocaine epidemic waned considerably during the early 1990s, yet we observe an acceleration of prison growth over the course of this decade. Moreover, we find considerable growth in incarceration prior to the onset of the crack epidemic and not much evidence of an increase in the growth rate following that onset.

To be sure, the crack cocaine epidemic may have had an important indirect effect on the nation's incarceration rate through the policy responses that it elicited. The most salient policy response was federal legislation that enacted mandatory minimum sentences that were particularly tough on those charged with crack-related offenses.

Chapter 7 focuses on the relationship between incarceration and crime rates. Incarceration has an impact on crime through three broad channels. First, incarceration incapacitates the criminally active. Second, the threat of incarceration may deter those who might otherwise commit crime. Finally, an incarceration experience may either straighten someone out (often referred to as "specific deterrence") or enhance the criminal propensity of an incarcerated offender (often referred to as prison's "criminogenic" effect on former inmates). In either case, a specific incarceration spell will have an impact on crime, positive or negative, with a dynamic lag.

Existing empirical research on incarceration and crime for both the United States and other countries provides clear evidence of incapacitation and general deterrence effects on crime rates. However, this research also finds that crime-fighting effects diminish considerably as the incarceration rate increases. Specifically, as incarceration rates grow, the marginal impact on crime rates diminishes. In the United States today, this diminishing return to scale appears to be quite substantial: the marginal incarcerated offender incapacitates very little crime, and that crime is generally of a less serious nature. This is not too surprising considering that, in the U.S. context, where the incarceration rate has increased nearly fivefold, the average incarcerated offender today is serving a prison term for a considerably less serious crime than the average inmate of years past. This finding also suggests a great heterogeneity among those in prison and the potential for strategically and deliberately scaling back the use of incarceration. We discuss this relationship in great detail in chapter 7, along with what is known regarding the long-term effects of incarceration on a criminal who offends after release.

In our final chapter, we offer our thoughts about whether the United States is overusing incarceration in its national crime control strategy, and we present some ideas regarding alternative policy paths that states might fruitfully pursue. The chapter begins by discussing what an optimal—that is, efficient—crime control strategy would look like in terms of costs relative to benefits. We then provide a fuller accounting of the collateral social costs of the prison boom that have been documented by researchers over the past decade or so. The collateral consequences are many, and they include but are not limited to impacts on the employment prospects of former inmates, on racial education attainment differentials, on the spread of infectious diseases, on the children of the incarcerated, on political participation and the outcomes of electoral competition, and on racial inequality generally. We believe that the diminished crime-fighting effects of incarceration at high rates in conjunction with these high social costs clearly indicate that, as a nation, we're overdoing it. We close by discussing what would need to happen to bring down our incarceration rate and alternative crime control strategies that policymakers could adopt.

CHAPTER 2

Understanding and Documenting the Determinants of Incarceration Growth

There are several stylized facts about the U.S. prison population that the lay reader is likely to find surprising. First, prisons are often mischaracterized as places where we lock people up and throw away the key. In fact, the typical person admitted to prison on a new felony conviction is likely to be released after two years, with many offenders serving less time and some serving considerably more time. These relatively short terms have prompted the observation (and frankly, the admonition) by Jeremy Travis (2005), the president of the John Jay College of Criminal Justice, that "they all come back."

Second, few outside of those who work within the criminal justice system are aware of the degree of fluidity in the prison population—in particular the extent to which the prison population turns over from year to year. For example, on December 31, 2007, there were 1,598,316 inmates in state or federal prison. During the calendar year 2007, 751,593 inmates were admitted to prison (47 percent of the year-end population), while 725,402 were released from prison (roughly 45 percent of the year-end total). In some states, the degree of turnover is unusually high. For example, California, which, with 174,282 inmates at the end of 2007 held over 10 percent of the nation's prison inmates, released 135,920 inmates and admitted 139,608 that year.

To understand the factors driving growth in the U.S. incarceration rate, we need a framework for characterizing what determines the size at a given point in time of what is inherently a dynamic population. In our research on U.S. prisons, we have found the analogy of the student body at a university to be particularly useful. Suppose that we wish to start a four-year undergraduate institution from scratch. We build the buildings, hire the necessary professors and staff, and admit our first freshman class of 1,000 students. In our first year of operation, we thus have a relatively small student population of 1,000. In year two, our 1,000 freshmen become sophomores (assuming everyone progresses on schedule), and we admit a new class of 1,000 freshmen, increasing the student body to 2,000. Similar progression and new admissions in years three and four increases our student body to 3,000 and 4,000, respectively. In year five, however, the effect on our total student body of 1,000 freshman admissions is perfectly offset by the graduation of our original cohort of 1,000 students. Hence, beyond year four our student body stabilizes at a population of 4,000 with the number exiting (our graduates) exactly offset by the number entering (the new freshmen).

The eventual stability of our student body provides an example of a dynamic population reaching what is often referred to as the "steady state." When such a population is in a steady state, exits equal admissions and the population is constant from period to period. Of course, the members of the population change from year to year as the new freshmen replace the graduating seniors. However, our student body attains a predictable and stable total.

The usefulness of this analogy is in highlighting factors that would lead to long-run changes in the size of the student body. For example, suppose we decide to permanently increase freshman admissions to 1,100. In the first year following this change, this decision leads to an increase in the student body to 4,100 as freshman admissions more than offset graduating seniors. However, it takes four years for the full impact of this policy change to be realized. Eventually, there are 1,100 students in each year and the size of our student body shifts to a new steady state of 4,400. The change in the steady-state population caused by increased admissions exactly equals the number of new admissions multiplied by the number of years each new admission will study at the university.

Alternatively, suppose we are prompted to add one more year of study to the undergraduate program because the students do not seem to be learning enough in four years. With 1,100 admissions per year and five required years of study, our student population will eventually stabilize at 5,500. We can further complicate our analysis by adding different degree programs. For example, suppose we add a two-year master's program and a PhD program that typically takes six years to finish. Our student population will eventually reach a level equal to the sum of the steady-state populations of each of these programs. Moreover, the effect of a change in admissions on the steady-state student population is larger for programs that take longer to finish. To be specific, a permanent increase in admissions by one person results in two extra students in the steady state for the master's degree program, five extra students for the undergraduate degree (assuming our longer five-year program), and six extra students for the PhD program.

While prisons and universities are certainly very different places,[1] the modeling parallel is quite clear. If prison admissions permanently increase, so does the prison population. Such an increase in admissions may result from higher crime rates or policy changes that increase the likelihood that a given offense results in a prison term. Similarly, if we enact policies that punish offenders with enhanced sentences (increasing the amount of time an offender can expect to serve), our prison population increases. An increase in admissions of offenders with very long sentences has larger long-term effects on the nation's incarceration rate than an increase in admissions of offenders with relatively short sentences. However, increasing admissions for relatively less serious felonies leaves a large proportion of former inmates among the non-institutionalized population. Finally, increases in both admissions and the length of prison sentences are mutually reinforcing in driving up incarceration rates.

In this chapter, we use this simple framework to identify and empirically document the factors driving the large increase in U.S. incarceration rates. We begin with a discussion of admissions to state prisons and changes in admissions rates over time. This is followed by estimates of how much time an offender can expect to serve conditional on being convicted of a specific offense. Finally, we discuss the growth in the federal prison incarceration rate separately.

CHANGES IN STATE PRISON ADMISSIONS RATES

Aggregate admissions into the nation's state prisons come from three broad sources. First, many inmates are admitted to prison following conviction for a new felony offense. Such admissions are referred to as "new court commitments" because the offender is being sent to prison immediately following the adjudication of his or her case.

A second major source of prison admissions is parole failures. Those on parole are former prison inmates who are conditionally released from prison and technically serving the remainder of their sentence in the community. Their conditional liberty can be revoked when they fail to meet the requirements defining their conditional release. Failing to show up to meetings with one's parole officer, using drugs or alcohol, leaving one's county of residence without permission, moving without informing the authorities, or being arrested for minor violations may result—and often does—in having one's parole revoked and being readmitted to prison. When parolees commit and are convicted of new felonies, they are admitted to prison on those new felony commitments, with new prison sentences, rather than as parole violators. This distinction is very important. Admissions rates for technical parole violations, which are generally under the discretion of policymakers, are quite high and thus an empirically important source of annual prison admissions. Moreover, being returned to custody for a technical parole violation does not officially involve the commission of a new felony, while being returned to custody with a new felony sentence does.

The third source of prison admissions operates through the nation's probation system. Each of the fifty states as well as the federal government has a probation system for convicted felons and those convicted of lesser offenses. Generally speaking, a sentence to a probation term is given in lieu of incarceration, although for those who do not meet their probationary conditions, a subsequent prison or jail spell is an option. Probation is sometimes combined with an initial short jail or prison sentence, but the majority of those on probation do not serve time in prison unless they violate the conditions of their probation or commit and are convicted of a new crime during their probationary period.[2] Like parolees who are returned to custody, those on probation can be admitted to prison for violating the terms of their probation or for committing a new felony offense.

Table 2.1 shows the distribution of admissions to prison by type of admission for the year 2004. We tabulate these admissions rates using data from the 2004 National Corrections Reporting Program. The NCRP provides annual microdata on all individuals admitted to and released from prisons within participating states. In 2004, thirty-four states participated in the program, with all of the largest states in the nation represented.[3] The first column of

Table 2.1   Distribution of Admissions to Prison, by Source of Admission, 2004

	Proportion of Total Admissions	Distribution of Admissions Within a Given Source, by Offense Category[a]		
		Violent Crime	Property Crime	Drugs and Other Crime
New court commitments	0.61	0.27	0.28	0.45
Parole revoked, new sentence	0.06	0.18	0.37	0.45
Parole revoked, no new sentence	0.24	0.24	0.33	0.43
Probation revoked, new sentence	0.01	0.14	0.37	0.48
Probation revoked, no new sentence	0.09	0.20	0.35	0.46

Source: Authors' tabulations from the Bureau of Justice Statistics, *National Corrections Reporting Program* (2004a).

Notes: The distribution of admissions by source excludes admissions records where the admissions source was missing and those admitted owing to transfers, return of escapees, or returns from appeal or bond. Similarly, the distribution of admissions within a source group excludes those admissions records where offense data are missing.

[a]Within source groups, these figures sum to 1.

figures presents the proportional distribution of prison admissions by source. New court commitments coming from those not incarcerated and not on parole or probation account for the largest source of prison admissions (61 percent). A substantial portion of admissions are generated from the nation's 700,000-plus parolees. Slightly less than one-third of prison admissions come from those on parole, with 24 percent of total admissions coming from technical parole violations and 6 percent from parolees convicted of new crimes. Approximately 10 percent of admissions come from the country's probation population. The lion's share of these admissions comes from those whose probation is revoked without a new term.

Table 2.1 also provides information on the offense committed for each source of prison admissions, splitting admissions from each category into those convicted of violent crimes, property crimes, or drug or other crimes. The data reveal several interesting patterns. First, those convicted for drug or other offenses represent a disproportionate share of new court commitments to prison (45 percent). As we will soon see, the proportional importance of drug offenders has increased considerably over the past few decades. Second, those admitted for parole violations are generally less likely to have been convicted for a violent offense, both because they tend to have shorter sentences and because they are less likely to have been convicted of a violent offense in the first place. Similarly, those being admitted for probation violations are less likely (relative to new court commitments) to have been convicted for violent offenses. Again, this is not surprising, because those convicted of violent felonies are relatively unlikely to receive probation in lieu of a prison sentence.

To analyze how prison admissions rates have changed over the past few decades we group prison admissions into two broad classes. First, we group together all people admitted for a new court commitment, a parole revocation involving a new felony commitment, or a probation violation. All such admissions are effectively entering prison for the first time for their most recent felony conviction. Thus, the amount of time they can expect to serve on the current admission equals the typical time served for the first commitment for inmates convicted of similar crimes. Second, we separately compare admissions rates for technical parole violators (those returned to custody without a new felony conviction). As we will soon see, while this category of admissions is numerically important, time served on admissions due to technical parole violations tends to be relatively short. We further disaggregate the first category of admissions into eleven categories defined by the most serious offense resulting in the current admission to prison.[4] Hence, throughout our discussion of state prison growth, we analyze admissions rates and time served for twelve mutually exclusive groups.

Figure 2.1 presents our estimates of state prison admissions rates in the United States at three points in time; 1984, 2004, and 2009.[5] The period between 1984 and 2004 coincides with enormous growth in the U.S. incarceration rate, while incarceration rates were relatively stable between 2004 and 2009 (see figure 1.1). For each year, admissions rates are expressed as state prison admissions per 100,000 U.S. residents, thus accounting for population growth over this period. Several general patterns stand out in figure 2.1. First, in most of the offense categories, the admissions rate increased considerably between 1984 and 2004. For example, the admissions rate in 2004 for rape or sexual assault was 1.64 times the comparable rate in 1984. Similarly, between 1984 and 2004 the admissions rates for aggravated assault and other violent crime increased by a factor of 2.65 and 4.21, respectively. Interest-

Figure 2.1   Admissions to Prison per 100,000 U.S. Residents, by
                Most Serious Offense, 1984, 2004, and 2009

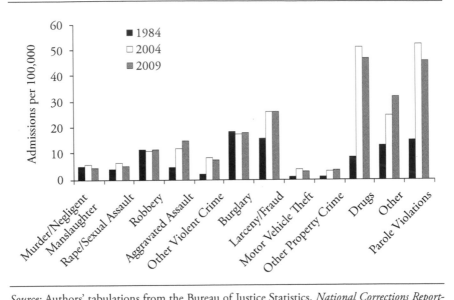

Source: Authors' tabulations from the Bureau of Justice Statistics, *National Corrections Report-ing Program* (various years).

ingly, there was only a small increase in the murder admissions rate and a slight decline in the admissions rate for robbery over this period. Both crimes are offenses that are more likely than not to result in a prison term for those convicted. Hence, the admissions rates for these crimes are more tightly tied to underlying crime trends than to changes in policy.

Turning to property crime, admissions rates for burglary were relatively stable between 1984 and 2004. However, admissions rates for larceny fraud, motor vehicle thefts, and other property crimes increased considerably (by factors of 1.66, 4.14, and 2.87, respectively).

By far the largest absolute and proportional increases in admissions rate were for drug offenses. While in 1984 drug-related prison admissions per 100,000 residents stood at 8.52, the rate had shot up to 51.10 by 2004 (increasing sixfold). There were also pronounced increases in admissions for other crimes (by a factor of 1.81) and for technical parole violations (by a factor of 3.49).

Overall the number of state prison admissions per 100,000 U.S. residents increased from 99 in 1984 to 221 in 2004. Between 2004 and 2009, total admissions remained constant. However, there were some slight changes within offense categories during this latter period—notably, a decline in drug admissions and parole violation admissions.

Higher Crime or an Increased Propensity to Punish with a Prison Spell?

The pronounced increase in prison admissions rates overall and within specific offense categories begs the question regarding the factors driving these increases. Of course, higher crime rates would mechanically result in higher prison admissions, holding all else equal, since the pool of offenders potentially eligible for a prison term would be larger. However, there are several links in the chain between the commission of a felony offense and a prison admission where policy has an impact on the likelihood that an offender will be sent to prison. For example, the amount of resources devoted to policing affects the likelihood that a given crime will be cleared by arrest. Moreover, sentencing policy is a factor in the likelihood that someone arrested and convicted will be punished with a prison term.

To delve deeper into the root causes of the increases in prison admissions, it is useful to formally articulate the relationship between prison admissions rates, crime and arrest rates, and the admissions rate to prison conditional on having been arrested. Specifically, if the prison admissions rate is defined as the number of admissions divided by the overall population, a bit of strategic manipulation of this ratio yields the following useful expression:

$$\frac{\text{Prison Admissions}}{\text{Population}} = \frac{\text{Crimes}}{\text{Population}} \times \frac{\text{Arrests}}{\text{Crimes}} \times \frac{\text{Prison Admissions}}{\text{Arrests}}$$

Or:

$$\text{Prison Admissions Rate} = \text{Crime Rate} \times \text{Clearance Rate} \times \text{Conditional Prison Admissions Rate}$$

This decomposition of the prison admissions rate for a specific criminal offense into the crime rate, the rate at which crimes of this sort are cleared by arrest, and the likelihood of being admitted to prison conditional on having committed and being arrested for this sort of crime sheds light on the exact sources of increasing prison admissions rates. If crime is driving the increases observed in figure 2.1, we should see higher crime rates in 2004 relative to

1984. Alternatively, if more effective policing (or just more policing) is driving admissions, we should see higher proportions of crimes cleared by arrest in 2004 relative to 1984. Finally, a greater propensity to punish offenders with prison due to changes in sentencing policy would lead to a higher ratio of prison admissions per arrest.

Table 2.2 presents our estimates of each of these component parts of prison admissions rates for specific crimes for 1984, 2004, and 2009. The table is limited to the seven felony offenses regularly reported by the U.S. Federal Bureau of Investigation (FBI) in the Uniform Crime Reports (UCR) series, as it is impossible to define an underlying crime rate for technical parole violations and drug offenses. (Nevertheless, we will analyze drug admissions in more detail shortly.) The first three columns present crime rates. Within each crime category, table 2.2 documents the enormous decline in crime rates between 1984 and 2004 and the continuing crime rate declines through 2009. The overall violent crime rate (the sum of the murder, rape, robbery, and aggravated assault rates) declined by roughly 20 percent between 1984 and 2009. Similarly, the overall property crime rate (the sum of the burglary, larceny or fraud, and motor vehicle theft rates) declined by 33 percent between 2004 and 2009. The lion's share of the decline in rates for both of these broad crime categories occurred between 1984 and 2004. Moreover, these declines occurred for each of the seven felony offenses listed in the table.

These crime trends suggest that increases in crime explain very little of the increase in prison admissions since the early 1980s. Of course, we might argue that the large increases in prison admissions account for the observed crime declines and that we might have experienced increases in crime rates if the incarceration rate had not increased. We return to this issue in chapter 3, where we present an overall assessment of the culpability of policy changes relative to criminal behavior in explaining the prison boom.

The second group of figures in table 2.2 present estimates of the ratio of the number of arrests for each crime to the number of crimes committed in the given calendar year.[6] Both the size and direction of change in these ratios vary across categories. For example, the clearance rates for murder as well as for sexual assault declined between 1984 and 2009, while the clearance rate for aggravated assault increased. For property crimes, clearance rates were relatively stable across the entire twenty-five-year period. In general, there is little support for the hypothesis that more effective policing or more policing is driving the large increases in incarceration.

Table 2.2   Decomposing Prison Admissions Rates for Part-1 Felony Offenses, 1984, 2004, and 2009

	Crimes per 100,000 Residents			Arrests per Crime			Prison Admissions per Arrest		
	1984	2004	2009	1984	2004	2009	1984	2004	2009
Murder and negligent manslaughter	7.9	5.5	5.0	1.05	0.73	0.81	0.59	1.39	1.15
Rape and sexual assault	35.7	32.4	28.7	0.38	0.22	0.24	0.28	0.89	0.76
Robbery	205.7	136.7	133.0	0.26	0.22	0.31	0.21	0.37	0.28
Aggravated assault	290.6	288.6	262.8	0.38	0.41	0.52	0.04	0.10	0.11
Burglary	1,265.5	730.3	716.3	0.13	0.11	0.14	0.11	0.22	0.19
Larceny and fraud	2,795.2	2,362.3	2,060.0	0.24	0.21	0.21	0.02	0.05	0.06
Motor vehicle theft	437.7	421.5	258.8	0.10	0.09	0.10	0.02	0.10	0.11

Source: Crime rates and arrest totals: FBI Uniform Crime Reports (1984, 2004, and 2009); prison admissions totals: authors' tabulations from the Bureau of Justice Statistics, *National Corrections Reporting Program* (1984, 2004a, and 2009).

Note: We apply the distribution of admissions across offense types for states participating in the NCRP to total admissions to state prison for the nation to arrive at offense-specific admissions rates.

This brings us to the conditional prison admissions rate. The final three columns in table 2.2 present our estimates of the ratio of prison admissions for specific crimes to arrests for specific crimes. We interpret this ratio as the probability that someone who has been caught for a specific crime will be sent to prison as a result. Here we observe enormous increases. For example, between 1984 and 2009 the conditional admissions rate for murder doubled, the rates for rape or sexual assault as well as aggravated assaults nearly tripled, and the conditional admissions rate for robbery increased by a factor of 1.33. We observe similar pronounced increases in the conditional prison admissions rate for property crimes: the rate nearly doubled for burglary, increased threefold for larceny or fraud, and increased more than fivefold for motor vehicle theft.

Table 2.2 creates a very strong impression. Crime rates are down. Arrests per crime exhibit little evidence of change since the early 1980s. However, conditional on being caught, one's chances of going to prison have increased tremendously. This last factor is determined, of course, by the adjudication outcomes and the types of punishments levied, and changes therein must be driven by changes in policy regarding what society deems to be offenses meriting a spell in prison. We postpone the enumeration of these policy changes until chapter 4. However, it is worthwhile noting the overwhelming role of this particular link in the causal chain in explaining our current relatively high prison admissions rates.

Drug Offenses

The largest relative and absolute increases in prison admissions rates have occurred for drug offenses. Unfortunately, it is impossible to decompose the drug prison admissions rate into its component crime rates, arrest rates, and conditional admissions rates, because there is no official count of reported drug crimes that we could use to estimate a "drug crime rate." Nonetheless, we can decompose drug offenses further by whether the offense involved trafficking, manufacturing, possession, and so on, and at least assess what has happened to arrest rates (equal to the product of the first two components of the equation in the previous section) and the rate at which offenders are admitted to prison conditional on being arrested. Of course, an increase in arrest rates can be driven by either more offending or enhanced policing efforts targeted at drug enforcement. Most conspicuously, the "War on Drugs" commenced, accelerated, and endured during the period that we are studying

Table 2.3   Comparison of Drug Arrest Rates, Drug Prison Admissions Rates, and Prison Admissions per Drug Arrest, 1984, 2004, and 2009

	1984	2004	2009
Drug arrests per 100,000 U.S. residents			
All drug offenses	300.4	596.0	541.9
Sales, manufacturing, or trafficking	67.8	111.4	101.1
Possession or nature unspecified	232.7	484.6	440.7
Drug-related prison admissions per 100,000 U.S. residents			
All drug offenses	8.5	51.1	47.0
Sales, manufacturing, or trafficking	4.5	21.2	19.5
Possession or nature unspecified	4.0	29.9	27.5
Drug-related prison admissions per drug-related arrest			
All drug offenses	0.03	0.09	0.09
Sales, manufacturing, or trafficking	0.07	0.19	0.19
Possession or nature unspecified	0.02	0.06	0.06

Source: Arrest data from the FBI Uniform Crime Reports (1984, 2004, and 2009) and prison admissions data from the Bureau of Justice Statistics, *National Corrections Reporting Program* (1984, 2004a, and 2009).

here, and thus we have reason to believe that higher arrest rates in large part reflect this policy and its various incarnations across the country.

Table 2.3 focuses on the determinants of drug-related prison admissions rates. We present figures for all drug offenses as well as for sales, manufacturing, and trafficking offenses and for drug offenses that are due to possession or where the nature of the offense is unspecified. The first set of figures show drug arrests per 100,000 U.S. residents for the three years 1984, 2004, and 2009. Unlike the seven felony offenses that we have already analyzed, here we observe very large increases in drug arrest rates: from 300 to 596 per 100,000 U.S. residents between 1984 and 2004 for all drug arrests. The majority of this increase is attributable to an increase in arrests for offenses classified as "possession/nature unspecified." However, the arrest rate for trafficking or manufacturing increased by roughly 65 percent over this period.

The second set of figures shows drug-related prison admissions rates for each year for all drug offenses and for our two subcategories of drug offenses. The numbers for all drug offenses correspond exactly to the admissions rates displayed in figure 2.1. The admissions rates by type of offense reveal an interesting reversal. In 1984 the admissions rate for trafficking- or manufacturing-related offenses was slightly higher than the admissions rate for possession offenses and offenses whose nature was unknown. By 2004 admissions rates for both categories had risen. However, the admissions rates for the relatively less serious drug offense category exceeded the admissions rate for the trafficking category (29.9 per 100,000 for possession or nature unspecified compared to 21.1 for sales, manufacturing, or trafficking). This pattern remained stable through 2009.

Most interesting are the patterns displayed in the last set of figures at the bottom of the table. The last three rows present our estimates of the number of drug-related prison admissions per drug-related arrest. Similar to our analysis of the serious violent and property offenses, we interpret these conditional admissions rates as the probability of being sent to prison conditional on being arrested for this type of offense. Here we see the pronounced effects of changes in sentencing policy in explaining the large increases in admissions rates for drug offenses. The ratio of admissions per arrest for all drug offenses tripled between 1984 and 2004 (from 0.03 to 0.09) and remained stable thereafter. Admissions per arrest for sales, manufacturing, or trafficking offenses increased by twelve percentage points, from 7 to 19 percent. Although admissions per arrest for offenses classified as possession or nature unspecified were notably lower in each year than the conditional admissions rate for trafficking offenses, the conditional admissions rate for these less serious offenses tripled. Moreover, given the much higher arrest rates for these relatively less serious drug offenses, this tripling in the conditional admissions rate translates into a large increase in the number of admissions per capita.

What About Parolees?

Perhaps the most difficult category of prison admissions to disaggregate and analyze are those admitted to prison for technical parole violations. Unlike drug offenses and all of the other offense categories we study here, technical parole violations do not require a felony offense to trigger the arrest and subsequent process leading to a prison admission. Spot checks by parole officers, instructions to law enforcement to search all parolees stopped for whatever reason, missed appointments, positive drug tests, and many other such factors may result in the revocation of one's conditional release and a return to prison. Moreover, changes in enforcement levels and the stringency with which violations are policed and punished depend on parole staffing levels, caseloads per officer, and the general degree of risk aversion among parole officers. It is nearly impossible to gauge the levels of such violations among parolees and the stringency with which such violations are sanctioned by the authorities.

Nonetheless, it is possible to make a few general points about the more than tripling of the prison admissions rates for technical parole violators. In general, parolees can be and are often returned to custody for violations that would not result in a prison term for someone who is not on parole. Hence, a larger proportion of the non-institutionalized population on parole translates directly into higher prison admissions rates for parole violations. Indeed, the size of the parole population has increased in conjunction with the prison population. Between 1984 and 2004, the population of adults on parole increased from 250,138 to 682,261. Expressed per 100,000 U.S. residents, this represents an increase in the parole rate from 106 to 233. The sheer increase in the size of the parole population certainly accounts for a portion of the increase in prison admissions for parole violations.

Holding constant the size of the parole population, policy regarding the manner in which prisoners are released may also contribute to subsequent admissions for technical parole violations. Many states have greatly curtailed the discretion of parole boards in making decisions regarding early release. As a result, fewer inmates are released as the result of a parole board review than in years past, while more are released through what is known as "mandatory parole": inmates being released according to an administrative schedule based on sentence length and good time credits earned. This shift is documented in figure 2.2, which displays the proportion of prison releases for 1984 and 2004 occurring under the discretion of a parole board, occurring under a mandatory parole regime, being triggered by the expiration of a sentence, or occurring through some other form of conditional release. A considerably smaller proportion of inmates were released through a parole board's decision in 2004 than in 1984 (a decline from 46 to 22 percent). Conversely, the proportions being released through mandatory parole or the expiration of their sentences increased.[7]

A key issue in the debate regarding the relative merits of discretionary versus mandatory parole is the question of whether affording discretion to corrections authorities to decide who and when to release leads to better postrelease outcomes. To the extent that parole boards are good at distinguishing those at low risk of reoffending from those at high risk, or that in-

Figure 2.2   Comparison of the Distribution of Releases from State
                Prison, by Type of Release, 1984 and 2004

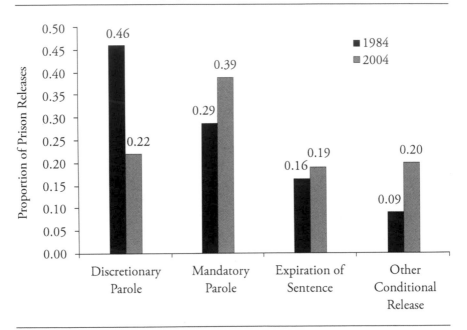

Source: Authors' tabulations from the Bureau of Justice Statistics, *National Corrections Reporting Program* (various years).

mates make more effort to rehabilitate in order to win early release from a
parole board, the shift away from discretionary parole may lead to higher
parole failure rates. Indeed, parole failure rates (as gauged by the proportion
of parolees returned to custody over the course of a year) have increased since
1984. Figure 2.3 compares the proportion of parolees who successfully completed their parole term, who were returned to custody, or who unsuccessfully
exited parole owing to other causes, such as absconding from authorities or
dying, for 1984 and 2004 (Bureau of Justice Statistics 1986b, 2005a). The
proportion who successfully completed parole terms declined by nine percentage points, while the proportion returned to custody increased by seven
percentage points, and the proportion with unsuccessful outcomes for other
reasons increased by six percentage points.

In chapter 4, we discuss in greater detail the effects of the broad shift from
discretionary to mandatory parole and what current research tells us about the
types of release from prison and the subsequent likelihood that former inmates

Figure 2.3   Comparison of Transition Rates Out of Parole, 1984 and 2004

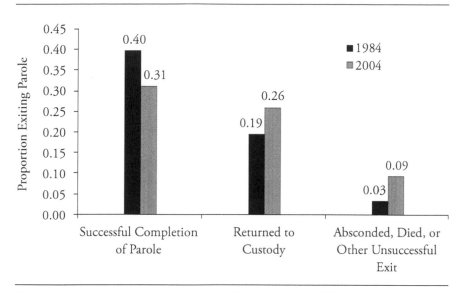

Source: Authors' tabulations based on Bureau of Justice Statistics (1986b, 2005a).

will succeed in reentering non-institutional society. For the moment, however, we note that both the increase in the absolute and relative size of the parole population and the higher failure rate relative to past years drive the large increases in admissions for parole violation that we have documented here.

Admissions and the Changing Composition of the Prison Population

The large increases in prison admissions rates, coupled with the disproportionate contribution of drug offenses and other relatively less serious offenses to this increase, have altered the internal composition of the prison population. Figure 2.4 shows the distribution of prison inmates across our twelve offense categories for the years 1986 and 2004.[8] The proportion of inmates serving time for violent offense declined from 53 percent in 1986 to 46 percent in 2004. There was a larger decline in the proportion serving time for a property offense (from 28 to 17 percent). In contrast, the proportion of inmates serving time for a drug offense increased from 8 to 20 percent, while the proportion serving time for other crimes doubled from 6 to 12 percent.

Despite the fact that prison admissions rates for parole violations in 2004

Figure 2.4   Distribution of State Prison Inmates, by Offense,
Resulting in the Current Incarceration Spell, 1986
and 2004

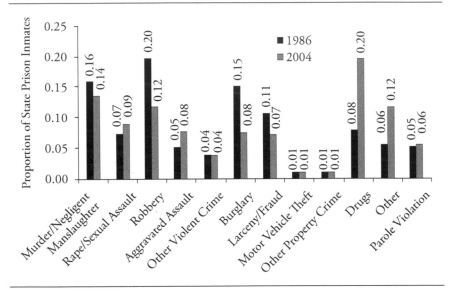

Source: Authors' tabulations of national inmate surveys conducted by U.S. Census Bureau.

were three-and-a-half times the admissions rates for 1984, the proportion of prisoners serving time for a parole violation increased only slightly (from 5 to 6 percent, or by one percentage point). This relatively modest contribution reflects the fact that technical parole violators tend to serve very short spells for their violation, and indeed, the length of these spells actually declined slightly over the period in question. This fact, combined with pronounced increases in the amount of time that those admitted for more serious offenses could expect to serve, kept the contribution of parole violators to the average daily population of prisons relatively modest.

To summarize, prison admissions rates have increased considerably over the past few decades, with relatively modest increases for violent crimes and property crimes and pronounced increases for drug offenses, parole violations, and other less serious crimes. These increases cannot be attributed to higher crime or higher clearances of crimes by arrest and thus are driven almost entirely by an increase in the likelihood of going to prison conditional on being caught for committing specific crimes. Returning to our analogy of the size of a university's student body, the change in prison admissions rates is equivalent to increasing the admissions rates into all of the degree programs in our hypothetical university (with larger increases in some programs relative to others). Such increases certainly will cause increases in the nation's steady-state incarceration rate.

Of course, the other key factor influencing the size of the prison population is the effective length of prison sentences, to which we turn in the next section.

DOCUMENTING TRENDS IN TIME SERVED

Gauging time served and how it has changed over the years is a tricky business. Ideally, we would have access to longitudinal data on those admitted to prison and we would be able to observe actual entry and exit dates. Even with such data, however, we would still face the problem of estimating time served for those serving very long sentences and for those sentenced to life. This limitation is especially problematic if we want to gauge the amount of time that inmates recently admitted to prison will eventually serve. Regardless, there currently are no publicly available longitudinal data sets that would permit such analysis.

An alternative would be to analyze how sentences meted out have changed over time: presumably changes in sentence length would be indicative of changes in the amount of time an inmate could expect to serve for a specific offense. This too is a problematic strategy. First, the sentences of offenders sentenced under indeterminate sentencing regimes include a minimum sentence and a maximum sentence, and the difference between the two is often quite large. The state's parole board exerts great influence in determining the length of these inmates' actual prison spells, which may bear little resemblance to either the maximum or minimum sentences. Although fewer and fewer offenders are sentenced under indeterminate sentencing, this was the dominant sentencing regime at the beginning of the period that we study in this chapter.

Even in determinate sentencing regimes, actual time served is not perfectly related to the official sentence: the strength of the link between these two variables depends on state policy choices, which vary from state to state. For example, many states have truth-in-sentencing laws requiring that inmates serve a minimum fraction of their sentence. Not only does the existence of such laws vary from state to state, but so does the statutory minimum fraction. Moreover, states vary with regard to rules governing good time credits and other administrative formulas that ultimately determine the date of earliest possible release. Finally, there is some evidence that judges may have responded to truth-in-sentencing laws by adjusting sentences downward in an attempt to hold constant actual time served. In some of our earlier research (Raphael and Stoll 2009), we found that maximum sentences declined considerably during the period when state after state enacted truth-in-sentencing statutes. We also found, however, that actual time served increased during the same period.

Fortunately, there is a simple indirect way to estimate actual time served for different inmates. To illustrate, let's revisit our student body example. When our university's student population is in steady state, one-fourth of the undergraduates (the seniors) will leave each year and be replaced by new freshmen. Alternatively stated, the annual exit rate when our undergraduate population is in steady state is one-fourth. A simple rule of thumb for estimating time spent earning the undergraduate degree is to take the reciprocal of the exit rate. Hence, if one-fourth of the students graduate each year, the typical undergraduate spends four years at the university. Similarly, if half of the master's students graduate each year, then the master's degree takes two years.

We can apply this rule of thumb to prison populations. If we know the number of inmates released each year, the controlling offenses for these inmates, and the base population of prison inmates, we can estimate time served by calculating the exit rate and then taking the reciprocal.[9] In table 2.4, we present such estimates for our twelve offense categories. Here we present figures only for 1984 and 2004 because 2004 is the most recent year for which the U.S. Census Bureau conducted a national survey of prison inmates. Since we need these data to estimate the base prison population by offense, we are constrained to studying the period from 1984 to 2004. Nonetheless, we have already documented a stabilizing of the prison population around 2005, and thus the results for 2004 are likely to be representative of more recent years.

Table 2.4 reveals pronounced increases in the amount of time that someone admitted to prison can expect to serve. We observe the largest increases among inmates who have committed violent felony offenses (murder, rape, robbery, and aggravated assault). For example, in 1984 an inmate convicted of murder or manslaughter could expect to serve 9.2 years. By 2004 this figure had increased to 14.27 years. For those convicted of a rape or sexual assault, time served increased from 5.05 years in 1984 to 8.09 years in 2004. Concurrently, time served for robbery and time served for aggravated assault increased by 1.5 and 0.9 years, respectively. We observe a decline in time served in only one violent crime category: "other." Given that this category

Table 2.4   Comparison of Expected Value of Time Served, by Crime Type, 1984 and 2004

Offense	1984	2004	Ratio 2004/1984
Murder and negligent manslaughter	9.20	14.27	1.55
Rape and sexual assault	5.05	8.09	1.60
Robbery	3.51	5.04	1.44
Aggravated assault	2.20	3.12	1.42
Other violent crime	3.56	2.29	0.64
Burglary	1.62	1.95	1.21
Larceny and fraud	1.26	1.31	1.04
Motor vehicle theft	1.93	1.51	0.78
Other property crime	1.11	1.42	1.28
Drugs	1.87	1.75	0.94
Other	0.98	2.09	2.13
Parole violations	0.78	0.47	0.61

Source: Authors' tabulations from the Bureau of Justice Statistics, *National Corrections Reporting Program* (1983, 1984, 1985, 2003, 2004a); Bureau of Justice Statistics, *Survey of Inmates in State and Federal Correctional Facilities* (2004b); Bureau of Justice Statistics, *Survey of Inmates in State Correctional Facilities* (1986).

Notes: Time served was estimated by calculating the inverse of the release probability from prison for each offense. For 2004, we first summed all releases recorded in the 2003 and 2004 NCRP release files. We then estimated the distribution of releases by offense and applied the distribution to the average annual releases for the period 2003 to 2005. Similarly, for 1984, we summed all recorded NCRP releases for 1983, 1984, and 1985, calculated the distribution of releases across offense categories, and then applied the distribution to average annual releases from state prison for 1983 to 1985. We tabulated base prison populations by offense with data from the 2004 Survey of Inmates in State and Federal Correctional Facilities and the 1986 Survey of Inmates in State Correctional Facilities. We used these two microdata sets to estimate the distribution of the stock of inmates in these two years by offense. We then applied these distributions to the average state prison total for 1983 to 1985 and 2003 to 2005. The 1986 survey is the closest inmate survey to the starting year of 1984 for the study period.

accounts for a relatively small share of prison inmates (4 percent in 2004), the overall impression from table 2.4 is that inmates convicted of a violent offense are serving much longer prison spells today than in years past.

With the exception of aggravated assault, our finding that admissions rates for violent felonies were relatively stable between 1984 and 2004 suggests that admissions for such crimes did not contribute to growth in incarceration over this time period. However, the increases in time served certainly contributed to prison growth. When all is said and done, longer sentences for a given offense translate into more inmates serving time for that offense in the steady state. In the following chapter, we directly estimate the contribution of higher admissions relative to longer prison spells in explaining the growth in U.S. incarceration rates.

Table 2.4 reveals more modest increases in time served by inmates convicted of property crimes. For example, time served for burglary increased from 1.62 to 1.95 years between 1984 and 2004. The comparable figure for larceny or fraud is an increase from 1.26 to 1.31 years, while time served for other property crimes increased from 1.11 to 1.42 years. Although time served for motor vehicle theft declined slightly, inmates convicted of this crime accounted for a relatively small portion of inmates doing time for a property offense. Hence, for most inmates convicted of a property crime, time served increased over the twenty-year period under study.

Time served in state prison for drug offenses remained relatively stable (with the typical inmate serving slightly less than two years in both 1984 and 2004). Our analysis of admissions rates suggests, however, that the composition of the population of drug offenders admitted to prison has shifted toward less serious offenses. Hence, this stability in time served probably reflects the opposing effects of a shift in the composition of the population of drug offenders sentenced to prison toward less serious crime coupled with an increase in sentence length and effective time served. We observe a decline in time served for parole violators, from three-quarters of a year to half a year. This finding, frankly, is not surprising, since the composition of the population of those on parole has shifted toward less serious offenders (as has the composition of the prison population and prison admissions).

To summarize, an offender admitted to state prison today for a given offense can generally expect to serve more time than he would have served had he been convicted in years past. This is especially true for violent offenses, which show the largest proportional and absolute increases in expected time served, but we also find increases in time served among those convicted of property crimes.

COMPARING HIGH- AND LOW-INCARCERATION STATES

So far we have focused our attention on what distinguishes the present from the past. We have seen that we are currently admitting people to state prisons

Figure 2.5   Scatter Plot of State Incarceration Rates in 2007
               Against State Incarceration Rates in 1977

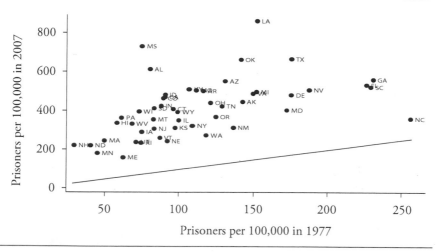

Source: Authors' tabulations from Bureau of Justice Statistics, *National Prisoner Statistics* data
(various years).
Note: Solid line is a forty-five-degree line.

at rates that far exceed those of past decades. In addition, we incarcerate those
we send to prison for relatively longer spells.

We could focus solely on the present and ask what distinguishes high-
incarceration states from low-incarceration states. It is certainly the case that
every state in the nation has experienced sizable increases in incarceration
rates. This is illustrated in figure 2.5, which presents a scatter plot of each
state's 2007 incarceration rate against its incarceration rate in 1977. The figure also displays a forty-five-degree line showing all points where the value on
the vertical axis equals the value on the horizontal axis. Any data point lying
above the line represents a state whose incarceration rate has increased over
this period. This is the case for all states.

Nonetheless, there was still a fair degree of heterogeneity in state incarceration rates in 2007. For example, state incarceration rates ranged from 159 per
100,000 (Maine) to 865 per 100,000 (Louisiana). There was also a big difference between the incarceration rate of the state at the twenty-fifth percentile
of this distribution (Kansas, with a 2007 incarceration rate of 312) and the
state at the seventy-fifth percentile (Arkansas, with a 2007 rate of 502).
Hence, in addition to comparing admissions and time served at two points in

Figure 2.6   Distribution of 2005 Incarceration Rates for the Twenty-
             Two States Reporting Information on Prisoners in the
             2005 NCRP

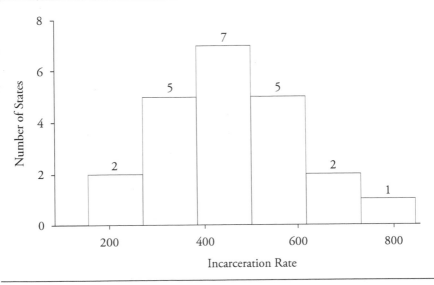

Source: Authors' tabulations from the Bureau of Justice Statistics, *National Corrections Report-ing Program* (2005a).

time, we can also make these comparisons for states with relatively high and low incarceration rates.

Unfortunately, data on incarceration, prison admissions, and prison releases by offense and for individual states are incomplete. For 2005, however, the necessary data are available for twenty-two states. For this subset, we classify the eleven states with the highest incarceration rates as high-incarceration states and the eleven states with the lowest incarceration rates as low-incarceration states and compare these states along a number of dimensions.[10] Figure 2.6 displays the distribution of incarceration rates for this subset of twenty-two states. Fortunately for us, the range of values is comparable to the range of values for all states combined.

Before comparing admissions rates and time served, it is instructive to analyze how incarceration rates for specific crimes vary across states. To do so, we tabulated offense-specific incarceration rates using five broad categories: violent crime, property crime, drug crime, parole violations, and serving time for other crimes. Figure 2.7 displays the distributions of these offense-specific incarceration rates across the twenty-two states. The incarceration rate with

Figure 2.7   Empirical Distributions of the 2005 Offense-Specific
Incarceration Rates for the Twenty-Two States Reporting
Data in the 2005 NCRP

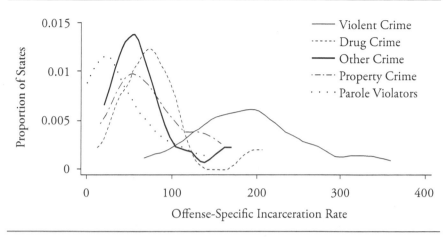

Source: Authors' tabulations from the Bureau of Justice Statistics, *National Correctional Reporting Program* (2005a).

by far the highest average, as well as the largest variance, is that for violent crime. This finding alone suggests that variation in violent crime incarceration explains a fair portion of the differences in incarceration rates that we observe across states. It also accords with our analysis in chapter 3, where we also show that enhanced sentencing for violent offenders is a principal driver of growth in state incarceration rates.

Property crime rates and drug crime rates also vary considerably across states. Incarceration rates for parole violations are generally quite low for all states, though a few states incarcerate technical parole violators at a rate equal to the overall incarceration rate in the United States prior to the current prison boom. However, the lower average and lower variance for parole incarceration rates means that this particular category does not contribute substantially to cross-state differences.

We can more formally assess the relative contribution of incarceration for specific crimes to cross-state difference in incarceration rates through a decomposition of variance. Specifically, given that a specific state's incarceration rate equals the sum of the incarceration rates for specific offenses (violent, property, drugs, and so on), cross-state variation in incarceration rates can be decomposed into cross-state variation caused by state differences in incarceration rates for specific crimes as well as a series of components reflecting the

Table 2.5   Contribution to Cross-State Variance in the Overall
Incarceration Rate of Incarceration Rates for Specific
Offense Categories and the Covariance in Incarceration
Rates Across Offense Categories, 2005

	Violent Crime	Property Crime	Drugs	Parole Violation	Other and Unknown
Violent crime	0.21	—	—	—	—
Property crime	0.17	0.07	—	—	—
Drugs	0.13	0.12	0.09	—	—
Parole violation	0.05	0.03	0.04	0.06	—
Other and unknown	−0.02	−0.01	−0.01	−0.01	0.07

Source: Stock data from the Bureau of Justice Statistics, *National Corrections Reporting Program* (2005a).

Notes: Figures in the table sum to 1. The figures pertain to the twenty-two states that reported stock data for prison inmates in the 2005 NCRP. These states accounted for 75 percent of state prison inmates in 2005.

degree to which offense-specific incarceration rates co-occur with one another (for example, the degree to which states with higher violent crime incarceration rates also have higher property crime rates).[11]

Table 2.5 presents a matrix displaying the results from decomposing cross-state variation in incarceration rates into the components attributable to variation in offense-specific rates as well as the components attributable to covariance across states in different crime-specific incarceration rates. Figures on the diagonal of the table show the proportional contribution of variance in a crime-specific incarceration rate. Figures below the diagonal show the relative contribution of various covariance values. The table reveals that cross-state heterogeneity in violent crime incarceration rates is by far the largest contributor to cross-state variation in overall incarceration (accounting for one-fifth). However, states with high violent crime incarceration rates also have high property and drug crime incarceration rates. There is also a positive association between property crime incarceration rates and drug crime incarceration rates, as well as positive yet relatively weak covariance between all of the above and parole incarceration rates. Notably, variance in parole incarceration rates explains little of the cross-state heterogeneity, probably because, even though states differ greatly in admissions rates for parole violators, the expected prison spell length for parole violators is generally quite short.

An interesting way to summarize the patterns in table 2.5 is to ask what proportion of the total variation in state incarceration rates can be explained by variation in offense-specific rates as opposed to the degree of covariation across offense-specific rates. Adding the figures on the diagonal reveals that roughly half of the differences we observe across states can be attributed to differences in incarceration rates for specific types of offenses; this finding suggests that the remaining half is explained by the generally positive association between incarceration rates of different types. In other words, although the specifics of crime and sentencing for violent crime, drug crimes, and so on, distinguish high-incarceration from low-incarceration states, states with a tough sentencing policy for one type of crime tend to have tough sentencing policies for all types of crime.

Finally, we compare prison admissions rates and expected time served in high- versus low-incarceration states. Figure 2.8 displays the ratio of either the expected time served or the prison admissions rate in high-crime states to low-crime states for each of the twelve offense categories. Values in excess of 1.00

Figure 2.8   **Comparison of Time Served and Prison Admissions Rates, by Offense, for High-Incarceration States Relative to Low-Incarceration States, 2005**

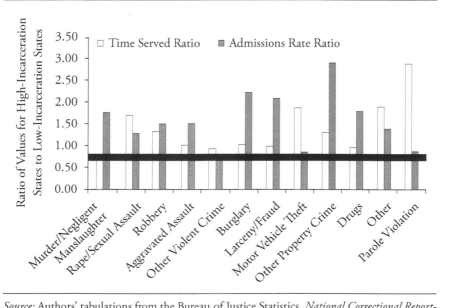

Source: Authors' tabulations from the Bureau of Justice Statistics, *National Correctional Reporting Program* (2005a).

Note: Bars equal ratio of high-incarceration-state average to low-incarceration-state average.

(indicated with the thick horizontal bar) indicate tougher policy in the high-incarceration states. The figure reveals generally higher time served in high-incarceration states, though expected time served for murder stands out as a notable exception. In nearly all comparisons, prison admissions rates are substantially higher in high-incarceration states relative to low-incarceration states.

THE FEDERAL PRISON SYSTEM

The federal government administers the largest and fastest-growing prison system in the United States. In 1980 roughly 24,000 inmates were under the jurisdiction of the Federal Bureau of Prisons. By 2000 this population had increased to 145,416, and by 2010 the population had increased further to roughly 210,000 (more than an eightfold increase since 1980). The federal prison population has grown at a rate that far exceeds that of the U.S. resident population as well as that of the population of state prisoners. In 1980 there were 11 federal prison inmates per 100,000 U.S. residents. By 2010 this rate had increased over sixfold to 67 per 100,000. Today 13 percent of the U.S. prison population is accounted for by federal prisoners—that is to say, roughly one of every eight prison inmates is doing time in a federal prison.

The federal prison system differs from the fifty state correctional systems in a number of ways. First, federal prisoners are arrested for violating federal law, and specific punishments are often set by federal legislation. Recent decades have witnessed a drift toward greater "federalization" of criminal activity: offenses that would have been adjudicated in state courts in the past are increasingly being handled in federal court and prosecuted by U.S. attorneys (U.S. Sentencing Commission 2011). We discuss this development in detail in chapter 4.

Second, there is a tighter association between sentence length and time served in the federal system than in many of the state prison systems, especially in recent years. Although the federal system does permit sentence reductions for serving "good time," such good time credits are relatively modest and applied across the board for sentences of varying severity. There is no early conditional release for good behavior, and nearly all inmates serve their complete sentences. In fact, the overwhelming majority of released federal prisoners are released unconditionally (as their sentences less any good time credits expire).

Third, while there are federal prison inmates serving time for all different types of crime, the distribution of prison inmates in the federal system largely reflects the mandates of federal law enforcement agencies. For example, drug offenders are a very large fraction of federal prisoners. Indeed, an entire federal agency, the Drug Enforcement Agency (DEA), is devoted to enforcing federal law prohibiting drug trafficking. Similarly, the enforcement of immigration law is a federal responsibility, under the purview of U.S. Immigration and Customs Enforcement, and it is not surprising that those doing time for immigration offenses are disproportionately represented in the federal prison population.

Finally, sentencing in federal courts across the country is governed by sentencing guidelines created and maintained by the U.S. Sentencing Commission, which defines, produces, and maintains a series of sentencing ranges that depend on the severity of an offense as well as the extent of a particular offender's criminal history record. Incorporated into these guidelines are any legislatively mandated mandatory minimum punishments (for example, a minimum of five years for possession of more than five grams of crack cocaine). Until recently, federal judges were bound by the sentencing ranges set by the U.S. Sentencing Commission, with few avenues for departing from those guidelines. We postpone our discussion of these policy changes until chapter 4, but here it is worthwhile to note the uniform and relatively structured regime within which federal sentences were handed down during the time period under study. It is also worth noting that the composition of the population of federal prison inmates and changes in that composition are linked quite closely to specific pieces of federal legislation often targeted at sentence enhancements for specific offenses.

In recent decades, the composition of the population of federal inmates has changed dramatically. Figure 2.9 shows a breakdown of the federal prison population in 1974, 1989, and 2004. To foster comparability to the earliest year in this period, we are forced to aggregate offenses into relatively broad categories. There are very clear trends in the data. Between 1974 and 2004, there was a large increase in the percentage of federal prison inmates serving time for drug offenses, from 28 to 55 percent. There was also a large increase in the proportion incarcerated for weapons offenses. Not surprisingly, these two offense categories have fairly stiff mandatory minimum penalties, enacted by federal legislation during the late 1980s and 1990s. In general, the percentage of federal inmates serving time for violent crimes was small relative to what we observe for state prisons, and it was stable through time. The percentage of federal inmates doing time for fraud and other property crimes dropped dramatically, from 22 percent in 1974 to 4 percent in 2004.

Table 2.6 provides a more detailed breakdown of the distribution of federal

Figure 2.9   Distribution of Federal Prison Inmates, by Offense
                Categories, 1974, 1989, and 2004

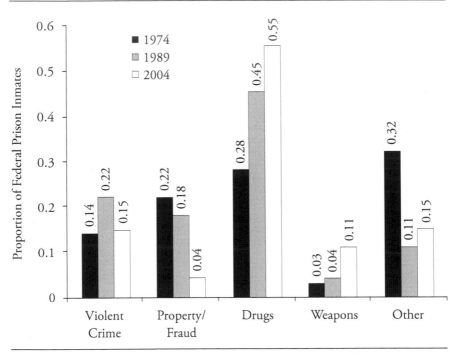

Source: Authors' compilation. 1974: Werner Cahalan (1986); 1989: Snell (1993); 2004: authors' tabulations from the Bureau of Justice Statistics, *Survey of Inmates in State and Federal Corrections Facilities* (2004b).

prisoners by offense for 2000 and 2010. Most federal inmates doing time for violent crime are convicted for robbery. Few who are prosecuted for homicide are convicted in federal court. Similarly, property crime offenders in federal prison tend to be those who have committed a fraud or embezzlement offense. One detail that stands out in table 2.6 is the relatively large proportion of federal inmates doing time for an immigration offense (11 percent in 2010). As we will soon see, there has been explosive growth in the last decade in the proportion of criminal suspects handled by U.S. attorneys for this offense category.

Similar to our analysis of state incarceration trends, understanding growth in the federal prison population requires a careful examination of changes in prison admissions as well as changes in expected time served for those admitted to prison. Relative to our study of what happened in the states, there are

Table 2.6   Distribution of Federal Prison Inmates, by Most Serious Offense, 2000 and 2010

Offense	2000	2010
All offenses	100%	100%
Violent offenses		
Homicide	1	1
Robbery	7	4
Other violent crime	2	2
Property offenses		
Burglary	0	0
Fraud	6	4
Other property crime	2	1
Drug offenses	56	51
Public-order offenses		
Immigration	10	11
Weapons	8	15
Other	6	8
Other unspecified	1	1

Source: Authors' tabulations based on Guerino, Harrison, and Sabol (2011).

several advantages to studying the federal system. First, the Bureau of Justice Statistics regularly produces detailed reports on the case processing flow of criminal suspects handled by U.S. attorneys that are comparable across time and quite detailed regarding the various steps between arrest, conviction, and sentencing. These data permit us to create a detailed portrait of the key contributors to federal prison admissions and changes in them over time. Another advantage is that sentences are more closely linked to time served in the federal system, a fact that greatly simplifies the task of gauging how time served has changed.

We begin with an analysis of the key rates determining admissions into the federal prison system. In our discussion of state prisons, we noted that the admissions rate into state prisons is given by the product of the crime rate, arrests per crime, and prison admissions per arrest, and we documented changes in each of these rates over time for specific offenses. The available data for the federal system permit a more detailed analysis of the admissions process at the midpoint of the case processing flow between crime commission and prison admission. However, the structure of the data requires that we aggregate two rates at the start of the flow. Specifically, for a given crime resulting in federal prison admission, the prison admissions rate—the number of people admitted to federal prison per U.S. resident—can be expressed as:

$$\frac{Crimes}{Population} \cdot \frac{Arrests}{Crimes} \cdot \frac{Prosecutions}{Arrests} \cdot \frac{Convictions}{Prosecutions} \cdot \frac{Prison\ Admissions}{Convictions}$$

Alternatively stated, the admissions rate into federal prisons is determined by the crime rate, the likelihood of being arrested conditional on committing a crime, the proportion of arrests resulting in prosecution, the conviction rates, and the proportion of the convicted sentenced to prison. By necessity, we must aggregate the first two terms to the number of federal arrests per U.S. resident, as there are no available crime statistics for federal offenses that would permit the estimation of base crime rates. However, we are able to decompose the remaining process from arrest to prison admission with federal data, a big improvement over what is feasible with data on state prison admissions.

Table 2.7 presents estimates of the rate at which criminal suspects are received by U.S. attorneys (our gauge of federal arrests per 100,000 U.S. residents), as well as the proportion of suspects prosecuted in U.S. district courts (the prosecution rate). For each of these links in the prison admissions chain, figures are presented for 1985, 2000, and 2009. Between 1985 and 2009, the federal prison admissions rate increased by a factor of 2.25, from 8 admissions per 100,000 to 18. Concurrently, the rate at which suspects were received by U.S. attorneys was roughly stable, if not declining, for property and violent offenses. However, this rate increased substantially for drug offenses, weapons offenses, and immigration offenses, with the largest absolute increases for drug offenses. Between 2000 and 2009, the table reveals a dramatic increase in the number of arrests for immigration offenses, from 6 per 100,000 to 28. The rates for all other offenses over this nine-year period exhibited relative stability.

The prosecution rate figures reveal little evidence of systematic change in the rate at which U.S. attorneys prosecuted criminal suspects. Hence, while part of the increase in admissions rates can be attributed to more arrests for drug, weapons, and immigration offenses, there is little evidence of a role for an enhanced propensity to prosecute.

By contrast, conviction rates increase discretely, as does the proportion of

Table 2.7 Criminal Suspects Processed by U.S. Attorneys and the Proportion of Criminal Suspects Criminally Prosecuted, by Offense, 1985, 2000, and 2009

Offense Type	Suspects in Criminal Matters Received by U.S. Attorneys per 100,000 U.S. Residents			Proportion of Suspects Prosecuted in U.S. District Court		
	1985	2000	2009	1985	2000	2009
Violent crime	2	2	2	0.682	0.603	0.581
Property, fraud	11	9	8	0.550	0.537	0.499
Other property crime	2	1	1	0.558	0.478	0.521
Drugs	8	14	12	0.803	0.781	0.767
Weapons	1	3	4	0.746	0.648	0.690
Immigration	3	6	28	0.340	0.833	0.319
Regulatory public-order crime	3	2	2	0.392	0.319	0.378
Other public-order crime	9	7	6	0.560	0.335	0.595

Source: Authors' compilation based on Bureau of Justice Statistics (1990, 2002a) and Motivans (2012).

Note: Prosecution rates pertain to all cases concluded in the corresponding fiscal year.

the convicted who are sentenced to a prison term. Table 2.8 presents figures for the proportion of criminal defendants convicted in federal court as well as the proportion of those convicted who were sent to prison, by offense. Again, we present figures for 1985, 2000, and 2009. For all offenses, there were discrete increases in the proportion of defendants found guilty between 1985 and 2000, and stability thereafter. For example, between 1985 and 2000 the percentage of drug defendants found guilty increased from 81.6 percent to 91.2 percent, while the percentage convicted among defendants charged with violent crimes increased from 82.7 percent to 90.3 percent. In fact, across all offenses the conviction rates increased by seven to ten percentage points. Of course, this occurred primarily through guilty pleas, since relatively small proportions of criminal defendants in both the federal and state systems actually go to trial.

Table 2.8 reveals an even larger increase in the proportion of convicted defendants who were sentenced to prison. Although there was little change for those convicted of violent offenses, the percentages sent to prison among those convicted of fraudulent property crimes increased by twenty-two percentage points, from 40.2 percent in 1985 to 62.8 percent in both 2000 and 2009. Between 1985 and 2000, the likelihood of being sent to federal prison increased by fifteen percentage points for those convicted of drug offenses, by twenty-seven percentage points for those convicted of a weapons offense, and by twenty-six percentage points for those convicted of an immigration offense. Again, the figures remained stable after 2000.

Clearly, higher conviction rates, a greater propensity to send convicted felons to prison, and higher arrest rates for drug and weapons offenses are a big part of the story behind the more than doubling of federal prison admissions rates. However, while admissions roughly doubled, the federal prison population increased by more than sixfold. Hence, changes in case processing outcomes through admissions to prison can only partially explain federal prison growth. The remainder must be attributable to changes in sentences and, by extension, time served.

Table 2.9 presents average sentences (in months) for those convicted of a federal crime and sentenced to prison, by offense. Focusing on the change between 1985 and 2009, there is little evidence of stiffer sentences for those convicted in federal court of violent and property offenses. In fact, average sentences for violent crimes declined by about 12 percent over this time period. For drug, weapons, and immigration offenses, however, there were pro-

Table 2.8 Proportion of Suspects Prosecuted in U.S. District Courts Who Are Convicted and Proportion of Those Convicted Who Are Sentenced to Prison, by Offense, 1985, 2000, and 2009

Offense Type	Proportion of Defendants Convicted			Proportion of Convicted Offenders Sentenced to Prison		
	1985	2000	2009	1985	2000	2009
Violent crime	0.827	0.903	0.918	0.813	0.831	0.831
Property, fraud	0.844	0.910	0.899	0.402	0.628	0.628
Other property crime	0.776	0.909	0.901	0.429	0.497	0.497
Drugs	0.816	0.912	0.928	0.750	0.904	0.904
Weapons	0.812	0.884	0.922	0.637	0.910	0.910
Immigration	0.880	0.959	0.969	0.574	0.834	0.834
Regulatory public-order crime	0.777	0.866	0.884	0.312	0.474	0.474
Other public-order crime	0.726	0.876	0.899	0.259	0.804	0.804

Source: Authors' compilation based on Bureau of Justice Statistics (1990, 2002) and Motivans (2012).

Note: Conviction rates and the proportion sentenced to prison pertain to all cases concluded in the corresponding fiscal year.

Table 2.9   Average Sentence Length (in Months) for Offenders
Convicted and Sentenced to Federal Prison, 1985,
2000, and 2009

Offense Type	1985	2000	2009
Violent crime	131.2	86.5	115.8
Property, fraud	30.6	22.5	31.9
Other property crime	34.4	33.2	35.3
Drugs	57.5	75.5	83.7
Weapons	38.8	91.4	87.2
Immigration	14.4	29.5	21.4
Regulatory public-order crime	42.2	28.4	36
Other public-order crime	32.7	43.3	71.3

Source: Authors' compilation based on Bureau of Justice Statistics (1990, 2002) and Motivans (2012).
Note: Sentence lengths pertain to all cases concluded in the corresponding fiscal year.

nounced increases in average sentence length. In 1985 the average convicted drug offender who was sentenced to prison received a sentence of fifty-eight months. By 2009 this figure had increased 46 percent to eighty-four months. The average sentence for weapons offenders sent to prison increased by 125 percent relative to the 1985 value, while sentences for immigration offenses increased by 49 percent. Similar to the changes in conviction rates and the proportions of the convicted sent to prison, most of these changes occurred between 1985 and 2000.

We should note that the increases in official sentence lengths by offense understate the increase in actual time served by most inmates admitted to federal prison. Over the time period studied, the Bureau of Justice Statistics estimates, the average proportion of the official sentence actually served in federal prison increased from 58 to 85 percent (Sabol and McGready 1999). In conjunction with the increases in official sentences documented here, it is undeniably the case that offenders currently sentenced in federal court can expect to serve more time than comparable offenders sentenced in years past.

CONCLUSION

The trends documented in this chapter paint an unambiguous portrait. The sentencing practices of the fifty state criminal justice systems and the federal criminal justice system have become tougher. We are more likely to send convicted criminal offenders to prison today than in the past. The composition of the prison inmate population has shifted toward less serious offenders, who are often those convicted of nonviolent drug crimes. Anyone we send to prison today can expect to serve a longer term. When released from prison, that individual is more likely to fail to meet the conditions of postrelease community supervision and be returned to custody. Although there are some notable differences between the federal and state systems, the general change in tenor is uniform: we have become much tougher with those who commit crime, and we have greatly expanded the definition of the offenses that merit forced removal from non-institutional society.

We have said little about the relative contribution of specific changes in sentencing practices to prison growth. For example, are longer sentences more important than higher admissions rates? Is drug policy crowding our prisons with people who would not have been in prison in years past? Or does prison growth reflect more intensive punishment for those who would surely have been admitted to prison for their serious offenses? In the following chapter, we turn to these questions.

CHAPTER 3

What Would Current Incarceration Rates Be Under Previous Sentencing Practices?

We have documented several empirical facts about changes in the U.S. criminal justice system. First, someone convicted of a felony today is considerably more likely to be sentenced to a prison term relative to someone convicted in years past. This is especially the case for those convicted of nonviolent felonies and those convicted of violent felonies that do not always result in a prison spell (for example, aggravated assault). Second, conditional on being convicted and sentenced to prison, a convicted felon is likely to serve a longer spell in prison than in years past. The effective length of sentences has increased for nearly all offense types, especially convictions for violent offenses. Finally, a larger proportion of the nation's population is on parole or some form of conditional postrelease supervision. In addition, these parolees fail at a higher rate than in years past and are more likely to be returned to custody (that is, to prison).

Not surprisingly, these changes in sentencing practices have coincided with massive increases in incarceration rates in every state as well as with rapid growth in the federal prison population. It is certainly the case that these changes in policy have contributed to incarceration growth, but by how much? Of course, a change in sentencing policies is not the only factor that could contribute to growth in the nation's prison population. Changes in crime and all of the determinants therein may also be driving these trends.

Moreover, over the period under study there have been a number of social developments that are commonly thought to have increased crime and, by extension, incarceration.

For example, the almost complete emptying and closing of the nation's mental hospitals between the 1950s and today has loosely coincided with explosive growth in the prison population. Untreated mental illness and violent crime are often linked in the media, usually through high-profile events such as the recent tragic mass shootings in a movie theater in Aurora, Colorado, and an elementary school in Newtown, Connecticut. Moreover, the policy responses to such events often pay particular attention to the role of untreated mental illness and the need to prevent such individuals from having access to firearms.[1] To the extent that the untreated mentally ill are at high risk of committing felonies, the change in mental health policy since the 1950s may have partially driven incarceration growth, sentencing policy changes notwithstanding.

The crack cocaine epidemic that ravaged inner-city communities throughout the country during the 1980s provided an alternative source of rising crime that is commonly cited to explain high U.S. incarceration rates. Emerging first in Northeastern cities around 1985 and then spreading to urban areas across the country, the crack cocaine epidemic had profound impacts on U.S. cities, through increased drug addiction, the violence associated with trafficking, and, perhaps most importantly, the policy changes it prompted.

Understanding the relative importance of crime trends versus sentencing policy changes in explaining the growth in the nation's prison population is important for framing the policy debate on crime control in the United States. Suppose that relatively high crime is the key factor explaining the fact that the U.S. incarceration rate is the highest in the world. In this case, the true problem faced by the United States would be relatively high crime rates, and the appropriate policy response would be to ask whether the nation could devise a crime control strategy that is more effective and has lower social costs than a strategy that relies heavily on after-the-fact punishment by confinement.

Alternatively, suppose that the explosive growth in the U.S. incarceration rate is explained predominantly by changes in U.S. sentencing policy rather than increases in crime. In this scenario, the growth in incarceration is driven largely by our policy choices and has little to do with policymakers' reactions to social developments beyond their control. In other words, high incarceration rates were not hoisted onto us by a crime wave but instead are the outcome of something like a large social experiment we chose to conduct. Although the experiment may have generated benefits in terms of lower crime (an issue addressed in detail in chapter 7), conducting it has also incurred substantial costs in the form of direct fiscal outlays and the adverse social costs associated with segregating, confining, and perhaps permanently stigmatizing a large minority of predominantly young African American and Latino men.

In this chapter, we assess the relative contribution of changes in sentencing practices and changes in criminal offending to the growth in U.S. incarceration rates in recent decades. We employ a simple model of incarceration rates to simulate what the incarceration rate today would be under various hypothetical sentencing practices. For example, we can ask what today's incarceration rate would be if sentencing practices in terms of prison admissions rates and time served reverted to those of the 1980s. Alternatively, we can ask what would happen if sentencing practices for specific crime categories were selectively rolled back. For example, what would the incarceration rate be if sentencing practices for drug crimes reverted to those of the early 1980s?

Our simulation results point to a stark finding. Even though we built assumptions into the simulations that should bias the analysis toward finding a role for changes in criminal behavior, our analysis demonstrates that nearly all (if not all) of the growth in state and federal prison populations can be attributed to tougher sentencing policy. There are some key differences between the state and federal systems. Although the lion's share of the growth in state prison populations can be traced to harsher sentencing for violent offenders, followed by the effect of harsher sentencing for drug offenders, the key factor explaining the growth in federal prison populations is tougher sentencing for drug offenders. There are also differences in the relative role of higher admissions rates and longer sentences. Despite these nuances, in both systems tougher sentencing outcomes relative to what was observed in the past are the primary drivers of the growth in incarceration in the United States.[2]

EXPLANATIONS FOR GROWTH IN STATE PRISON INCARCERATION RATES

In chapter 2, we described a simple framework for thinking about what determines the size of a dynamic population—that is, one in which admissions and exits constantly alter the members of the population and perhaps the size. In such a population, we noted, growth in admissions rates eventually leads to an increase in the size of the "steady-state" population, where the steady state is defined as exits equaling admissions and the population effectively stabilizing at a specific level. Similarly, a reduction in the rate of exit or release from the population—which corresponds in turn to an increase in the amount of time that an individual can expect to stay in the population—also increases the steady-state population level. Grafting this framework onto the prison population, we see that higher admissions rates and higher amounts of time served (that is, lower release rates) translate directly into higher incarceration rates.

In chapter 2, we also presented specific estimates of admissions rates to state prison for specific crimes as well as estimates of how much time an individual admitted to prison can expect to serve given the crime committed and the year of admission to prison. Here we make use of these empirical estimates to assess the contribution of sentencing changes to incarceration growth by calculating what the steady-state incarceration rate would be under several alternative scenarios. A useful way of thinking about our simulations would be to answer the following question: considering the rate at which we are admitting people to prison and the amount of time they serve, at what level will our incarceration rate eventually settle, given sufficient time? This stable level provides an estimate of the incarceration rate associated with a given set of admissions rates and effective sentence lengths.

Of course, the actual incarceration rate today may not equal the steady-state rate implied by today's admissions and time served values. For example, if we were to increase admissions rates today for an offense that carries a five-year sentence, it would be five years before the full effect of this policy change is reflected in the steady-state population. (Think of the example of the impact of increasing freshman admissions on the current population and eventual steady-state population of a university.) Hence, the steady-state incarceration rate that we would eventually reach given our new admissions rates would exceed the actual incarceration rate until the change in policy has had sufficient time to play itself out. Alternatively, if we were to reduce effective sentences for newly convicted violent offenders who are still given relatively lengthy prison terms, the effects of this change on the incarceration rate would not be realized for several years. Hence, the actual rate would exceed the steady-state rate until the system has had sufficient time to adjust.

Nonetheless, by comparing the implied steady-state incarceration rates using different sets of admissions rates and time served values from different time periods, we can simulate the relative contribution of changes in these gauges of sentencing practices. Moreover, with such a framework, we can ask questions regarding what would happen if we changed a specific set of sentencing practices, given sufficient time for our policy changes to bear fruit. The appendix to this chapter provides the technical details behind the simulation model that we employ to ask such questions. In this section, we provide a more intuitive description of our simulation results and what they suggest about the forces that have driven up U.S. incarceration rates.

We begin by assessing whether our simulation model does a good job of predicting the observed increase in the state prison incarceration rate between 1984 and 2004 (the period studied in chapter 2) based on observed changes in admissions rates and effective sentence lengths. Table 3.1 presents the results from our base simulations. The first column shows the actual number of state prisoners per 100,000 U.S. residents in 1984, the corresponding rate in 2004, and the change in the actual rate over this time period. As can be seen, the incarceration rate more than doubled, from 181 to 449 per 100,000, an increase of 268. The second column presents our estimates of the steady-state incarceration rates implied by the offense-specific prison admissions rates and the expected time served for each year that we presented and discussed in chapter 2. Interestingly, in both years the steady-state values from our simulations exceed the actual values, suggesting that in both years the national incarceration rate had yet to reach the steady-state incarceration rate and that prison populations would continue to grow in the years following (a prediction that was borne out in fact). Despite the differences in each year between the simulated steady-state incarceration rates and the actual rates, the predicted change in the steady-state incarceration rate of 273 per 100,000 is quite close to the actual increase in the state incarceration rate over this period (268). Hence, although the national incarceration rate was in steady state in neither 1984 nor 2004, the change in the implied steady-state values between these two years is a pretty good predictor of the change in incarceration rates that we actually observe.

Armed with this fact, which effectively validates the steady-state model as a predictor of changes in the national incarceration rate, we employ our simulation model to explore several hypothetical scenarios that selectively alter sentencing practices. First, we assess what the 2004 incarceration rate would be if sentencing practices were to revert to those of 1984. Second, we assess

Table 3.1   Actual State Incarceration Rates and Simulated Steady-State Incarceration Rates per 100,000 U.S. Residents, Using 1984 and 2004 Admissions and Time Served Estimates

	Actual Incarceration Rate	Simulated Steady-State Incarceration Rate	Ratio, Actual/ Simulated
1984	181	217	0.83
2004	449	491	0.91
Change from 1984 to 2004	268	273	0.98

Source: Figures tabulated from annual state-level incarceration totals from the *National Prisoner Statistics* data series, Bureau of Justice Statistics (various years).
Note: See appendix to chapter 3 for the simulation methodology.

what the 2004 incarceration rate would be if sentencing practices for specific crime categories were rolled back to 1984.

Rolling Back Sentencing Practices to 1984

We begin by assessing the cumulative effect of changes in sentencing practices between 1984 and 2004. By changes in sentencing practices we are referring to the relatively higher admissions rates per offense committed (our measure of how extensively prison is used to punish criminal offenders) and the longer sentences for those sent to prison (our measure of how intensely we punish criminal offenders) in 2004 relative to 1984. We use our simulation model to estimate what the incarceration rate would be in 2004 under 1984 sentencing practices. Comparing this hypothetical rate to our steady-state calculations for 1984 and 2004 permits us to assess the relative contribution of changing sentencing policy to incarceration growth.

A key challenge that we face in trying to calculate what current incarceration rates would be under past sentencing practices concerns the possibility that under more lenient sentencing crime rates would be higher. To be sure, there are several reasons to believe that this would in fact be the case. With lower incarceration rates, more individuals with a high propensity to commit crime would be on the streets and crime rates would likely be higher as a result. In the language of criminologists, there would be less incapacitation of the criminally active. Moreover, to the extent that potential offenders were deterred from committing crime by the threat and severity of punishment, lower incarceration rates might result in higher crime through less deterrence. For the purposes of our simulations, higher crime rates would translate directly into higher prison populations even under 1984 sentencing practices. This follows from the fact that prison admissions rates depend on both crime rates and sentencing practices. Thus, tabulating what the incarceration rate would be in 2004 with 1984 sentencing practices and actual 2004 crime rates is likely to overstate the role of policy changes in explaining incarceration growth over this period unless we account for the crimes prevented by incarceration growth.

We postpone a more detailed discussion of the relationship between prison and crime until chapter 7. For the purposes of our simulations, however, we need to account for the fact that crime rates would probably have been higher in 2004 under a lighter sentencing regime. To calculate such hypothetical crime rates we need estimates of the amount of crime prevented per prison year served and the degree to which the incarceration rate would be lower under the lighter sentencing practices. For our simulations, we estimate crimes averted per prison year served based on the empirical methods laid out in the appendix to chapter 7 for the time period between 1984 and 2004. In conjunction with the actual increase in incarceration rates between these two years, this allows us to estimate how much the lower crime rates in 2004 are due to the increase in incarceration since 1984. We then add these "crimes prevented" to the actual 2004 crime rates to estimate what crime rates would have been in 2004 had our sentencing practices remained more lenient.[3]

Table 3.2 presents these estimates. The first two columns present actual crime rates for serious felony offenses and show the large declines in crime over this time period that we have already discussed in chapter 2. The third column portrays "counterfactual crime" in 2004: our estimates of what crime rates would have been in 2004 had incarceration rates not changed since 1984. Comparing the counterfactual crime rates to actual 2004 crime rates, these estimates suggest that crime rates would have been substantially higher under more lenient sentencing practices. Yet for several crime categories (in particular, murder, robbery, and burglary), the counterfactual crime rates in 2004 are still well below the 1984 crime rates.

For crimes that are not incident-based (in the sense that they are not generated by a report to the police), generating comparable hypothetical crime

Table 3.2   Actual Crime Rates in 1984 and 2004 and the
             Counterfactual Crime Rate in 2004, Assuming No
             Increase in the Incarceration Rate (All Expressed as
             Reported Incidents per 100,000 U.S. Residents)

	1984 Actual Crime Rate	2004 Actual Crime Rate	2004 Counterfactual Crime Rate
Murder and manslaughter	7.9	5.5	6.1
Rape and sexual assault	35.7	32.4	38.9
Robbery	205.7	136.7	176.0
Aggravated assault	290.6	288.6	290.6
Burglary	1,265.5	730.3	905.8
Larceny and fraud	2,795.2	2,352.3	2,782.4
Motor vehicle theft	437.7	421.5	527.6

Source: Actual crime rates: FBI Uniform Crime Reports (1984, 2004). To calculate counterfactual crime rates, we first estimate the average effect of an additional inmate on each crime rate using state panel data for the period 1984 to 2004. (The details behind this estimation are discussed in greater detail in chapter 7.) We then use these estimates to calculate what crime rates would be in 2004 if the incarceration rate were rolled back to the 1984 level.

rates is more difficult. This is particularly problematic for drug offenses. One conservative strategy for estimating hypothetical drug crimes and admissions to prison would be to assume that the entire increase in drug arrests observed over our study period would have occurred regardless of policy changes. This is akin to assuming that the enormous increases in drug arrests are driven entirely by more prevalent drug use and drug trafficking activity. Such an assumption clearly biases our results toward finding a larger impact of behavioral change in explaining incarceration growth, since there has also been a notable increase in antidrug enforcement efforts over this period that probably explains the large increase in arrests. However, since our simulation results find little impact of behavioral change, we are willing to tolerate this bias.

Table 3.3 presents several alternative sets of prison admissions rates that we employ in our incarceration simulations. The first two columns present actual prison admissions rates for 1984 and 2004 and reproduce the results showing large increases in admissions, especially for less serious crime. The third column presents what prison admissions rates would be with crime rates equal to actual values for 2004 and admissions per crime equal to those for 1984. Not surprisingly, these counterfactual admissions rates are considerably lower

Table 3.3 Actual Prison Admissions Rates per 100,000 U.S. Residents for 1984 and 2004 and Hypothetical Admissions Rates for 2004, Using 1984 Admissions per Crime and 2004 Crime Rates and 1984 Admissions per Crime and 2004 Counterfactual Crime Rates

	1984 Actual Crime Rate	2004 Actual Crime Rate	Hypothetical 2004 Crime Rate Using 1984 Admissions per Crime and 2004 Crime Rates	Hypothetical 2004 Crime Rate Using 1984 Admissions per Crime and 2004 Counterfactual Crime Rates
Murder and manslaughter	4.9	5.6	3.4	3.8
Rape and sexual assault	3.8	6.2	3.5	4.1
Robbery	11.2	10.7	7.5	9.6
Aggravated assault	4.5	11.8	4.4	4.5
Other violent crime[a]	1.9	8.2	5.0	5.0
Burglary	18.2	17.3	10.5	13.1
Larceny and fraud	15.6	25.8	13.2	15.5
Motor vehicle theft	0.9	3.8	0.9	1.1
Other property crime[a]	1.1	3.1	1.8	1.8
Drugs[b]	8.5	51.1	16.9	16.9
Other crimes	12.9	24.6	14.1	14.1
Parole violations[c]	15.0	52.4	25.2	27.8

Source: Authors' compilation based on Federal Bureau of Investigation Uniform Crime Reports (1984, 2004).

[a] The table imputes crime rates for other property and other violent crime using the average admissions per crime for overall violent and property crime, respectively.

[b] The table assumes that drug crime rates are equal to drug arrest rates in each year and that these values would have been observed regardless of corrections policy.

[c] Hypothetical admissions rates for parole violations are set equal to 31 percent of the sum of admissions rates for all new crimes (the empirical proportional relationship between parole admissions rates and other admissions rates for 2004).

than actual admissions rates in 2004, with the lower values driven by both lower crime rates in this year and the lower admissions per crime from the earlier year. The final column presents hypothetical admissions rates assuming 1984 admissions per crime values and the 2004 counterfactual crime rates. Although these hypothetical admissions rates are larger than the hypothetical rates based on observed 2004 crime rates, they are substantially less than the actual prison admissions rates for 2004. Of course, this suggests that even after accounting for the likelihood of a higher crime rate, incarceration rates would be much lower today had sentencing practices not changed.

Armed with these alternative crime rates and hypothetical prison admissions rates, we can now simulate various changes in the nation's rate of incarceration in state prisons under alternative scenarios. Figure 3.1 summarizes the results from several simulations. The first bar shows the simulated change in the steady-state incarceration rates between 1984 and 2004 using the actual sentencing values and crime rates for each year. The increase of 273 per 100,000 corresponds exactly to the base simulations presented in table 3.1 and is provided as a benchmark against which we compare the other simulation results. The second bar shows the hypothetical change in incarceration that would have occurred using actual 2004 crime rates but assuming that admissions per crime and time served remained at 1984 levels. The simulations show that, under these assumptions, the incarceration rate in state prisons would have declined by 16 per 100,000. In other words, these simulations, conditional on observed 2004 crime levels, indicate that the entire increase in state incarceration over this time period was driven by changes in sentencing practices rather than changes in criminal behavior.

The third simulated change measures the change from 1984 that would have occurred assuming the higher hypothetical crime rates for 2004, 1984 admissions per crime, and 1984 time served values. In these simulations, incarceration in state prisons increases by 24 per 100,000 between 1984 and 2004. This increase amounts to slightly less than 9 percent of the increase in steady-state incarceration rates observed in our benchmark simulations, suggesting that 9 percent of the increase, at most, can be explained by a shift in criminal behavior. Moreover, since our hypothetical crime rates probably overestimate admissions for drug offenses under 1984 policy parameters, this 9 percent figure is likely to be an overestimate (or at a minimum, an upper-bound estimate of the truth). This is one of the principal findings of this chapter: changes in criminal behavior explain very little of the increase in

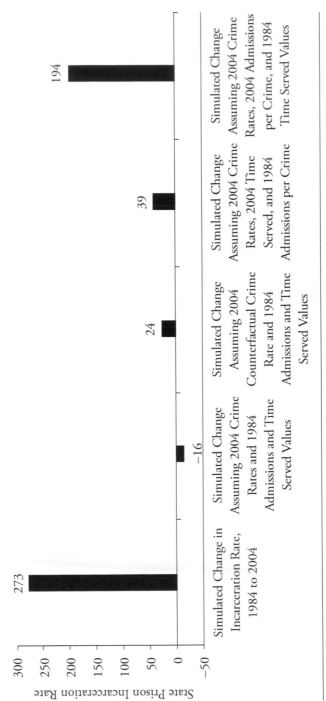

Figure 3.1 Simulated Changes in State Prison Incarceration Rates per 100,000 U.S. Residents Between 1984 and 2004 Under Various Scenarios Regarding Admission Rates, Time Served, and Crime Rates

Source: Figures derived from the authors' simulation model. See the appendix for simulation details.

state incarceration rates. By contrast, changes in sentencing practices are paramount.

We might ask these simulation models a set of related questions: which change in sentencing practice matters most? We have documented the policy expansion in the use of incarceration in both extent (an increased propensity to sentence convicted felons to prison) and intensity (an increase in how long a sentence is served by those admitted to prison). To what extent are these alternative margins of adjustment in our use of incarceration independently driving prison growth?

Of course, policy changes along these two margins have mutually reinforcing effects. For example, increasing time served for a typical offense by one year has a larger effect on the steady-state prison population when admissions rates are high. Similarly, an increase in admissions per crime has larger impacts on the eventual incarceration rate when expected time served is relatively long. Nonetheless, by selectively rolling back sentencing practices along each margin and simulating the impact on incarceration rates in 2004, we can get some sense of which aspect of sentencing policy is contributing more to incarceration growth.

The final two bars in figure 3.1 provide such results. The fourth bar in the chart shows by how much the steady-state incarceration rate would have changed over our study period if admissions per crime are held at 1984 values while time served per crime is permitted to increase to the values observed for 2004. The fifth bar shows the comparable change when time served is held to 1984 values while admissions per crime are permitted to increase to the actual levels observed in 2004. Since changes in behavior explain very little of overall incarceration growth, we employ actual 2004 crime rates in both of these final simulations. The results are quite similar when we perform these simulations using the higher hypothetical crime rates for 2004.

Had admissions rates been held to 1984 levels, the increase in effective sentence lengths would have driven up state incarceration rates by 39 per 100,000, amounting to roughly 14 percent of the total increase in our benchmark simulations. The final bar shows that, had effective sentence lengths been held at 1984 levels, the increase in admissions per crime between 1984 and 2004 alone would have generated an increase in the state prison incarceration rate of 194 per 100,000 (amounting to 71 percent of the overall increase in the steady-state incarceration rate over this period).[4]

Hence, our results indicate that changes in criminal behavior explain little to none of the growth in state prison incarceration rates since the early 1980s. One particular policy change, our enhanced tendency to sentence convicted felons to prison, is primarily responsible for incarceration growth, though setting longer sentences is also a contributing factor.

Selectively Rolling Back Sentencing Practices for Specific Offense Groups

Another set of questions that we might ask of these simulation models concerns the role of changing sentencing practices and policies pertaining to specific offense categories. We know, for instance, that states across the country have enhanced sentences for violent offenses and devoted considerably more resources to punishing drug offenders. Our cross-state comparison in chapter 2 suggested that state differences in incarceration for violent offenses account for a disproportionate share of interstate variation in incarceration rates. We also know that parole failure rates are higher today than in years past. What would incarceration rates in state prison be if we were to selectively roll back sentencing practices for specific offense categories?

Figure 3.2 presents the simulation results needed to answer these questions. The first bar shows the steady-state incarceration rate in 2004 using actual crime and sentencing practices in each year, while the second bar shows what incarceration would be in 2004 with 2004 crime rates and 1984 sentencing practices for all crimes. The difference in incarceration rates between the two simulations of 290 provides a benchmark against which we compare the effects of rolling back specific sets of sentencing practices. Changes in effective sentences for violent offenders have contributed the most by far to incarceration growth in state prisons over this period. Rolling back such sentences to 1984 levels would reduce the steady-state incarceration rate in 2004 to 352, a difference relative to the actual steady-state value of 139. Relative to the benchmark difference provided by the first two simulations, the results for violent offenses suggest that harsher sentencing for violent offenders explains roughly 48 percent of incarceration growth in state prisons over this time period.

Harsher sentencing for drug offenders is also responsible for a fair share of the increase in state incarceration, though to a lesser degree than enhanced sentences for violent offenders. Rolling back sentences for drug offenders reduces the steady-state incarceration rate in 2004 to 427, a difference relative to the steady state using actual values for 2004 of 64 inmates per 100,000 U.S. residents. Relative to the benchmark change in incarceration, the policy

Figure 3.2 Simulated 2004 Incarceration Rates in State Prisons per 100,000 U.S. Residents, Rolling Back Admissions per Crime and Time Served for All Offenses and for Specific Offense Categories

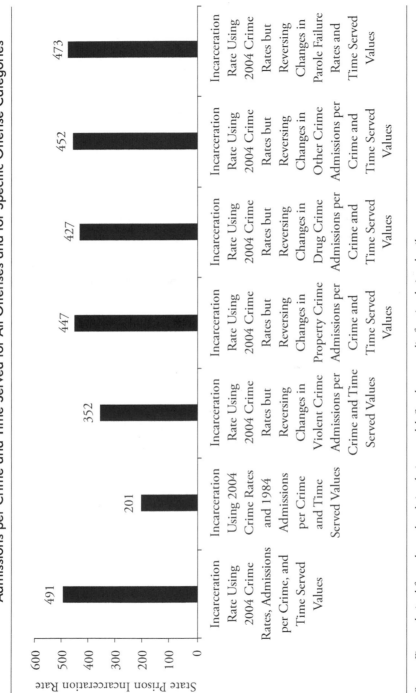

Source: Figures derived from the authors' simulation model. See the appendix for simulation details.

of handing out tougher sentences for drug offenders explains approximately 22 percent of the increase.

Tougher sentences for property crimes and for other crimes each explain approximately 15 percent of the increase observed in our benchmark simulations. Changes in parole failure rates and time served explain very little of the increase. Rolling back punishment parameters for parole violators would reduce the steady-state incarceration rate by 18 per 100,000, or slightly more than 6 percent of the increase observed in the first two simulations. Hence, while admissions rates for parole violators have by far increased the most over this period and account for a disproportionate share of all admissions, the relatively short prison stays of parole violators limit the contribution of this change to incarceration growth over the time period.

EXPLANATIONS FOR GROWTH IN THE FEDERAL PRISON INCARCERATION RATE

Our descriptive analysis of federal sentencing practices in chapter 2 revealed several key differences relative to sentencing outcomes in state courts throughout the country. First of all, there are large differences in the types of offenses that are typically adjudicated in federal courts, where a disproportionate share are convicted of drug offenses, weapons offenses, and other public-order offenses, such as immigration. Second, we were able to document a sizable increase for many offenses in the proportion of cases pursued by U.S. attorneys that result in conviction, an empirical pattern suggestive of a shift in the balance of power toward federal prosecutors. Third, for select crimes, the increased official sentences handed down are very long and have increased sharply in recent decades. In conjunction, these factors imply that the policy changes driving growth in the federal prison system are likely to differ qualitatively from the particulars of the changes in sentencing practices driving growth in state prison incarceration.

Parallel to our discussion of state incarceration, we begin our analysis of the federal system by discussing the results of some base simulations in which we use actual sentencing practice values for specific years to tabulate the implied steady-state federal incarceration rate. Table 3.4 presents these simulation results for the years 1985 and 2009. The first column presents figures for the actual number of federal prisons per 100,000 U.S. residents in each year. Over this twenty-four-year period, the federal prison incarceration rate increased from 17 to 68 per 100,000, a change of 51. The second column presents our tabulations of the steady-state incarceration rate in each year implied

Table 3.4   Actual Federal Incarceration Rates and Simulated Steady-State Federal Incarceration Rates per 100,000 U.S. Residents, Using 1985 and 2009 Admissions and Time Served Estimates

	Actual Incarceration Rate	Simulated Steady-State Incarceration Rate	Ratio, Actual/ Simulated
1985	17	24	0.71
2009	68	98	0.69
Change from 1985 to 2009	51	74	0.69

Source: Authors' compilation based on Bureau of Justice Statistics, *National Prisoner Statistics* (various years).
Note: See appendix to chapter 3 for the simulation methodology.

by the admissions rates and effective sentences handed down for those years. In our simulations, we assumed that prisoners admitted in 1985 would serve 58 percent of their official sentence while prisoners admitted in 2009 would serve 85 percent of their sentence.[5] In both years, the implied steady-state rate exceeds actual incarceration rates, with the ratio of the latter to the former equal to roughly 0.7 in each year. Unlike the state-level simulations, whose predicted change in incarceration based on steady-state tabulations is quite close to the actual change, our simulations for the federal system predict a change in the federal incarceration rate (of 74 per 100,000) that is somewhat larger than the actual change over this time period (51 per 100,000).

This disparity between the predicted steady-state change and the actual change in the federal incarceration rate could be driven by several factors. First, the higher steady-state values relative to actual values in each year imply that the actual incarceration rates are not at stable levels and are likely to increase toward the higher steady-state values in subsequent years. This was certainly the case in 1985. Whether the federal incarceration rate will continue to grow today (as is implied by the relatively high steady-state rate in 2009) remains to be seen. It is noteworthy, however, that between December 31, 2009, and March 12, 2012, the federal prison population grew by 4.6 percent (from 208,118 to 217,769), while over the same period the state prison population actually declined.[6] To the extent that the relatively high steady-state value for 2009 is a true reflection of sentencing outcomes in the federal system, then the higher increase has basically yet to be realized.

Alternatively, our simulation model may be doing a poor job of predicting growth in the federal system. The problem here might lie with our underlying data. For the federal system, we cannot observe actual releases from prison by offense category, a key input to estimating time served in our state simulations. Rather, we observe average sentences handed down by offense category and approximations of the average time served for all offenses combined. To the extent that these two indirect proxies lead us to overestimate expected time served by offense, our simulation overstates the eventual growth in the federal incarceration rate due to changes in sentencing practices over the period studied.

Despite this caveat, to a first approximation the change in steady-state incarceration rates is qualitatively similar to the actual change: in both instances the federal incarceration rate increased roughly fourfold over the period studied. Since we are primarily interested in qualitatively describing which changes in sentencing practices are the most likely culprits behind this quadrupling, we believe that the simulation exercises discussed here are informative under either of the possible explanations for the higher steady-state change observed in table 3.4.

Thus, we proceed along the same lines as our analysis of the state system. We first explore the extent to which the federal incarceration rate would have changed had sentencing practices been held at 1985 levels. In particular, we evaluate the steady-state incarceration rate in 2009 using 2009 crime rates (measured by the rates at which suspects were referred to U.S. attorneys by offense) and 1985 values for admissions per crime and time served. We then explore the effects on the federal incarceration rate of selectively rolling back sentencing practices for specific crime categories. One departure from our analysis of state incarceration rates is that here we do not attempt to estimate what the "crime rate" as measured by cases taken on by U.S. attorneys would have been in the absence of a sentencing change. In the federal system, several key pieces of legislation have greatly enhanced penalties for specific federal crimes (drug crimes in particular) and increased the resources devoted to arresting offenders and trying such cases in federal court. In this instance, we feel confident that the assumption that offending levels in 2009 would have been at 2009 levels in the absence of changes in federal sentencing practices is a conservative assumption biased toward finding a larger role for behavior relative to policy. Again, in light of the findings we are about to present, we are willing to tolerate an assumption biased in this direction.

Figure 3.3 presents the results from several simulations. The first bar shows the difference between the federal steady-state incarceration rates in 2009 and 1985 using actual values from each year for offending rates and for sentencing practices. The figure displays the predicted increase in the federal incarceration rate of 74 per 100,000 already discussed in table 3.4. The second bar displays the counterfactual increase in the federal incarceration rate assuming 2009 offending levels and sentencing parameters from 1985. The models imply that, under such a scenario, the federal incarceration rate would have increased by only 9 per 100,000, amounting to 12 percent of the full increase in steady-state incarceration from our benchmark simulation. The third and fourth bars show the predicted increase in federal incarceration rates assuming (1) 2009 crime rates and time served values and 1985 admissions per crime, and (2) 2009 crime rates and admissions per crime and 1985 time served values. In contrast to our results for state incarceration rates, the relative responsibility of higher admissions and longer time served is more even. Each of these changes would individually increase the federal incarceration rate by about 30 percent of the actual change in the benchmark simulations (by 22 per 100,000 for the change in time served and 21 per 100,000 for the change in admissions per crime). The remaining one-third of the increase is explained by the larger impact of an increase in sentence length on the prison population when admissions rates are high, while the impact of increases in admissions rates are larger in the presence of long sentences.

Figure 3.4 presents simulated steady-state incarceration rates for 2009 with sentencing practices (in terms of both admissions per crime and expected time served) rolled back to 1985 levels for individual offense categories while sentencing values for all other offense categories are held at 2009 levels. The results here contrast sharply with what we observed for state incarceration rates. For reference, the first two bars present (1) the steady-state rate in 2009 using actual 2009 values, and (2) the rate in 2009 using 2009 offense rates but 1985 sentencing practices. The goal of this figure is to assess the degree to which rolling back sentencing practices for a specific offense brings us from the value depicted in the first bar to the value depicted in the second. Tougher sentencing practices for violent and property offenses explain very little of the increase in incarceration over this period. Specifically, our simulations indicate that rolling back violent crime sentences and admissions per crime to 1985 levels lowers the steady-state incarceration rate to 96, a difference of only 2 per 100,000 relative to the benchmark value for 2009. The similar figure for property offenses is 95, with a difference of only 3 per 100,000 relative to the

Figure 3.3 Simulated Changes in Federal Prison Incarceration Rates Between 1985 and 2009 Under Various Scenarios Regarding Admissions Rates and Time Served

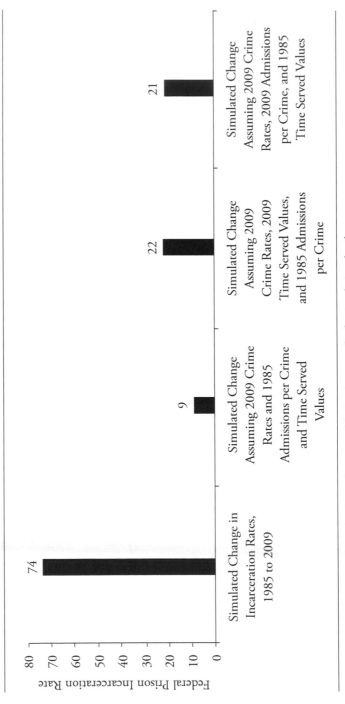

Source: Figures derived from the authors' simulation model. See the appendix for simulation details.

Figure 3.4 Simulated 2009 Federal Incarceration Rates Rolling Back Admissions per Crime and Time Served for All Offenses and for Specific Offense Categories

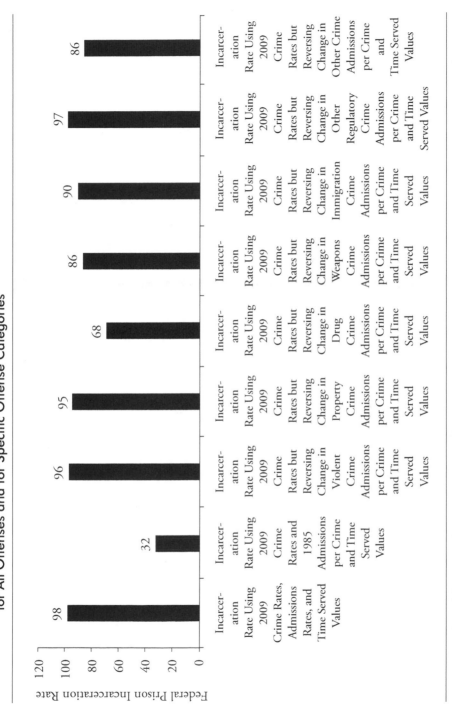

Source: Figures derived from the authors' simulation model. See the appendix for simulation details.

benchmark. Hence, tougher sentencing for violent and property offenders is relatively unimportant in explaining the growth in the federal system.

For drug offenses, however, we have an entirely different story. Rolling back admissions per drug offense and expected time served for drug offenses to 1985 values would yield a steady-state incarceration rate in 2009 of 68 per 100,000. This is a difference of 30 per 100,000 relative to the base simulation for 2009, and it amounts to 45 percent of the difference in incarceration rates between the first two simulations in the figure. Moreover, this is likely to be a downwardly biased estimate of the complete role of changes in drug policy. Over this time period, suspects received by U.S. attorneys for drug offenses increased by 50 percent. This most certainly reflects in part increased drug enforcement efforts in addition to trends in drug use and the extent and scope of drug markets. We return to this question in chapters 4 and 6.

Although the differential sentencing of drug offenders explains the lion's share of growth in the federal system, several other categories make sizable, if smaller, contributions to the simulated change in incarceration rates between the years. First, rolling back sentences for weapons offenses (mostly offenders who are convicted for being felons in possession of a firearm) yields a 2009 incarceration rate of 86 per 100,000. This implies that 18 percent of the difference in incarceration rates between the two base simulations in figure 3.4 is attributable to tougher sanctions for this offense. Similar in magnitude, the effect of tougher sentencing for those violating immigration law explains about 12 percent of this difference. Specifically, rolling back admissions per offense and expected time served for immigration offenses would reduce the incarceration in 2009 from 98 to 90 per 100,000.

CONCLUSION

Sentences for criminal offenders have gotten tougher for both those adjudicated in state court and those adjudicated in federal court. There is very little evidence that a higher propensity among U.S. residents to commit crime is the reason behind the explosive growth in both federal and state prison populations. By contrast, there is overwhelming evidence that the observed growth is driven primarily by changes in sentencing policy. These changes have occurred along both the extensive margin (a greater propensity to send the convicted to prison) and the intensive margin (to send them for longer periods when we do). Hence, why are so many Americans in prison? The short answer to this question is that we have decided to incarcerate so many people through our collective choices regarding criminal sentencing.

The results of this chapter do reveal some very interesting differences between the factors driving growth in the state prison population and the factors driving growth in the federal prison population. First, in the state systems higher admissions rates to prison appear to be the principal factor driving up incarceration rates in recent decades, though longer time served also plays a substantial, if smaller, role. In the federal system, increases in admissions per crime and longer expected time served more evenly share responsibility for the quadrupling of federal prison incarceration rates.

Second, there are large differences between the federal and state systems in the relative culpability of changes in sentencing practices for specific offenses. In both systems a more extensive and intensive use of prison as punishment for drug offenders contributes substantially to prison growth. However, in the federal system this is the key set of sentencing changes, with tougher drug sentences explaining roughly half of the increase in the federal prison incarceration rate.

Tougher sentences for drug offenders account for one-fifth of the growth in state prison incarceration rates, a sizable contribution. However, the big-ticket offense category is violence. We have documented large increases in both admissions per crime and time served for violent offenses, and we have also documented that this has little to do with higher clearance rates by arrest. These effective sentence enhancements for violent offenders explain half of the increase in state prison incarceration rates over the past few decades.

Having thoroughly documented the end results of tougher sentencing and pinned incarceration growth on these particular policy changes, we can ask the obvious next question: which changes in sentencing policies are driving these empirical patterns? This is the subject of chapter 4.

APPENDIX: SIMULATION METHODS

This chapter presents several simulation results from our exploration of what incarceration rates would be today if we were to reverse many of the changes in sentencing policy that have taken place since the early 1980s. The simulations rely on a simple steady-state model of the national incarceration rate that takes the rates at which people are admitted to and released from prison for specific offense categories and mathematically solves for the incarceration rate that will eventually be reached given sufficient time and stable admissions and release rates. In this appendix, we lay out the mathematics behind these simulations and discuss the specifics of the data sources and the simplifying assumptions that we make to derive the results presented here.

Key to the steady-state model of incarceration rates is the set of transition probabilities that gauge the rate at which individuals in society flow between different possible criminal justice statuses. Table 3A.1 displays a simple example. The table describes six possible criminal justice categories, which are listed in both the stub of the table and the top row of the table: (1) not incarcerated/not on parole, (2) incarcerated for a violent felony, (3) incarcerated for a property felony, (4) incarcerated for a drug felony, (5) incarcerated for a parole violation, and (6) on parole. Each element in the matrix represents the probability of transitioning from the status measured on the stub to the status measured along the top row over a given time period (for example, one year). For example, the likelihood of transitioning from "not incarcerated, not on parole" to "incarcerated for a drug felony" is given by Ad, while the comparable likelihood of transitioning to "incarcerated for a violent felony" or "incarcerated for a property felony" is Av and Ap, respectively. Some of the transition probabilities in the matrix are zeroed out. For example, one cannot transition directly from "not incarcerated, not on parole" to "on parole," since parole is a post-prison release status. In addition, the transition probabilities in each row must sum to 1. In the table, this is reflected by the transition probabilities measuring the likelihood of remaining in one's current status into the next period being set equal to 1 minus all other transition probabilities in the row.

As discussed in chapter 2, the admissions rates (presented in the first row of the transition probability matrix) reflect both the offense-specific crime rate as well as prison admissions per crime. The release rates (presented in the second, third, and fourth rows of the matrix) are inversely proportional to typical time served. For example, adding the unconditional release rate for a violent crime (Rv1) and the conditional release rate for a violent crime (Rv2) gives the overall release rate for the period. The reciprocal of this overall release rate gives the expected value of time served for a violent offense.

Our simulations involve solving for the eventual steady-state incarceration rate that will be reached given sufficient time and stable admissions and release probabilities. The details behind these simulations are as follows. Define the vector Pt as

$$P_t = \begin{bmatrix} P_t^1 & P_t^2 & P_t^3 & P_t^4 & P_t^5 & P_t^6 \end{bmatrix}, where \sum_j P_t^j = 1 \qquad (3A.1)$$

where t indexes time periods and the index values indicate the six potential states of being not in prison and not on parole ($j = 1$), in prison for a violent

Table 3A.1 Transition Probabilities Describing Movements Between the Incarcerated, the Non-Incarcerated, and the Parole and Probation Populations

	Destination State					
Origin State	Not Incarcerated, Not on Parole	Incarcerated for a Violent Felony	Incarcerated for a Property Felony	Incarcerated for a Drug Felony	Incarcerated for a Parole Violation	On Parole
Not incarcerated, not on parole	$1 - A_v - A_p - A_d - A_{parole}$	A_v = violent crime rate × admissions rate per violent crime committed	A_p = property crime rate × admissions rate per property crime committed	A_d = drug crime rate × admissions rate per drug crime committed	A_{parole} = parole violation rate × parole admissions per violation	0
Incarcerated for a violent felony	R_{v1} = unconditional release rate for inmates convicted of violent crimes	$1 - R_{v1} - R_{v2}$	0	0	0	R_{v2} = conditional release rate for inmates convicted of violent crimes
Incarcerated for a property felony	R_{p1} = unconditional release rate for inmates convicted of property crimes	0	$1 - R_{p1} - R_{p2}$	0	0	R_{p2} = conditional release rate for inmates convicted of property crimes

Table 3A.1   (Continued)

Origin State	Destination State					
	Not Incarcerated, Not on Parole	Incarcerated for a Violent Felony	Incarcerated for a Property Felony	Incarcerated for a Drug Felony	Incarcerated for a Parole Violation	On Parole
Incarcerated for a drug felony	R_{d1} = unconditional release rate for inmates convicted of drug crimes	0	0	$1 - R_{d1} - R_{d2}$	0	R_{d2} = conditional release rate for inmates convicted of drug crimes
Incarcerated for a parole violation	R_{pa1} = unconditional release for inmates incarcerated for a parole violation	0	0	0	$1 - R_{pa1} - R_{pa2}$	R_{pa2} = conditional release of those incarcerated for a parole violation
On parole	R_{par} = rate of successful transitions off parole	$A_{v,par}$ = admissions rate for parolees committing new violent felonies	$A_{p,par}$ = admissions rate for parolees committing new property felonies	$A_{d,par}$ = admissions rate for parolees committing new drug felonies	$A_{p,par}$ = admissions rate for parolees violating parole conditions	$1 - R_{par} - A_{v,par} - A_{p,par} - A_{d,par} - A_{p,par}$

Source: Authors' compilation.

offense ($j = 2$), in prison for a property offense ($j = 3$), in prison for a drug offense ($j = 4$), in prison for a parole violation ($j = 5$), and on parole ($j = 6$). Define the transition probability matrix T as

$$T = \begin{bmatrix} T^{11} & T^{12} & T^{13} & T^{14} & T^{15} & T^{16} \\ T^{21} & T^{22} & T^{23} & T^{24} & T^{25} & T^{26} \\ T^{31} & T^{32} & T^{33} & T^{34} & T^{35} & T^{36} \\ T^{41} & T^{42} & T^{43} & T^{44} & T^{45} & T^{46} \\ T^{51} & T^{52} & T^{53} & T^{54} & T^{55} & T^{56} \\ T^{61} & T^{62} & T^{63} & T^{64} & T^{65} & T^{66} \end{bmatrix}, where\ 0 \leq T^{ij} \leq 1, \forall i, j\ and\ \sum_j T^{ij} = 1, \forall j \tag{3A.2}$$

where each element, T^{ij}, gives the probability of transitioning from state i to state j over a given time period. Here we are assuming that the transition matrix is stable over time, although this need not be the case. The matrix T corresponds to the matrix detailed in table 3A.1.

The proportional distribution of the U.S. population across the six states in any given year can be rewritten as a linear function of the state distribution in the previous year and the transition probability matrix, or

$$P_{t+1} = T' P_t \tag{3A.3}$$

The system reaches the steady state when applying the transition matrix to the population share vector at the beginning of the year yields the same population distribution at the beginning of the subsequent year. That is to say, in steady state, it must be the case that

$$P_t = P_{t+1} = P \tag{3A.4}$$

where we drop the time subscript to indicate the steady-state value. When combined with equation 3A.2, this gives the steady-state condition

$$P = T^T P \tag{3A.5}$$

Solving for P in equation 3A.5 requires that we incorporate the constraint that the population shares across the six states sum to 1 and that we rearrange the six equations in 3A.5 in a manner that lends itself to a simple algebraic solution. Explicitly writing out the six equations in 3A.5 gives

$$P^1 = T^{11}P^1 + T^{21}P^2 + T^{31}P^3 + T^{41}P^4 + T^{51}P^5 + T^{61}P^6$$
$$P^2 = T^{12}P^1 + T^{22}P^2 + T^{32}P^3 + T^{42}P^4 + T^{52}P^5 + T^{62}P^6$$
$$P^3 = T^{13}P^1 + T^{23}P^2 + T^{33}P^3 + T^{43}P^4 + T^{53}P^5 + T^{63}P^6$$
$$P^4 = T^{14}P^1 + T^{24}P^2 + T^{34}P^3 + T^{44}P^4 + T^{54}P^5 + T^{64}P^6 \qquad \text{(3A.6)}$$
$$P^5 = T^{15}P^1 + T^{25}P^2 + T^{35}P^3 + T^{45}P^4 + T^{55}P^5 + T^{65}P^6$$
$$P^6 = T^{16}P^1 + T^{26}P^2 + T^{36}P^3 + T^{46}P^4 + T^{56}P^5 + T^{66}P^6$$

The constraint that the shares sum to 1 can be incorporated by substituting this summation constraint for the last equation of the system. Making this substitution for the sixth equation and rearranging slightly gives the system

$$0 = (T^{11} - 1)P^1 + T^{21}P^2 + T^{31}P^3 + T^{41}P^4 + T^{51}P^5 + T^{61}P^6$$
$$0 = T^{12}P^1 + (T^{22} - 1)P^2 + T^{32}P^3 + T^{42}P^4 + T^{52}P^5 + T^{62}P^6$$
$$0 = T^{13}P^1 + T^{23}P^2 + (T^{33} - 1)P^3 + T^{43}P^4 + T^{53}P^5 + T^{63}P^6$$
$$0 = T^{14}P^1 + T^{24}P^2 + T^{34}P^3 + (T^{44} - 1)P^4 + T^{54}P^5 + T^{64}P^6$$
$$0 = T^{15}P^1 + T^{25}P^2 + T^{35}P^3 + T^{45}P^4 + (T^{55} - 1)P^5 + T^{65}P^6$$
$$1 = P^1 + P^2 + P^3 + P^4 + P^5 + P^6$$

which can be rewritten as

$$
\begin{bmatrix} 0 \\ 0 \\ 0 \\ 0 \\ 0 \\ 1 \end{bmatrix}
=
\begin{bmatrix}
T^{11}-1 & T^{21} & T^{31} & T^{41} & T^{51} & T^{61} \\
T^{12} & T^{22}-1 & T^{32} & T^{42} & T^{52} & T^{62} \\
T^{13} & T^{23} & T^{33}-1 & T^{43} & T^{53} & T^{63} \\
T^{14} & T^{24} & T^{34} & T^{44}-1 & T^{54} & T^{64} \\
T^{15} & T^{25} & T^{35} & T^{45} & T^{55}-1 & T^{65} \\
1 & 1 & 1 & 1 & 1 & 1
\end{bmatrix}
\begin{bmatrix} P^1 \\ P^2 \\ P^3 \\ P^4 \\ P^5 \\ P^6 \end{bmatrix}
\qquad \text{(3A.7)}
$$

If we name the column vector on the left side of the equation V and the square matrix involving the transition probabilities A, the system in equation 3A.7 can then be rewritten compactly as

$$V = AP \qquad (3A.8)$$

Solving for P gives the solution

$$P = A^{-1}V \qquad (3A.9)$$

Calibrating the model to actual data requires that we estimate the individual elements of the transition probability matrix. Since these elements are equal to prison admissions rates and prison release rates (the reciprocal of time served), we are able to use the estimates of these values presented in chapter 2 to calibrate the model to actual U.S. data. Simulating hypothetical situations requires that we estimate what the transition probability matrix would be under various alternative scenarios. Here we discuss the specifics of the values used for these alternative simulations.

To start, our simulations differ slightly from the model presented in equations 3A.1 through 3A.9. Our simulations for state prison incarceration rates employ fourteen criminal justice categories, including not incarcerated and not on parole, on parole, and being incarcerated for each of the twelve offense categories discussed in detail in chapter 2. Our simulations for federal prison incarceration rates employ nine criminal justice categories, including not incarcerated and being incarcerated for each of the eight controlling offense categories for federal prisons discussed in chapter 2.

Our first set of simulations calibrates the model to actual transition and release probabilities. For state prison incarceration rates, we employ the admissions and release probability estimates from the 1984 and 2004 NCRP data. These probabilities correspond exactly to those presented in chapter 2. For federal prisoners, we employ the implied admissions probabilities given the case processing statistics presented in chapter 2 (the product of the rate at which suspects are received by U.S. attorneys, the prosecution rate, the conviction rate, and the proportion sent to prison by offense). To estimate release probabilities, we assume that inmates in 1985 serve 58 percent of their sentence while inmates in 2009 serve 85 percent of their sentence (in accordance with the empirical findings presented in Sabol and McGready 1999). The reciprocal of these estimates of time served provides our release probability estimates.

Our hypothetical simulations roll back either all or select admissions and release probabilities to their values at the beginning of the study period. In all simulations, we roll back values for admissions rates by substituting admissions per crime in the early year for admissions per crime in the latter year. To roll back time served, we simply substitute release rates from the early year for release rates for the latter year. Regarding admissions rates, since the overall admissions rate for a given offense category equals the crime rate times the admissions per crime, our counterfactual simulations must choose a crime rate to employ when simulating admissions rates under a less punitive sentencing system. In many of our simulations, we simply assume that crime in 2004 would equal empirically observed values for that year. For one state incarceration simulation, we estimate a counterfactual crime rate based on empirical estimates of the number of crimes prevented per prison year served for the period 1984 to 2004. These estimates are based on state-level panel data regressions employing an instrumental variables strategy detailed in Johnson and Raphael (2012). These results are discussed in detail in chapter 7, and the explicit estimation methods are discussed in the appendix to chapter 7.

CHAPTER 4

The Policy Changes Driving Incarceration Growth

The explosive growth of the U.S. prison population since the mid-1970s stands in stark contrast to the relative stability of the prison population during the preceding half-century. In a widely cited article, the criminologists Alfred Blumstein and Jacqueline Cohen (1973) noted the remarkable stability of the U.S. incarceration rate and posited natural predetermined levels of crime and corresponding incarceration that might fluctuate from year to year yet would generally hover around stable rates. The stability of U.S. incarceration rates over this period was certainly a function of the stable policy regime governing sentencing in the states and the dominant ethos among criminal justice officials regarding the social role of penitentiaries. Conversely, identifiable changes in these sentencing regimes as well as a notable shift in ethos among policymakers are largely responsible for the changes we have observed since.

Through the mid-1970s, all state prison sentences and the actual amount of time that a criminal offender would serve were governed by a set of sentencing practices often referred to as "indeterminate sentencing." Under indeterminate sentencing, judges specify a minimum and maximum sentence and actual time served falls within this range. Once an inmate has been sentenced and admitted to prison, actual time served is determined by parole boards, with the decision to release governed by interviews with inmates, behavior while incarcerated, elements of the offense, demonstrable remorse, evidence of rehabilitation, and perhaps the personal biases of parole board members pertaining to the specific characteristics of the inmate in question. In principle, indeterminate sentencing reserves prison and long prison sentences in particular for those who commit the most serious crimes and those who pose the greatest threat to society. Such a sentencing regime is characterized by a high degree of discretion afforded to criminal justice actors and to judges and parole boards in particular (Tonry 1996).

The indeterminate sentencing practices that dominated through the late 1970s reflected the belief that sentences should be individualized with the ultimate aim of rehabilitating the offender in question. Presumably, by leaving the exit date an open question, inmates faced a strong incentive to take the necessary steps to hasten an early release. Moreover, with criminal justice officials explicitly in charge of population relief valves (judges deciding whether to send a convicted felon to prison and parole boards deciding whether to release), the stability of U.S. incarceration rates in this early period is perhaps not too surprising.

Shortly after the publication of Blumstein and Cohen's 1973 article, several high-profile studies of crime and the U.S. corrections systems articulated dissatisfactions with the status quo and, in retrospect, presaged the drastic changes to come. First, in 1974 Robert Martinson published a highly influential essay in *The Public Interest* that summarized the results of an exhaustive review of evaluation research on rehabilitation programs conducted over previous decades. The essay was extremely pessimistic about the effectiveness of such interventions and all but concluded that nothing works when it comes to publicly financed efforts to rehabilitate criminal offenders. Although Martinson qualified his conclusions with the usual caveats regarding the quality of the research studies reviewed and the potential effectiveness of programs whose evaluation studies were not included in the review owing to weak research methodologies, he ultimately concluded: "I am bound to say that these data, involving over two hundred studies and hundreds of thousands of individuals as they do, are the best available and give us little reason to hope that we have in fact found a sure way of reducing recidivism through rehabilitation" (Martinson 1974, 49).

To be sure, Martinson's essay and the larger literature review on which it was based (Lipton, Martinson, and Wilks 1975) have since sparked a revisionist literature as well as a wealth of new research on the determinants of criminal offending. Although it is certainly the case that most informed ob-

servers have a sober view of the prospects for rehabilitating the active criminal, it is also safe to say that today such a pessimistic assessment of rehabilitation efforts as characterized by the 1974 Martinson essay does not constitute
the conventional wisdom (see, for example, the thoughtful review in Cullen
and Gendreau [2000] or Mark Kleiman's 2009 treatise on policy options for
controlling crime). Nonetheless, Martinson's work is often cited as a damning
evaluation of U.S. rehabilitation efforts and a turning point, owing to its high
profile, in the thinking of many policymakers.

A further indictment of U.S. corrections and crime control policy was
presented by the sociologist James Q. Wilson in his 1975 book *Thinking
About Crime.* A careful reading of this highly influential work reveals that it
was as much an indictment of contemporary academic research as a critique
of U.S. correctional policy. Wilson lambasted those social scientists and social
commentators who argued that effective crime control policy requires addressing the "root causes" of crime.[1] Wilson advocated instead for a policy
agenda that recognizes the limits of government intervention in influencing
human nature and that takes into account the fact that many crimes reflect to
some degree rational choices that weigh benefits against costs. Wilson made a
utilitarian case for incapacitating the criminally active and developed an argument akin to the rational microeconomic model of crime first articulated by
the Nobel laureate economist Gary Becker (1968), which emphasizes the calculating nature of some criminals and the potential for policymakers to deter
such offenders from committing crime in the first place. Wilson bemoaned
the low rate at which convicted offenders were sentenced to prison at the time
and placed blame squarely on a system that afforded judges great discretion in
determining sentence severity. This indictment of the correctional system at
the time is summarized quite succinctly in the closing lines of the book:

> Wicked people exist. Nothing avails except to set them apart from innocent
> people. And many people, neither wicked nor innocent, but watchful, dissem-
> bling, and calculating of their opportunities, ponder our reaction to wicked-
> ness as a cue to what they might profitably do. We have trifled with the wicked,
> made sport of the innocent, and encouraged the calculators. Justice suffers, as
> do we all. (Wilson 1975, 209)

Whether Martinson's review or Wilson's book actually influenced policymakers and public opinion or simply reflected the existing intellectual and

political currents of the time is, for our purposes, unimportant. Both pieces provide thorough critiques of the indeterminate sentencing systems that existed in most states as well as the rehabilitation-centered approach to corrections that in many ways provided motivation for subsequent policy changes. Moreover, the messages in these treatises coincided with a shift in public sentiment toward greater punitiveness and a reactionary political climate in which the tough-on-crime message resonated with the public and crime control policy became highly politicized. The decades that followed witnessed increases in the likelihood of being sent to prison conditional on committing a crime, longer sentences, a great reduction in the discretion afforded to judges in sentencing and parole boards in their release decisions, a substantial strengthening of the hands of prosecutors across the country, and soaring incarceration rates.

What specific changes in state and federal sentencing policy have driven up the nation's incarceration rate? Moreover, what are the social and political factors that led to these changes? In this chapter, we address these questions.

THE EVOLUTION OF STATE SENTENCING POLICY

Prior to the explosive growth in the U.S. incarceration rate, state sentencing practices were characterized by more uniformity in process, though probably greater variation in official sentences and actual time served among inmates convicted of similar crimes. Today sentencing practices vary to a greater degree across states. Despite this increase in heterogeneity, several common qualitative patterns describe many of the changes observed over the past three decades. First, judges generally have less discretion today than in the past in deciding which inmates would be sent to prison and the length of effective sentences. Second, release decisions are more constrained by administrative rules pertaining to good time credits, by a diminished role of parole boards in release decisions, and by laws that mandate minimum time served requirements. Third, states have implemented a number of reforms intended to increase uniformity in sentencing for inmates convicted of similar offenses. Fourth, through legislation targeted at specific offenders and offenses, as well as legislation reforming overall sentencing, sentences have become considerably more structured. Finally, sentencing practices have become increasingly punitive.

Given that there are fifty states, and given the large amount of legislative activity focused on criminal justice practices, completely characterizing changes in sentencing practices is a terribly difficult task. The best such effort, in our view, is presented in the work *Of Fragmentation and Ferment* by Don Stemen, Andres Rengifo, and James Wilson (2006). These authors describe several sets of sentencing practices through which many if not all states have formally altered the operation of their criminal justice systems. Specifically, they focus on:

- *The shift from indeterminate to determinate sentencing:* Determinate sentencing laws specify fixed sentences for offenses (or relatively narrow minimum and maximum ranges), in contrast to the broad ranges handed down under indeterminate sentencing policies. A key factor that distinguishes determinate sentencing from indeterminate sentencing is the greatly curtailed release discretion afforded to parole boards (and in some instances the abolishment of parole boards). This constraint on parole boards ensures that the sentence served is determined primarily by the sentencing judge and not, ultimately, through the release decisions of parole boards. Stemen and his colleagues (2006) find that by 2002 nineteen states had adopted determinate sentencing regimes. Many states also adopted additional policy reforms that increased the determinacy of sentencing practices, as we discuss later.

- *The introduction of greater structure in sentencing through voluntary and presumptive sentencing guidelines:* The term "structured sentencing" refers to sentencing practices that impose either mandatory structure on the sentences handed down by judges or attempts to impose structure through official advice regarding sentencing for specific classes of offenders. In general, judges have less discretion under structured sentencing. Stemen and his colleagues (2006) distinguish between states with structured sentencing according to several aspects of practice. First, they distinguish states that mandate presumptive sentences involving fixed sentences for specific offenses (or perhaps narrow sentencing ranges) from states with sentencing guidelines that enable judges to impose sentences from within a specified sentencing range (defined by a minimum and maximum) that varies with both the offense and the criminal history of the offender. Actual guidelines are usually determined by a state sentencing commission, with guideline sentences that increase in severity for more severe offenders and more severe offenses. Within the set of states that have adopted sentencing guidelines, Stemen and his co-authors also distinguish between states with voluntary and presumptive structures. Presumptive sentencing structures require that the judge sentence within the guideline range or offer justification for departing from it. Upward departures are subject to appeal by the defense, while downward departures are subject to appellate review at the request of the prosecution. Deviations from voluntary sentencing guidelines are not subject to appellate review.

- *Truth-in-sentencing laws:* Truth-in-sentencing laws extend the actual time served by requiring that certain subsets of offenders serve a minimum proportion of their sentences (Ditton and Wilson 1999; Sabol et al. 2002). For states with determinate sentencing, this provision usually applies to the fixed sentence imposed by the judge. In indeterminate sentencing states, the provision may apply to either the maximum or minimum sentence, as prescribed by law. Truth-in-sentencing laws figured prominently in the Violent Crime Control and Law Enforcement Act of 1994. In addition to providing federal funds to augment the number of local police throughout the country, the legislation created federal matching grants under the Violent Offender Incarceration and Truth-in-Sentencing (VOI/TIS) program, which was directed toward expanding the capacity of state prisons and local jails (Ditton and Wilson 1999). A condition for receiving funds from the VOI/TIS program was that states had to have a truth-in-sentencing provision that violent offenders were required to serve a minimum of 85 percent of their sentence. The number of states with truth-in-sentencing laws has increased over the past three decades. Moreover, as Stemen and his colleagues (2006) show, in states that base their time served requirements on either the maximum sentence (in indeterminate sentencing states) or the fixed sentence (in determinate sentencing states), the average time served requirement has increased considerably, especially in 1994 with the creation of the VOI/TIS grant program. By 2008, twenty-eight states had truth-in-sentencing laws that met the federal 85 percent requirement for violent offenders.

- *Repeat offender laws:* Repeat offender laws refer to sentence enhancements for criminal offenders who repeatedly commit the same crime. The laws are often described using the baseball metaphor "three strikes and you're out," conveying the idea that those who serially offend may ultimately face life terms. Stemen and his colleagues (2006) distinguish repeat offender laws from habitual offender laws. The latter refers to provisions that enhance the sentences of those with any prior felony conviction.

Repeat offender laws often apply to those who repeatedly commit a targeted offense or who have committed a particularly serious offense in the past. Most states had habitual offender laws in place at the beginning of the current prison boom, though many states have increased the severity of punishment and scope of these laws in the years since. Repeat offender laws first appeared in most states during the early to mid 1990s under the label of "three strikes," with the first in the state of Washington in 1993. By the close of the twentieth century, one-half of all states had such provisions in their sentencing systems. The provisions of actual repeat offender laws vary considerably across states. For example, in California a "second striker" (someone with a prior conviction for a violent offense convicted of a second felony) receives a sentence equal to twice the sentence normally handed down for the second offense. Until recently, all "third strikers" (those with two prior violent felony convictions) were given an indeterminate sentence of twenty-five years to life for any further felony offenses.[2] By contrast, Pennsylvania's "three strikes" law is triggered only when an offender who has already been convicted of two prior felonies is subsequently convicted of one of eight specified offenses. Moreover, the law gives the sentencing court the discretion to increase the sentence for the underlying offense by up to twenty-five years.

- *Mandatory minimum sentences:* Mandatory sentencing laws specify minimum prison sentences for specific offenses or offenses with aggravating circumstances that are targeted by specific legislation. Stemen and his colleagues (2006) note that mandatory minimum sentences usually constrain both the decision regarding whether an offender should be sentenced to prison and the minimum amount of time that an inmate must serve. Between 1975 and 2002, every state adopted some form of mandatory minimum sentencing targeted at a specific offense. Nearly three-quarters of all states and the federal government enacted mandatory minimum sentences for possession or trafficking of illegal drugs. Mandatory minimum penalties are also often encountered for violent offenses, offenses involving weapons, carjacking, offenses victimizing minors, and offenses committed in close proximity to schools. Federal law is riddled with mandatory minimum sentences, an issue we return to shortly.

In theory, many of these sentencing innovations, considered in isolation, might serve to either increase or decrease prison populations. Consider, for example, the move toward determinate sentencing. A judge determined to not increase the amount of time served could simply assign fixed sentences that in conjunction with a specific good-time-credit formula result in an actual sentence equal to what would have been served under a discretionary parole system, effectively neutralizing any effect of the policy change. However, judges may feel pressure to assign long terms when a fixed sentence is handed out and the blame for a short sentence cannot be passed on to a parole board. A key factor that may come into play is the fact that corrections officials do not control the release flow from prison. In the face of overcrowding, parole boards with broad discretion may adjust prison populations through selective release. Determinate sentencing eliminates this possibility, effectively dulling the responsiveness of releases to crowding conditions.

As an additional example, consider structured sentencing. The structured sentencing reforms described earlier should not necessarily lead to higher incarceration rates. Sentencing guidelines may be developed with an eye to using prison beds sparingly and a focus on shorter or alternative sentences for the least-threatening felons and longer sentences for those who commit the most serious crimes or who exhibit a high degree of incorrigibility. Of course, voluntary sentencing guidelines can be ignored altogether by judges who wish to impose their will. Since sentencing decisions under such systems are not subject to appellate review, there is no official bite to the guideline recommendations.

On the other hand, sentencing guidelines may provide the scaffolding on which to hang mandatory minimum sentences and thus open sentencing up to the political forces that affect state electoral politics. To the extent that guidelines provide such infrastructure, their greater use in recent decades may have fueled the growth in incarceration rates. Even within voluntary guideline states, sentencing recommendations may carry particular weight in the sentencing decisions of judges. In a particularly novel and clever analysis of Maryland's advisory guidelines, Shawn Bushway, Emily Owens, and Anne Morrison Piehl (2012) assess the effects of calculation errors in sentencing recommendations on the actual sentence handed down by judges. In a painstaking analysis of actual sentencing worksheets, these authors identify a set of cases in which the sentencing recommendation to the judge erroneously deviated from what should have been recommended according to the provisions of the advisory guidelines. They find that positive errors (sentencing recommendations that were erroneously too long) resulted in longer actual sentences, while negative errors (sentencing recommendations that were too short as a result of human calculation error) resulted in shorter sentences. This is particularly striking considering that the recommendations in this instance were only advisory. Although the impacts of such errors in each direction tend not to be extreme, the study reveals the influence that even advisory sentencing recommendations have on the sentencing decisions of judges.

As a final example, the effect of truth-in-sentencing laws as well as mandatory minimums could technically be undone through prosecutorial behavior as well as the sentencing decisions of judges. Prosecutors who believe that a particular sentence would be too harsh may file charges that avoid a specific mandatory minimum or that evade a truth-in-sentencing requirement. David Bjerk (2005) finds evidence, for example, that California prosecutors alter charges to avoid unduly harsh sentences for offenders who are eligible for sentence enhancement under California's "three strikes" law. This conclusion is driven by a comparison of arrest charges and the charges filed by prosecutors for a large set of felonies adjudicated in California counties. For their part, judges could neutralize the effects of truth-in-sentencing provisions by lowering the base sentence against which the minimum percentage requirement is levied, assuming that judges operate in a system that affords such discretion.

Of course, Bjerk's findings may be interpreted in a different light. To the extent that the threat of a second- or third-strike conviction strengthens the bargaining position of prosecutors, the plea deals to lesser offenses obtained under the "three strikes" law may result in stiffer sentences compared with comparable plea deals that were obtained prior to the law's passage and implementation. Hence, the down-charging that Bjerk observes may reflect tougher sentencing compared to the plea-bargaining outcomes from years past. A telling analysis of judicial reaction to the implementation of truth-in-sentencing laws and the impact on sentencing outcomes finds evidence consistent with this conjecture. Emily Owens (2011) finds no effect of the implementation of truth-in-sentencing on average sentences given to convicted felons whose offenses are covered by the legislation, suggesting that judges do not compensate for the requirement that a higher minimum percentage of the sentence be served by handing down lower sentences. Most tellingly, Owen finds that the laws increase the sentence lengths of those who are initially charged with a crime subject to a truth-in-sentencing requirement yet who ultimately plead down to a lesser offense. This is certainly consistent with the idea that truth-in-sentencing laws strengthen the bargaining position of prosecutors in plea deals.

A number of studies have attempted to link specific changes in sentencing policy to changes in incarceration rates. An early example is provided by Patrick Langan (1991), who notes that many of the earlier sentence enhancements were geared toward either repeat offenders or violent offenders, a development that, if binding, should have increased the proportion of such offenders among the incarcerated population and among prison admissions. Langan finds no such change in the data through 1988. Moreover, Langan demonstrates a relatively stable distribution of maximum sentences as well as stability in the median time served among recently released inmates. Based on these patterns, Langan concludes that these policy changes bear little responsibility for increases in incarceration, at least through 1988. However, a stable sentencing distribution coupled with a shift in the composition of the inmate population toward less violent and less serious offenders implies that sentences must have increased (a fact we demonstrate in chapter 2). Failing to account for the change in the offense composition of admissions and the prison population misses this fact.

Thomas Marvell (1995) explores the effects of sentencing guidelines on prison growth, and he and Carlisle Moody (Marvell and Moody 1996) assess the effects of the move to determinate sentencing and the abolishment of parole boards. In both studies, the authors find little evidence that these policy changes correspond to higher-than-average prison growth; indeed, prison populations actually grew more slowly in many states that adopted these sentencing regimes. Two cross-sectional studies of the determinants of incarceration (Taggert and Winn 1993; Sorensen and Stemen 2002) fail to find evidence that states with limited judicial and parole board discretion have higher incarceration rates. Of course, all of these studies focus on the contemporary effects of changes in policy on changes in incarceration rates—that is to say, the effects of the change in policy between two given years on change in incarceration rates in the corresponding years. The impact on incarceration rates of many of the changes discussed earlier that increase the effective sentence length of those sent to prison does not play out for years. Hence, it is difficult to place too much faith in cross-sectional comparisons or even longitudinal analyses that do not adequately model the dynamic multi-period relationship between the policy changes and state incarceration rates.

More recent studies that address some of the weaknesses of this earlier research conclude that sentencing reform plays a much bigger role in explaining incarceration growth. For example, in using panel data methods to estimate the effect of sentencing guidelines on incarceration rates, Sean Nicholson-Crotty (2004) distinguishes between those states with sentencing commissions that are mandated to calibrate guidelines to resources and those that are not. Confirming the earlier analysis of this question in Tonry (1996), Nicholson-Crotty finds that states with such resource guidelines have had lower incarceration growth while guideline states that do not consider resources have had higher-than-average growth. Using a similar empirical strategy, Stemen and his colleagues (2006) find that states with more mandatory sentencing laws tend to have higher incarceration rates. Although neither study models the dynamic lagged effect of these laws on incarceration rates, their analyses of long panel data sets and tests for heterogeneity in the effects of sentencing reforms on incarceration represent substantial improvements over previous research attempts.

The research studies that we find to be the most convincing are those that analyze the relationship between changes in sentencing policy and specific policy determinants of the steady-state incarceration rate. For example, the Owens (2011) analysis of truth-in-sentencing provisions provides evidence of a direct link between a specific policy and the severity of sentencing outcomes for those who plead down to lesser offenses. Although this link is probably one effect of the policy change on prosecutorial bargaining power, the research clearly shows that those who avoid the truth-in-sentencing requirements receive longer sentences, as do those who are sentenced and subject to the requirements. (This latter effect operates through the laws' lack of impact on sentencing distributions.)

Additional direct evidence of the impact of policy changes on key sentencing parameters is provided in a thorough analysis of truth-in-sentencing laws by scholars from the Bureau of Justice Statistics and the Urban Institute (Sabol et al. 2002). One of the key aims of this analysis is to assess the extent to which the incentives created by the federal VOI/TIS program drove adoption of truth-in-sentencing programs across states. An exhaustive analysis of existing state law as well as the details from VOI/TIS grant applications concludes that this particular policy fad was already racing through the states when the 1994 crime bill was passed and that most states would probably have adopted such laws regardless. There is a notable uptick, however, in the percentage requirements that states imposed on violent offenders around 1994, suggesting that the federally created prison funding incentives increased the stringency of these laws. Moreover, the BJS and Urban Institute authors present simulation results suggesting that the letter of the law in most states is likely to have contributed substantially to prison growth during the 1990s and beyond.

As a final example of research testing for the effects of sentencing reforms on key determinants of the incarceration rate, Daniel Kessler and Anne Morrison Piehl (1998) present evidence consistent with a positive effect of mandatory minimums on actual sentences subject to the minimums, as well as on sentences not covered by a mandatory minimum that are factually similar to those that are. Kessler and Piehl analyze the effects of the passage of an early 1980s California proposition that enhanced sentences for a subset of violent offenses. They find a significant increase in sentences for the covered offenses, no comparable increase for other offenses, and significant increases in sentences for offenses that are similar to those covered by the proposition. Kessler and Piehl interpret this finding as evidence of enhanced prosecutorial bargaining power, since the alternative uncovered offenses are likely to be those to which an individual charged with an eligible offense would plead down.

THE EVOLUTION OF FEDERAL SENTENCING POLICY

Changes in federal sentencing policy have to some degree paralleled what has been observed among the states. Although there are some key differences pertaining to the centrality and salience of federal corrections and the changing division of labor between federal and state criminal law, federal sentencing has moved decisively toward greater structure and determinacy and is increasingly governed by tough mandatory minimum penalties. Moreover, it could be argued that the political signals sent from Congress, as well as the actual incentives created by federal legislation, may have contributed to prison growth at the state level (with the VOI/TIS grants perhaps the most obvious example).

During the 1980s, the federal government moved from a system in which federal judges were afforded great discretion in sentencing toward a presumptive guideline system in which the actual sentencing structure was determined by a federal sentencing commission. The 1984 Sentencing Reform Act mandated that the new U.S. Sentencing Commission establish a set of sentencing guidelines that would be "consistent with all pertinent provisions of any Federal statute," that would take into account "the nature and degree of harm caused by the offense," "the community view of the gravity of the offense," "the public concern generated by the offense," "the deterrent effect a particular sentence may have on the commission of the offense by others," and "the current incidence of the offense in the community and in the Nation as a whole" (U.S. Sentencing Commission 2011, 40). In carrying out this mandate, the U.S. Sentencing Commission created and continues to update a sentencing grid in which actual sentences vary with the severity of the offense and the criminal history of the offender.

To be specific, the guidelines classify offense severity based on the actual offense plus any aggravating or mitigating circumstances into forty-three separate severity levels, with higher values of the offense severity score corresponding to the graver offenses. Offenders are further classified according to their criminal history into one of seven categories, with higher numbers corresponding to more extensive and serious criminal histories. Each offense level and criminal history pairing is scored according to an associated sentencing range that specifies minimum and maximum sentences. These sentencing guidelines are summarized in a two-dimensional grid whose rows correspond to offense severity and columns correspond to criminal history. Each cell in the grid, corresponding to specific offense severity and criminal history levels, contains the presumptive sentencing range. Until 2005, judges were required to impose a sentence from within these ranges unless the defendant provided information that aided in the prosecution of others or met certain criteria to qualify for relief from unduly harsh sentences under the guidelines.

Similar to debates at the state level, the passage of the 1984 Sentencing Reform Act and the creation of the sentencing grid were prompted by large differences between judges, and in some instances within-judge disparities, in sentencing outcomes for offenders convicted of similar offenses. Indeed, researchers have found that the introduction of the federal sentencing guidelines have reduced such disparities. James Anderson, Jeffrey Kling, and Kate Stith (1999) compare cross-judge variation in sentencing outcomes for like offenders for the two years preceding the implementation of the federal sentencing guidelines to such variation during the first six years of implementation. They find a 20 percent reduction in the expected difference between any two judges in the sentences of like offenders, a pattern directly attributable to the introduction of the sentencing grid. David Mustard (2001) demonstrates that many of the racial and gender disparities observed among offenders in the postreform period are attributable to corresponding differences in the distribution across the sentencing grid categories (that is, differences in the offense severity and criminal history scores), though significant difference remains for offenders with similar scores. Moreover, Mustard finds evidence of a differential propensity to depart downward for sentencing recommendations that appears to favor white defendants.

These mandatory guidelines governed federal sentencing for nearly twenty years. In 2005, however, the Supreme Court ruling in United States v. Booker rendered the sentencing recommendations voluntary. Specifically, the Supreme Court ruled that since not all of the information used to determine a defendant's position in the sentencing grid was argued and proved beyond a reasonable doubt before a jury, sentencing under the provisions of the 1984 Sentencing Reform Act violated the Sixth Amendment right to a jury trial (U.S. Sentencing Commission 2011). United States v. Booker does not affect sentences in instances where federal mandatory minimums apply, because specific offenses trigger the mandatory minimum and an adjudication process that establishes guilt for a specific offense also establishes whether an offender qualifies for the mandatory minimum penalty.

Federal criminal law is loaded with mandatory minimum sentences created by direct acts of Congress. Many of the most salient mandatory minimums that contribute disproportionately to the federal prison population were passed during the mid to late 1980s and 1990s. The Anti–Drug Abuse Act of 1986 created the notorious "100-to-1" rule for punishments associated with trafficking of crack cocaine. In particular, the law specifies a five-year mandatory minimum penalty for a trafficking offense involving at least five grams of crack cocaine and a corresponding mandatory minimum of five years for trafficking offenses involving at least five hundred grams of powder cocaine. This sentencing disparity is particularly grave considering that powder cocaine and crack cocaine have the exact same chemical composition and pharmacological impact on users (Hatsukami and Fischman 1996).[3] The 1986 act was followed in 1988 by federal legislation that applied the five-year mandatory minimum to possession offenses and expanded the scope of the mandatory minimum sentence to include conspiracy to commit drug crime (U.S. Sentencing Commission 2011, ch. 2). Congress eventually recognized the unjust sentencing disparities created by these two acts and in 2010 raised the minimum quantities of crack needed to trigger the mandatory minimum sentences. Congress stopped well short, however, of equalizing the punishment ratios for crack and powder cocaine, reducing the relative punishments from 100-to-1 to 28-to-1.

Additional examples of mandatory minimum penalties created or enhanced over the last three decades include mandatory minimums of five years for the use of a firearm in the commission of a crime (passed in 1984), for carrying or using a firearm in connection with a drug crime (enacting legislation in 1986), and for being a felon in possession of a firearm (enacting legislation in 1986). Congress also passed numerous laws from 1978 through 2003 that were aimed at enhancing penalties for the sexual exploitation of children. Not surprisingly, the lion's share of federal prison inmates comprise drug offenders, those convicted of weapons offenses, and those convicted of sexual exploitation of minors, with drug offenders by far the largest group.

In the domain of drug offenses, there is a complex interaction between mandatory minimum penalties and the sentencing grid that tends to increase sentence length and time served for those offenders who are convicted for drug offenses but do not qualify for the mandatory minimum sentence. For example, prior to 2010, five grams of crack cocaine was needed to trigger the five-year mandatory minimum penalty for such an offense. What then is the sentence for an offense involving 4.75 grams? In practice, the U.S. Sentencing Commission uses the mandatory minimum penalty to anchor the sentences for offenses involving quantities below the mandatory minimum (Vincent and Hofer 1994; U.S. Sentencing Commission 2011). Hence, the offender caught with 4.75 grams of crack would receive a sentence of 4.75 years.

One qualitative trend in federal sentencing that has received much attention and is discussed prominently in the most recent U.S. Sentencing Commission report on mandatory minimums is the increasing federalization of criminal law in the United States. Between 1980 and 2010, the size of the federal prison population increased nearly ninefold, from 24,000 to 210,000. This greatly exceeds the rate of increase of the state prison population and signals the increasing importance of federal corrections as a contributor to high incarceration in the United States. As our discussion of mandatory minimums and our empirical analysis in the early chapters reveal, this expansion largely reflects increased admissions and longer sentences for drug offenses, weapons offenses, and certain types of sex crimes. Many of these offenses are crimes that are routinely adjudicated in state courts and often result in state prison sentences. Hence, the particularly quick expansion of the federal prison population implies that some offenders currently adjudicated in federal courts would have been adjudicated in state courts in years past.

Perhaps the most salient example of federalization is observed in programs designed explicitly to divert certain firearms offenses into federal court. For example, Richmond's Project Exile, implemented in the mid-1990s, diverted all felons found in possession of a firearm into federal courts for prosecution, where the mandatory minimum penalty combined with no early parole release results in considerably harsher penalties (Raphael and Ludwig 2003). This program was replicated in many localities across the country and was similar in spirit to the federal Operation Triggerlock program, which encouraged coordination between local district attorneys and U.S. attorneys to identify criminal cases that could be prosecuted in federal court.

As evidence of the increasing federalization of crime, the U.S. Sentencing Commission notes the increases in the number of offenses covered by the U.S. criminal code. Between 1980 and 2000, the number of such offenses increased from 3,000 to 4,000. By 2008 the number of offenses had increased further, to 4,450. The U.S. Sentencing Commission notes that much of the federal legislation generating this expansion addresses criminal offenses that were already addressed by other federal laws and that overlap to a great extent with existing state penal codes. The commission notes concerns at the highest level regarding federalization, directly quoting from Chief Justice William Rehnquist's 1998 year-end report:

> The trend to federalize crimes that traditionally have been handled in state courts not only is taxing the Judiciary's resources and affecting its budget needs, but it also threatens to change entirely the nature of our federal system.... Federal courts were not created to adjudicate local crimes, no matter how sensational or heinous the crimes may be. State courts do, can, and should handle such problems. (U.S. Sentencing Commission 2011, 65)

Hence, greater determinacy through sentencing guidelines, increases in the number of mandatory minimum laws constraining judicial sentencing practices, and an expanded scope for federal criminal law characterize the evolution of federal sentencing policy over the last three decades. Moreover, frequent direct legislation of punishments for specific criminal offenses in highly charged political settings, as well as the high time-served requirements that characterize federal corrections, have been mimicked, at least superficially, by states across the country. Whether the federal government, through example, has prompted such activity at the state level or whether federal policy trends reflect a broader social consensus regarding a turn toward tough-on-crime policies is an open question. It is undeniably the case, however, that both federal law and state sentencing practices have decisively shifted toward tougher punishment.

WHY DID SENTENCING PRACTICES BECOME TOUGHER?

We have documented the cumulative effects of these policy changes and reviewed the research on the specific policy shifts that have marked our very large departure from the indeterminate sentencing practices and focus on rehabilitation of the 1970s and before. This review naturally leads to several questions: Why did these changes occur? Why did we not see more direct legislation of criminal sanctions, moves to constrain the discretion of judges and parole boards, and calls for greater uniformity during the 1960 or the 1950s? Why have these changes not been occurring in other countries?

One simple story is that rising crime during the 1960s sparked a reevaluation of American corrections and criminal justice policy akin to the discussion in the introduction to this chapter. In his 1975 book, Wilson outlines the rising crime experienced during the 1960s and the degree to which the U.S. experience deviated from contemporary trends overseas. Higher crime rates coupled with a change in beliefs regarding the effectiveness of rehabilitation efforts may certainly have set the stage for the policy choices that followed. This would especially be the case if crime trends translated into heightened public concern about crime and demands that elected officials do something. This "democracy at work" hypothesis, first articulated in the seminal work of Katherine Beckett (1997), suggests that policy changes are simply responses to the will of the people.

Beckett presents evidence, however, that our shift in policy toward greater punitiveness was hardly a response to higher crime rates. To start, while official crime statistics collected from the FBI Uniform Crime Statistics (UCR) show rising crime during the 1960s and 1970s, many believe that this trend was in part illusory. Crime data collected and reported by the FBI are based on victim reports to local police departments and then police department reports to the FBI (usually through the host state's attorney general's office). During the 1960s and 1970s, more and more police departments were participating in this data collection effort and the completeness of the data reported was increasing as well; as a result, the proportion of crimes actually being counted was growing. Many also suspect that for certain crimes, sexual assault in particular, the propensity of victims to report the crime to the police was also trending upward, as was the propensity of the police to count such incidents as actual offenses. It is indeed the case that very well measured violent crime rates (homicide in particular) were increasing during this period. However, the overall increases in crime, in particular property crime and poorly reported violent crimes, were certainly overstated by improvements in coverage of the UCR statistics.

Second, as Katherine Beckett and Theodore Sasson (2004) demonstrate, from 1970 onward, trends in public opinion regarding the relative importance of crime and drugs revealed no secular increase in concern over these issues. Their analysis of public opinion does reveal, however, that public sentiments regarding the importance of the crime issue appear to be quite sensitive to the message crafted by political elites and transmitted through media coverage. For example, Beckett and Sasson demonstrate a sharp increase in the proportion of Americans identifying drugs or drug abuse as the nation's most important problem that coincides with President George H. W. Bush's first televised national address in 1989. The entirety of the address was devoted to the problem of illegal drugs, and President Bush used the address to announce the creation of the position of the national drug czar to oversee antidrug policy for the federal government as well as an expanded role for the military in combating drug trafficking. Most memorably, President Bush displayed on camera a bag of cocaine purchased "in the shadow of the White House" (Beckett and Sasson 2004, 109). The proportion of the public citing drugs as the most serious problem facing the nation began to increase in the weeks before the speech as media coverage of the drug issue increased, largely in response to signals from the White House that this would be the topic of the president's first national address. This proportion peaked with the presentation of the speech, but then quickly dropped back to previous levels as the televised address faded from memory.

Beckett and Sasson also document a similar response of public opinion to the legislative debate surrounding the passage of the 1994 Violent Crime Control and Law Enforcement Act during the first Clinton administration. Public opinion regarding the severity of the crime problem over the previous fifteen or so years displayed no discernible trends, and consistently fewer than 10 percent of Americans identified crime or violence as the nation's most important problem. This figure shot up abruptly to over 50 percent with the passage of the 1994 legislation and the media coverage surrounding additional funding for local police, federal funds for new prison construction, and the truth-in-sentencing requirements attached to these funds. Following passage of the act, and with the decline in media coverage, the proportion of Americans citing crime as the nation's most pressing problem dropped discretely to below 30 percent and then continued to decline over the subsequent years to the low levels that prevailed prior to the legislative debate.

Beckett and Sasson do document a trend in public opinion toward greater punitiveness—primarily increasing support for the death penalty since the mid-1970s. This is consistent with a shift in perspective on the nature of criminal offending from a social theory emphasizing poverty, racial discrimination, and other environmental determinants of crime toward a vision of crime as the rational choice of the calculating offender, the latter view being a reorientation advocated by James Q. Wilson in 1975. However, the disconnect between public concern over crime and public opinion regarding the nature and determinants of crime led Beckett and Sasson and other scholars to look elsewhere for an explanation of policy shifts in our corrections policy, especially purely political explanations.

A growing body of social science research traces the origins of the colossal shift in U.S. sentencing policy to the political conflict surrounding the civil rights movement. This research points to key efforts by political elites to exploit crime and criminal justice policy either to pursue political gain or to push a segregationist agenda that was no longer considered a legitimate point of debate following the passage of civil rights legislation. For example, several researchers, including Naomi Murakawa (2005), Vesla Weaver (2007), and Michelle Alexander (2010), point to efforts by Southern politicians to redefine civil disobedience and other direct actions taken by civil rights activists as criminal. The contention here is that by reframing the civil rights movement as a law-and-order issue rather than a debate over race, segregation, and Jim Crow, Southern politicians could employ the criminal justice system to maintain the pre–civil rights social order. Moreover, such a strategy was cloaked in a race-neutral veil, even though the policy reforms it begot would prove to have racially disparate impacts that were severe. Weaver (2007) argues that this redefinition was hardly a reaction, or backlash, to the civil rights movement but rather a strategic and deliberate effort to adapt an existing agenda to the new federal law of the land (what Weaver refers to as a "frontlash" strategy).

At the federal level, several scholars point to the destruction of the New Deal coalition between ethnic white communities in Northeastern metropolitan areas and poor Southern whites, a coalition that had provided the key constituency of the Democratic Party in the pre–civil rights era (see, in particular, the discussions in Beckett 1997 and Alexander 2010). The Democrats' support for civil rights legislation was perceived as a betrayal by poor and working-class whites in Southern states, and also perhaps by working-class whites in the North, who now faced stiffer competition from African Americans for jobs and public resources. Seeing the opportunity to win over these disaffected Democrats, the Republican Party followed what is often referred to as the "Southern Strategy": national politicians appealed to Southern whites by pursuing policies that did not mention race and were ostensibly race-neutral, yet were thinly veiled attacks on the civil rights movement and the attendant gains won through federal legislation.

Key to the Southern Strategy was an emphasis on law and order. According to Michelle Alexander's (2010) account of this development, the call for tough-on-crime policies appealed to the sense of disorder created in the South by the direct actions of civil rights activists as well as the fears of whites throughout the country following urban riots in the mid-1960s and the spate of riots following the assassination of Dr. Martin Luther King Jr. This strategy may have been first manifested in national politics with the emphasis on crime and the need to crack down on criminals in Barry Goldwater's unsuccessful 1964 bid for the presidency. Emphasizing law and order was also part of Nixon's political strategy, and it figured prominently in the War on Drugs that began in 1982 under President Ronald Reagan.

Beckett (1997) was the first to advance an interesting hypothesis about the way in which political competition at the federal level manifested in an explicit and harsh focus on drug abuse and drug trafficking. Historically, maintaining law and order and punishing criminal offenders have been the responsibilities of state and local governments. The federal court system, which punishes those who violate federal law, traditionally has had a narrow focus on white-collar crime, organized crime, and threats to national security. The federal government has always played a large role, however, in drug trafficking. Beckett notes the dilemma faced by early national politicians attempting to exploit the law-and-order issue for political gain—they could run on a tough-on-crime platform, but there was little precedent and few existing mechanisms for a federal role in combating street crime.

Combating drug trafficking and drug abuse was clearly within the purview of federal authorities, though not a particularly pressing priority until the 1980s. With the announcement of the War on Drugs in 1982 (several years, it should be noted, before the onset of the crack epidemic), the federal government greatly stepped up drug enforcement, finding a clear path to make good on campaign promises to crack down on street criminals. Moreover, as we have already documented, subsequent congressional legislation fostered greater federalization of street crime, extending the reach of the federal criminal justice system into the realm of punishing certain sex offenders, repeat offenders using firearms, and other offenders who would have been adjudicated at the state level in the past.

Clearly the politics surrounding crime and sentencing is thoroughly asymmetric. A politician simply neutralizes a tough-on-crime political opponent by also being tough on crime. Opposing tough-on-crime policies, however, is going out on a limb that is easily sawed off by an opponent. The politicization of crime policy may have begun with segregationist politicians in the South and the Republican Southern Strategy, but by the close of the twentieth century, not surprisingly, members of both political parties were generally supportive of punitive sentencing reforms. Perhaps the starkest example of bipartisan support is the 1994 crime bill: introduced by the Clinton administration, it created incentives for states to increase sentence lengths by providing in exchange federal funds to build more prisons.

Of course, this story only partially explains the nation's shift in sentencing regimes: the lion's share of increasing incarceration was driven by growth in state prison populations and thus by shifts in state sentencing policy. However, we can easily identify a number of ways in which the national debate has had an impact on sentencing reform legislation and prison populations throughout the country. First, on several occasions since 1980 the federal government has created direct incentives for state and local governments to increase their enforcement activities. The 1994 legislation creating grants for prison capacity expansion in exchange for adopting stiff truth-in-sentencing laws is one example. Another is federal legislation during the 1980s that authorized local use of the forfeited assets seized in narcotics busts. Certainly, the federalization of crime control policy and the increasing focus of the national political process on crime created many such incentives for state lawmakers and local criminal justice officials to step up enforcement and enhance penalties.

Aside from these direct incentives, the politicization of crime at the federal level most certainly demonstrates the political salience of crime as an issue and the potential political benefits for those who are tough on criminals. Such debates figure prominently in statehouses across the country. As the review by Stemen and his colleagues (2006) shows, there has been no shortage of state legislative activity targeted at making sentencing practices tougher over the past twenty-five years.

Several scholars who have searched for root causes for the shift in sentencing policy emphasize the role of race and the history of race relations in the United States. It is certainly the case that African Americans—and in particular, African American men—have borne the brunt of sentencing reforms. The extreme racial disparities in incarceration rates and in the proportion of men who have ever been incarcerated has led the sociologist Loïc Wacquant to hypothesize that the modern U.S. penal system represents a form of ethno-racial-social control, akin to slavery, the system of Jim Crow laws, and Northern ghettos, that is explicitly designed to control poor African American men: "The ghetto is a manner of 'social prison' while the prison functions as a 'judicial ghetto.' Both are entrusted with enclosing a stigmatized population so as to neutralize the material and/or symbolic threat that it poses for the broader society from which it has been extruded" (Wacquant 2000, 378). Michelle Alexander (2010) draws a direct comparison between the daily lives of African American inmates and African American former prisoners and the restrictions on association, voting rights, and eligibility for public resources and the differential access to opportunities of all sorts in the Jim Crow South.

Support for harsh punishment and sentencing laws may also reflect larger societal assumptions about the criminal nature of African Americans. Several scholars have demonstrated that support for specific types of crime legislation partially stems from the general public perception of blacks as the sole perpetrators of crime and of violent crime in particular (Hurwitz and Peffley 2005; Cohn, Barkan, and Halteman 1991). This is akin to other work that has demonstrated the impact of negative evaluations of African Americans on policies targeted at welfare spending (Gilens 1999; Peffley, Hurwitz, and Sniderman 1997).

These racially prejudiced stereotypes about black offenders are often perpetuated and reinforced through the media. A number of scholars have shown how news programming influences general public opinion regarding crime prevalence, the need for an increased police presence, and the type of punishments that offenders should receive (Surette 1998; Barille 1984). In typical news stories, when perpetrators are shown as black (rather than white), the public tends to indicate being more fearful and to advocate for harsher punishments. In their examination of crime news scripts from local television sources, Franklin Gilliam and Shanto Iyengar (2005) experimented by alternating the race of the perpetrators in typical newscast frames. The result: respondents were more likely to fear crime and to support harsher punishments when the victim of the crime was white and the perpetrator was black.

A particularly provocative thesis concerns the general lack of public outrage as our current state of affairs persists. Glenn Loury (2002, 2008) argues that persistent racial inequality along a number of dimensions in the United States is facilitated by the failure of the majority to acknowledge the common humanity of African Americans, in particular African American men. A subtle propensity to specify black males as "other" or "less than worthy" permits acceptance of racial disparity and, in the instance at hand, acceptance of the racially disparate impact of our correctional policies. This thesis is duly illustrated by the following question. Would American society accept current corrections policy or deem the current state of affairs a necessary evil if a white male child born today faced a one-third lifetime chance of serving time in a state or federal prison? Presumably the answer to such a question would be a resounding no. So why do we observe no outcry in response to the fact that African American male children born today face these odds of incarceration?

Much of the scholarship discussed here draws on detailed historical analysis, and our discussion summarizes our interpretation of the politics driving corrections reforms over the past four decades. It is, of course, impossible to present precise statistical tests of the thesis that the Republican Southern Strategy opened the gate for punitive reforms in any one state, or that the U.S. prison boom has been partly a reaction and adaption to civil rights legislation by those seeking to push a segregationist agenda.

That being said, our empirical analysis in chapter 2 revealed very strong indicators of punitive shifts in sentencing policy and little evidence of an increase in crime over the past few decades. Our analysis in chapter 3 demonstrated that even if we take into account the crimes averted by the massive increase in incarceration over the past quarter-century, crime trends cannot explain the explosive growth in our prison population. It can also be noted that incarceration rates have increased the most in the very states that were the battlegrounds of the civil rights movement. (Figure 1.2 shows that Louisiana, Mississippi, and Alabama are among the states experiencing the largest increases in incarceration rates since 1977.) Moreover, there is little empirical support for the contention that increasing public concern about crime has driven our policy response: historical analysis of public opinion reveals little evidence of any such rising alarm. In general, the empirical results and historical and social analysis presented here strongly suggest that the origins of our shift toward punitive policy are essentially political and have little to do with the actual threat of crime.

CHAPTER 5

Deinstitutionalization of the Mentally Ill and Growth in the U.S. Prison Population

Chapters 1 through 4 were devoted to explaining the increase in the nation's incarceration rate since the mid-1970s.[1] The empirical decomposition and review of policy history yield a clear answer to the question posed in the title of this book. Namely, policy choices that have expanded the range of offenses to which incarceration is applied and the severity of prison sentences handed down explain nearly all, if not all, of the increase in incarceration. While harsher sentencing for drug offenders is a big contributor to prison growth, tougher sentencing for those convicted of violent offenses plays a particularly large role. In short, our incarceration rate has grown to such high levels because we have chosen, through changes to our sentencing policy, to have a high incarceration rate.

This and the next chapter focus on the factors that are commonly thought to have contributed to prison growth yet upon careful inspection are revealed to be minor contributors. Although the following analysis reinforces the conclusions that we draw from the analysis in the first four chapters, it also allows us to touch upon several important aspects of U.S. corrections and the conditions inside and outside of prisons faced by those most likely to serve time. In this chapter, we present a detailed analysis of the relationship between the deinstitutionalization of the mentally ill and growth in U.S. incarceration rates.

As we mentioned in chapter 1, mental health problems are extremely prevalent among U.S. prison and jail inmates (James and Glaze 2006). Over half of state prison inmates, slightly fewer than half of federal prison inmates, and over 60 percent of jail inmates report having mental health problems or symptoms indicative of mental illness. The relative prevalence of severe mental illness is particular high among the incarcerated (nearly five times that of the general adult population). Applying these prevalence rates to the 2008 incarcerated population yields an estimate of 316,000 severely mentally ill people in the nation's prison and jails (approximately 115,000 jail inmates and 201,000 state and federal prison inmates). By contrast, there are currently fewer than 60,000 inpatient residents in state and county mental hospitals. In other words, the population of incarcerated severely mentally ill is over five times the inpatient mental hospital population.

That the incarcerated mentally ill population exceeds the inpatient population of mental hospitals is a relatively new development. As shown in figure 5.1, at midcentury the number of mental hospital inpatients per 100,000 U.S. residents greatly exceeded the *overall* prison incarceration rate. The figure presents state and county mental hospital inpatients per 100,000, state and federal prisoners per 100,000, and the sum of these two series for the years between 1930 and 2000.[2] During the 1950s, the mental hospital inpatient rate was approximately three times the prison incarceration rate. The trend toward deinstitutionalization of the mentally ill began in earnest during the 1960s. Thereafter, the inpatient rate declined precipitously, falling below the incarceration rate in the mid-1970s and then continuing to decline. The positive difference between the prison incarceration rate and the mental hospital inpatient rate widened quickly during the 1980s and 1990s as the country experienced a nearly fivefold increase in incarceration rates. By the end of the twentieth century, the overall institutionalization rate (prisons and mental hospitals combined) was not appreciably different from what it was during the peak years for the mental hospital population.

The deinstitutionalization of the mentally ill, juxtaposed against the increase in incarceration rates and the current high incidence of severe mental illness behind bars, begs the question of whether the mentally ill have simply been transferred from mental hospitals to prisons and jails. Of course, we do not literally mean that residents of the nation's mental hospitals were physically relocated to prisons and jails. To be more precise, the declining likelihood of being committed as a mental hospital inpatient, due to policy changes that we discuss shortly, may have increased the relative risk of incarceration for the mentally ill. With less inpatient treatment, the severely mentally ill may be at a higher risk of committing a crime and ending up wards of state

Figure 5.1   Prisoners per 100,000 U.S. Residents, Mental Hospital Inpatients per 100,000 U.S. Residents, and Total Institutionalized Population per 100,000 U.S. Residents, 1930 to 2000

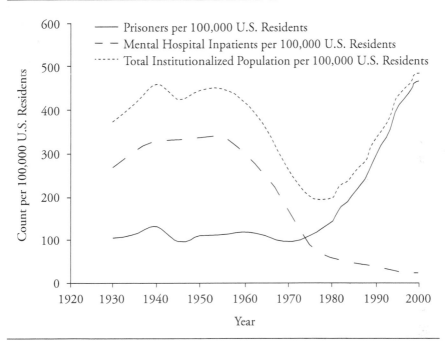

——— Prisoners per 100,000 U.S. Residents
– – Mental Hospital Inpatients per 100,000 U.S. Residents
······· Total Institutionalized Population per 100,000 U.S. Residents

Source: Prison data come from the Bureau of Justice Statistics, *National Prison Statistics Series* (various years). Data on mental hospital inpatients come from Palermo, Smith, and Liska (1991) and Raphael (2000).

or federal corrections authorities. To the extent that deinstitutionalization was not offset by sufficient expansion of outpatient mental health services, the closing of U.S. mental hospitals may have contributed to the drastic increase in U.S. incarceration rates over the past several decades, with prisons and jails becoming de facto mental institutions. Moreover, the untreated mentally ill may be at particularly high risk of incarceration today relative to past years owing in part to a much more punitive sentencing environment, which we documented in the first half of the book.

In this chapter, we assess the merits of this proposition. We analyze U.S. census data covering the period from 1950 to 2000 to assess the degree to which the mentally ill who would have been in mental hospitals in years past are now in prisons and jails. We begin with a detailed descriptive analysis of the population of state, county, and private mental hospitals as of midcentury (essentially the population deinstitutionalized over the subsequent fifty years). We document the fact that many of those who were institutionalized in the 1950s and 1960s and who were subsequently deinstitutionalized did not experience large increases in incarceration. In particular, the deinstitutionalization of women (who comprised nearly half the mental hospital population at its peak) and the elderly (who were nearly 30 percent of the mental hospital inpatient population) did not lead to substantial increases in incarceration for these groups. On the other hand, those who were most likely to be incarcerated as of the 2000 census experienced pronounced increases in overall institutionalization between 1950 and 2000, with particularly large increases for black males. Thus, the impression created by the aggregate trends in figure 5.1 is misleading, since the composition of the mental hospital population has differed considerably from the demographic composition of prison and jail inmates.

We also estimate the rate at which individuals who would have been institutionalized in years past have been transferred into prisons and jails—that is to say, the extent to which deinstitutionalization should be more accurately characterized as "transinstitutionalization" from hospitals to prisons and jails. We find no evidence of transinstitutionalization for any of the demographic groups analyzed prior to 1980. We do, however, find evidence that declining mental hospitalization rates after 1980 are related to growth in U.S. incarceration rates, especially for white men.

Regarding the numerical contribution of deinstitutionalization to prison growth, our estimates suggest that at most 3 to 6 percent of incarceration growth between 1980 and 2000 can be attributed to deinstitutionalization. Although this is a relatively small contribution to prison growth overall, the results do suggest that a sizable portion of the mentally ill behind bars today would not have been incarcerated in years past.

DEINSTITUTIONALIZATION AND THE CRIMINAL JUSTICE SYSTEM

Policies, Innovations, and Legal Decisions Driving Deinstitutionalization

The term "deinstitutionalization" refers to the set of policies and treatment innovations that drove the more than half-million-person decrease in the population of state and county mental hospitals between 1955 and the present. Although some of these policy choices were explicitly and deliberately aimed at reducing the use of mental hospitals, the cumulative decline also reflects pharmacological innovations and changes in the delivery of health care and the inherent budgetary incentives created for states (Johnson 1990). Initial declines during the late 1950s are often attributed to the introduction of medications, particularly phenothiazine, to control psychotic symptoms and possibly permit more effective outpatient treatment for the least severe cases of mental illness. A further impetus toward reduction of use of mental hospitals came with the 1966 introduction of the Medicaid and Medicare programs. Under these programs, the federal government's commitment to a 50 percent match for treatment costs in nursing homes created an incentive for states to transfer all eligible residents of mental hospitals (primarily the elderly mentally ill and those suffering from dementia) to nursing homes and other facilities. The reaction to this incentive by states accounts for much of the decline in the inpatient census during the 1960s and 1970s (Mechanic and Rochefort 1990).

The one policy change that embraced deinstitutionalization as an explicit goal was made under the Kennedy administration. The 1963 Community Mental Health Service Act established community mental health centers (CMHCs) to provide outpatient, emergency, and partial hospitalization services for the mentally ill. The legislation embodied the shift in professional opinion among service providers that favored outpatient care and residence in the community above traditional inpatient treatment in state mental hospitals.[3] A further force reducing inpatient population counts was the 1975 U.S. Supreme Court decision in O'Connor v. Donaldson, a key element of which was the finding that mental illness alone is not sufficient grounds for involuntary commitment. In subsequent years, most states changed their involuntary commitment statutes to require that an individual be a danger to himself or herself or to others, with varying evidentiary requirements. Most informed observers believe that involuntary commitment has become considerably more difficult as a result (Ross, Rothbard, and Schinnar 1996; Werth 2001).

To the extent that outpatient mental health services are inadequate, deinstitutionalization exposes severely and chronically mentally ill individuals to a number of competing risks. The risk that has received the most attention from academics and the press is the risk of homelessness among those with untreated mental illness (Jencks 1994; Torrey 1997). A competing risk that has received less attention is the probability of incarceration. The magnitude of the incarceration risk faced by the untreated mentally ill depends on the degree to which they are likely to commit crimes. Moreover, whether the mentally ill are incarcerated in jail or prison depends on the severity of the offenses they commit.

E. Fuller Torrey (1997) notes that the mentally ill are often arrested for minor crimes, such as shoplifting, engaging in publicly lewd behavior, or failure to pay for a restaurant meal, that are likely to result in a jail spell. Torrey also cites several instances of local authorities putting the mentally ill in jails so that they have a place to stay while awaiting psychiatric services and more suitable housing.[4]

A prison sentence, on the other hand, requires being convicted of a serious felony. Several studies address the issue of whether the mentally ill commit violent acts at a higher rate than the rate observed for the general public. An early review of this research documents the consistent finding that discharged mental patients are arrested and convicted for violent crimes at a rate that exceeds that of the general adult population (Godwin-Rabkin 1979).[5] The more recent literature reviews provided by John Monahan (1992) and Richard Frank and Thomas McGuire (2011) arrive at similar conclusions; these authors note the robustness of the relationship between severe mental illness and violence to alternative methodological approaches to measuring this relationship.[6]

The Prevalence of Mental Illness Among Prison and Jail Inmates

Analysis of recent inmate surveys reveals an overrepresentation of the seriously mentally ill among prison and jail inmates. Moreover, the fact that there is little indication that the incarcerated mentally ill are overly concentrated among jail inmates suggests that the criminal justice interactions of the untreated mentally ill extend beyond being jailed for safekeeping. Table 5.1 presents estimates of the lifetime prevalence of various mental illnesses from the 2004 Survey of Inmates in State and Federal Corrections Facilities and the 2002 Survey of Inmates in Local Jails. These estimates are based on questions about whether inmates have ever received a diagnosis of a specific mental illness from a health care professional. Certainly, these figures underestimate actual lifetime prevalence, since there are likely to be many mentally ill inmates who have never been diagnosed.[7] For comparison, the table also presents two sets of prevalence estimates for the general adult population.[8] Although we could not find comparable estimates for each condition included in the inmate surveys, these studies do provide lifetime prevalence estimates

Table 5.1   Lifetime Prevalence of Mental Illness Among Prison and Jail Inmates and the General Population

Have you ever been told by a mental health professional such as a psychiatrist or a psychologist that you have . . .	Prison		Jail	Non-Institutionalized	
	State, 2004	Federal, 2004	2002	All Persons Age Eighteen and Over, 2000 to 2002	All Males Age Fifteen to Fifty-Four, 1990 to 1992
. . . a depressive disorder?	0.191	0.108	0.194	0.166	0.121
. . . manic depression, bipolar, or mania?	0.097	0.041	0.101	0.039	0.016
. . . schizophrenia or another psychotic disorder?	0.046	0.020	0.046	0.007[a]	0.006[a]
. . . post-traumatic stress disorder?	0.057	0.033	0.051	0.068	—
. . . another anxiety disorder such as panic disorder?	0.071	0.046	0.071	0.057[b]	0.036[b]
. . . personality disorder such as antisocial or borderline?	0.060	0.033	0.051	—	—
. . . any other mental or emotional condition?	0.019	0.008	0.020	—	—
Any of the above?	0.248	0.144	0.250	—	—

Source: Prevalence levels for prison inmates are based on our analysis of the 2004 *Survey of Inmates in State and Federal Corrections Facilities* (Bureau of Justice Statistics 2004b), and prevalence estimates for jail inmates are based on our analysis of the 2002 *Survey of Inmates in Local Jails* (Bureau of Justice Statistics 2002b). Prevalence estimates for the total non-institutionalized population are based on analysis by Kessler et al. (2005) of the *National Comorbidity Survey* replication conducted between 2001 and 2003; the data are nationally representative of all non-institutionalized English-speaking residents of the United States over eighteen years of age. The estimates for men fifteen to fifty-four come from Kessler et al. (1994) and are based on analysis of the original *National Comorbidity Survey.* This data set pertains to all non-institutionalized persons between fifteen and fifty-four years of age and was conducted from 1990 through 1992.

[a] For the non-institutionalized, prevalence is measured for all individuals with a history of non-affective psychosis, including schizophrenia, schizophreniform disorder, schizo-affective disorder, delusional disorder, and atypical psychosis. See Kessler et al. (1994) for details. Note that the figures in this cell pertain to the earlier *National Corrections Reporting Program* survey and thus measure the lifetime prevalence of non-affective psychoses as of the early 1990s.

[b] For the non-institutionalized, prevalence is measured for those indicating that they have generalized anxiety disorder.

for the most severe mental illnesses (manic depression, schizophrenia, and other psychotic disorders).

Lifetime prevalences of mental illness for state prison inmates and for local jail inmates are nearly identical, with one-quarter of each group indicating at least one diagnosis. The prevalence of severe mental illness (manic depression and bipolar disorder or a psychotic disorder) among state prisoners and local jail inmates is very high (nearly 15 percent of each population, or 3.1 to 6.5 times the rate observed for the general adult population). The rates of mental illness among federal prison inmates are somewhat lower. Federal prison inmates account for only 13 percent of the prison population, however, so the overall prevalence of mental illness among prison inmates is much closer to the figures for state prisoners.

Tables 5.2, 5.3, and 5.4 present tabulations of average demographic as well as criminal history characteristics for state prisoners, federal prisoners, and jail inmates, respectively, by mental health status. Each table provides tabulations for all inmates, for inmates with no diagnosed mental illness, for inmates with any diagnosis, and for inmates diagnosed with bipolar disorder or manic depression or a psychotic disorder. There are several notable patterns in table 5.2. First, although males and racial and ethnic minorities are heavily over-represented among state prison inmates relative to the overall U.S. adult population, this is less the case among mentally ill inmates, especially among the severely mentally ill. For example, while 93 percent of state prison inmates are male, approximately 85 percent of severely mentally ill inmates are male. Similarly, while whites account for 49 percent of all inmates, the comparable figure for the mentally ill is 63 percent.

These patterns are consistent with the body of research documenting differences in the prevalence of mental illness across demographic and socioeconomic groups. In their review of fifty years of research on the topic, Richard Frank and Shelly Glied (2006) find relatively comparable lifetime prevalence rates of severe mental illness for men and women and for different racial groups. While adults of low socioeconomic status (SES) are overrepresented among the mentally ill (whether measured by their own income and education or by parental characteristics), it is difficult to rule out the possibility that their mental health condition is responsible for their relatively low SES.[9] In any event, since mental illness does not discriminate by race and gender, it is noteworthy that the demographics of the incarcerated mentally ill are closer to the demographics of the general adult population than are those for the incarcerated overall.

Table 5.2   Characteristics of State Prison Inmates by Whether They Indicate Having Been Diagnosed with a Mental Illness, 2004

	All State Prison Inmates	No Diagnosed Mental Illness	Diagnosed Mental Illness	Diagnosed with Bipolar, Manic, or Psychotic Disorder
Male	0.932	0.953	0.868	0.846
Married	0.164	0.167	0.154	0.142
Any children	0.555	0.558	0.546	0.555
Homeless prior to arrest	0.086	0.065	0.151	0.173
Latino	0.181	0.199	0.125	0.110
White	0.488	0.444	0.619	0.633
Black	0.430	0.466	0.321	0.317
American Indian	0.252	0.047	0.067	0.075
Offense				
Murder, homicide, or manslaughter	0.139	0.139	0.140	0.123
Sexual assault	0.107	0.102	0.124	0.099
Robbery	0.127	0.129	0.120	0.135
Assault	0.086	0.082	0.098	0.103
Other violent crime	0.020	0.019	0.024	0.023
Burglary	0.082	0.080	0.088	0.085
Fraud or larceny	0.078	0.072	0.096	0.114
Auto theft	0.012	0.011	0.016	0.020
Other property crime	0.010	0.010	0.012	0.013
Drugs	0.213	0.230	0.161	0.155
Weapons	0.025	0.027	0.018	0.019
Other	0.101	0.100	0.104	0.112
Parent or stepparent served time	0.201	0.247	0.247	0.263
Age				
Twenty-fifth percentile	27	26	27	27
Fiftieth percentile	34	34	35	35
Seventy-fifth percentile	42	42	42	42
Age at first arrest				
Twenty-fifth percentile	15	15	14	14
Fiftieth percentile	17	17	17	17
Seventy-fifth percentile	21	21	20	20

Source: Authors' tabulations from the 2004 *Survey of Inmates in State and Federal Prisons* (Bureau of Justice Statistics 2004b).

A second notable pattern among state inmates is that the mentally ill are only slightly more likely to be serving time for a violent crime (50.6 percent of all mentally ill compared to 47.1 percent of inmates without a diagnosis). The severely mentally ill are considerably more likely to be serving time for a property crime (six percentage points more likely), and are somewhat less likely to be doing time for a drug offense.

Finally, mentally ill prison inmates are more likely to indicate that they suffered a spell of homelessness in the year preceding the arrest leading to their current incarceration.[10] While 17.3 percent of inmates with severe mental illness experienced homelessness prior to their current arrest, the comparable figure for inmates with no diagnosed mental illness is 6.5 percent.

We observe similar demographic patterns for federal prison inmates, with lower proportions male, higher proportions white, and lower proportions Latino and black among the severely mentally ill (see table 5.3). We also observe a strong relationship between mental illness and the likelihood of being homeless prior to arrest. Mentally ill federal inmates are considerably more likely to be held for violent crime than are inmates with no diagnosis (28 percent for the severely mentally ill compared with 14 percent for inmates with no diagnosis) and considerably less likely to be serving time for a drug crime. One pattern that is unique to the federal system concerns the proportion serving time for a weapons violation. Inmates with severe mental illness are eight percentage points more likely to be incarcerated for a weapons violation than are inmates with diagnosed mental illness. Under federal law, individuals who have been "adjudicated mentally defective" or "committed to a mental health institution" are prohibited from purchasing firearms (Daly 2008). This differential treatment of the mentally ill under federal law may explain this disparity.

The comparisons for jail inmates largely conform to the patterns observed for state and federal prison inmates. We see similar patterns with regard to gender and race (table 5.4). Over one-fifth of severely mentally ill inmates were homeless prior to arrest. Severely mentally ill inmates are also nearly twice as likely to have been arrested for a violent crime relative to inmates with no such diagnosis. One interesting finding that jumps out from this table is the relatively small proportion of inmates who are being held for safekeeping. Only half a percent of all inmates are described in this manner. Although the proportion of the mentally ill being held for safekeeping is three times that for inmates who are not mentally ill, only 1 percent of jail inmates with severe mental illness are being held for this reason.[11]

Table 5.3   Characteristics of Federal Prison Inmates by Whether They Indicate Having Been Diagnosed with a Mental Illness, 2004

	All Federal Prison Inmates	No Diagnosed Mental Illness	Diagnosed Mental Illness	Diagnosed with Bipolar, Manic, or Psychotic Disorder
Male	0.929	0.943	0.847	0.834
Married	0.259	0.266	0.221	0.167
Any children	0.643	0.653	0.589	0.527
Homeless prior to arrest	0.037	0.026	0.100	0.154
Latino	0.249	0.261	0.179	0.112
White	0.435	0.412	0.575	0.574
Black	0.463	0.489	0.327	0.356
American Indian	0.040	0.036	0.064	0.044
Offense				
Murder, homicide, or manslaughter	0.029	0.029	0.026	0.029
Sexual assault	0.009	0.008	0.014	0.004
Robbery	0.085	0.077	0.134	0.205
Assault	0.017	0.017	0.019	0.029
Other violent crime	0.006	0.004	0.013	0.015
Burglary	0.005	0.004	0.008	0.021
Fraud or larceny	0.034	0.032	0.043	0.053
Auto theft	0.001	0.001	0.003	0.009
Other property crime	0.001	0.002	0.007	0.016
Drugs	0.552	0.575	0.418	0.339
Weapons	0.110	0.099	0.175	0.192
Other	0.150	0.151	0.140	0.089
Parent or stepparent served time	0.148	0.140	0.199	0.233
Age				
Twenty-fifth percentile	29	29	29	27
Fiftieth percentile	35	35	36	34
Seventy-fifth percentile	44	44	44	43
Age at first arrest				
Twenty-fifth percentile	16	16	15	13
Fiftieth percentile	18	18	18	17
Seventy-fifth percentile	23	23	22	22

Source: Authors' tabulations from the 2004 *Survey of Inmates in State and Federal Prisons* (Bureau of Justice Statistics 2004b).

Table 5.4   Characteristics of Jail Inmates by Whether They Indicate Having
Been Diagnosed with a Mental Illness, 2002

	All Jail Inmates	No Diagnosed Mental Illness	Diagnosed Mental Illness	Diagnosed with Bipolar, Manic, or Psychotic Disorder
Male	0.883	0.913	0.792	0.781
Married	0.161	0.169	0.142	0.124
Any children	0.552	0.552	0.554	0.546
Homeless prior to arrest	0.127	0.102	0.207	0.228
Latino	0.184	0.208	0.114	0.105
White	0.500	0.462	0.614	0.617
Black	0.430	0.456	0.337	0.336
American Indian	0.045	0.041	0.057	0.053
Reason held				
Awaiting arraignment	0.109	0.114	0.096	0.097
To stand trial	0.259	0.244	0.302	0.309
Awaiting parole or probation hearing	0.095	0.096	0.095	0.099
For safekeeping	0.005	0.003	0.010	0.009
As a witness	0.002	0.001	0.005	0.002
For contempt of court	0.014	0.014	0.001	0.016
Awaiting sentencing	0.109	0.103	0.128	0.114
Serving a sentence	0.353	0.362	0.325	0.302
Awaiting transfer	0.072	0.071	0.075	0.085
Other reason	0.067	0.068	0.064	0.066
Defining offense				
Violent offense	0.082	0.079	0.090	0.149
Property offense	0.251	0.261	0.218	0.183
Violation for financial gain	0.068	0.065	0.076	0.076
Drug offense	0.032	0.035	0.025	0.016
Public-order offense	0.568	0.560	0.591	0.575
Parent or stepparent served time	0.212	0.192	0.272	0.289
Age				
Twenty-fifth percentile	23	23	24	24
Fiftieth percentile	31	30	32	32
Seventy-fifth percentile	39	39	40	40
Age at first arrest				
Twenty-fifth percentile	15	16	15	15
Fiftieth percentile	18	18	17	17
Seventy-fifth percentile	21	22	21	20

Source: Authors' tabulations from the 2002 *Survey of Inmates in Local Jails* (Bureau of Justice Statistics 2002b).

The prevalence rates in table 5.1 and the comparisons of inmate characteristics in tables 5.2 to 5.4 clearly indicate that the mentally ill are at relatively high risk of experiencing incarceration. Moreover, mentally ill inmates are often serving time for quite serious, often violent crimes, while on any given day there are relatively few being held for safekeeping. To be sure, a high propensity among the mentally ill to commit violent acts and a relatively high incidence of mental illness among prison inmates do not imply that the closing of mental hospitals contributed significantly to growth in prison populations. If the difference in the propensity to commit violent acts is slight, deinstitutionalization may not cause notable increases in prison populations. Moreover, it is plausible that the incidence of mental illness among criminal offenders has always been high and that the mentally ill who would have been hospitalized in the past and the mentally ill who commit crime are separate populations.

There are two studies that directly correlate prison populations with mental hospital populations. Lionel Penrose (1939) was probably the first to raise the issue. Analyzing data from eighteen European countries, Penrose found a negative correlation between the size of the prison and mental hospital populations. Based on this negative relationship, Penrose advanced what he labeled the "balloon theory": assuming a stable population in need of institutionalization, squeezing the population of one institution (for example, closing mental hospitals) will cause a ballooning of the other as the displaced population is transferred. Although the statistical analysis in this early study was simplistic by modern standards, it is interesting to note that the inverse relationship observed in figure 5.1 existed in a different time and place.[12]

A more recent study by George Palermo, Maurice Smith, and Frank Liska (1991) analyzes national data for the United States between 1926 and 1987. This research also reveals a significant negative correlation between the size of the nation's mental hospital population and its prison and jail populations. Although these authors make no attempt to control for other possibly important variables, the documented empirical relationship is quite strong.

WHAT IS THE MAXIMUM POSSIBLE CONTRIBUTION OF DEINSTITUTIONALIZATION TO PRISON AND JAIL GROWTH?

The research findings regarding the relationship between severe mental illness and criminal activity, combined with the overrepresentation of the mentally ill behind bars, suggest that deinstitutionalization was an important contributor to U.S. prison growth during the last few decades of the twentieth century.

Table 5.5   Distribution of Institutional and Non-Institutional Populations Across Age Groups, Race-Ethnicity Groups, and Gender, 1950 to 1980

	1950			1960		
	Mental Hospital	Prison and Jails	Non-institutional	Mental Hospital	Prison and Jails	Non-institutional
Age groups						
Under ten	0.85	0.84	19.51	0.43	0.03	22.03
Ten to seventeen	1.06	11.10	11.51	1.66	2.85	14.21
Eighteen to twenty-five	5.31	27.54	12.13	5.03	30.01	9.86
Twenty-six to thirty	6.32	17.28	8.19	4.30	16.38	6.13
Thirty-one to thirty-five	8.02	12.88	7.54	5.94	13.76	6.73
Thirty-six to forty	8.40	8.69	7.45	7.36	11.86	6.90
Forty-one to forty-five	8.34	7.23	6.53	8.32	8.39	6.39
Forty-six to fifty	11.16	5.24	6.08	9.52	6.40	5.89
Fifty-one to fifty-five	11.69	4.08	5.20	10.11	4.78	5.28
Fifty-six to sixty-four	18.54	3.25	7.75	18.61	4.50	7.71
Sixty-five and over	20.30	1.88	8.10	28.72	.03	8.88
Race-ethnicity						
White	87.62	62.20	87.99	85.03	58.86	86.63
Black	10.52	33.40	9.90	12.73	35.57	10.47
Other	0.43	1.26	0.43	1.00	1.87	0.89
Hispanic	1.43	3.14	1.68	1.24	3.69	2.01
Gender						
Male	52.55	90.79	49.60	53.23	95.10	49.01
Female	47.45	9.21	50.40	46.77	4.90	50.99
Population estimate (in thousands)	621	315	151,274	698	356	178,247

Source: Authors' tabulations from U.S Census Bureau (1950, 1960, 1970, and 1980).

However, a careful analysis of the characteristics of those in mental hospitals during their peak period of use reveals large differences between the characteristics of those who were subsequently deinstitutionalized and those who were incarcerated at high rates.

Prison and jail inmates in the United States are overwhelmingly male, disproportionately minority, and relatively young. The same cannot be said for mental patients at midcentury. Table 5.5 uses U.S. census data for 1950 through 1980 to characterize mental hospital inpatients, prison and jail in-

Table 5.5   (Continued)

	1970			1980	
Mental Hospital	Prison and Jails	Non-institutional	Mental Hospital	Prison and Jails	Non-institutional
0.57	0.15	18.48	0.73	0.04	14.77
3.59	3.43	16.18	6.26	2.23	13.69
9.09	39.67	12.76	14.63	43.15	14.80
6.13	16.67	6.43	9.18	21.66	8.41
5.75	11.24	5.50	9.02	12.90	7.41
6.50	9.15	5.51	6.91	7.65	5.97
8.04	6.69	5.85	6.95	4.60	5.06
8.02	5.34	5.90	5.81	2.67	4.91
9.00	3.29	5.28	7.76	2.41	5.20
18.33	3.35	8.11	12.52	1.63	8.54
24.99	1.03	10.00	20.24	1.06	11.24
82.80	54.67	85.52	79.40	47.14	81.50
15.45	40.29	11.03	17.15	42.65	11.65
0.93	1.82	1.18	1.95	5.14	3.41
0.82	3.23	2.27	1.50	5.07	3.45
55.95	94.84	48.45	60.79	94.10	48.37
44.05	5.16	51.55	39.21	5.90	51.63
440	341	202,257	246	461	226,024

mates, and the non-institutionalized population.[13] Beginning in 1950, there were several notable differences between the inpatient and correctional populations. First, the mental hospital population was considerably older, with larger proportions over forty and a population age sixty-five and over that was more than ten times the comparable figure for the correctional population. Second, the proportion black or Hispanic was not appreciably larger than the comparable proportion for the non-institutionalized population, while minorities were very much overrepresented in prisons and jails at midcentury.

One of the most pronounced disparities is the gender composition. In 1950 nearly half of the mental hospital population was female, while only 9 percent of those in prison or jail were women.

Between 1950 and 1980, the mental hospital inpatient population became younger, proportionally more minority, and more male, although the elderly and women still constituted larger proportions of the population of mental hospital inpatients than they did of prison and jail inmates. These changes suggest that deinstitutionalization proceeded in a nonrandom fashion, with institutionalization rates declining first for those who were perhaps the least likely to end up in prison or jail (women and the elderly), followed by subsequent declines in mental hospital institutionalization among groups who subsequently experienced increases in incarceration (young men and racial and ethnic minorities). Although we cannot characterize further changes in the composition of the mental hospital population beyond 1980, we know from aggregate statistics that by 2000 the mental hospital population had become trivially small. Hence, the mental hospital population depicted in 1980 largely represents the demographics of those released from mental hospitals over the subsequent two decades.

These demographic differences between prison and jail inmates and mental hospital patients suggest that the potential impact of deinstitutionalization on prison growth is substantially less than what we might infer from comparisons of aggregate time series. Although figure 5.1 reveals a decline in mental hospital institutionalization rates of a comparable order of magnitude to the late-century increase in incarceration, a pattern that suggests that we are simply rehousing the mental patients of 1950 in current prisons and jails, the demographic dissimilarities in table 5.5 indicate that we should be cautious before drawing such a conclusion.

To illustrate the importance of these compositional differences, we pose the following two questions. First, how has the overall institutionalization risk (in either mental hospitals or prisons and jails) for those who demographically resemble the incarcerated in 2000 changed since 1950? Second, how did the institutionalization risk for those who resemble mental hospital inpatients in 1950 change over the subsequent half-century? To the extent that we have simply transferred the same types of people from one institution to another, the 2000 institutionalization risk of those likely to be incarcerated in the year 2000 should resemble their comparable institutionalization risk at midcentury. Similarly, the institutionalization risk of those institutionalized in men-

Figure 5.2   Institutionalization Rates for Adults Age Eighteen to
                Sixty-Four Between 1950 and 2000, Actual Rates, Rates
                for Those Who Resemble 1950s Mental Hospital
                Patients, and Rates for Those Who Resemble the
                Incarcerated in 2000

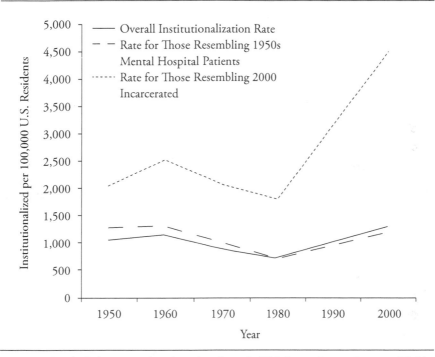

Source: Authors' tabulations are based on data from the U.S Census Bureau Integrated Public Use Microdata Samples of the U.S. Census of Population and Housing for census years 1950–2000.

tal hospitals in 1950 should be comparable in magnitude to the comparable risk in 2000.

To answer these questions, we use census data to estimate (1) the institutionalization rate for those most likely to be institutionalized in a mental hospital in 1950 for each year between 1950 and 2000, and (2) the institutionalization rate for those most likely to be institutionalized in a prison or jail in 2000 for each year between 1950 and 2000. The details of these tabulations are presented in the appendix. Figure 5.2 presents the results of this exercise when we analyze all adults age eighteen to sixty-four. The solid line shows the actual institutionalization rate (prisons, jails, and mental hospitals combined) for each year. The overall institutionalization risk exhibits a pattern comparable to that in figure 5.1: a substantial decline between 1960 and 1980 from 1,156 per 100,000 U.S. residents to 716 per 100,000, followed by a more than offsetting increase to 1,309 per 100,000 in 2000.

The long-dashed line shows the institutionalization rates for individuals with demographic characteristics most like those who were institutionalized in mental hospitals in 1950. Not surprisingly, the institutionalization risk for this group exceeded the overall risk in the peak mental hospital years of 1950 and 1960 by 14 percent. By 2000, however, the institutionalization risk for this group had fallen short of the overall institutionalization rate by 7 percent. In other words, those who were most likely to be institutionalized in a mental hospital in 1950 were less likely than average to be institutionalized by 2000.

The short-dashed line presents comparable results for individuals with demographics that match those of the typical person institutionalized in a prison or jail in the year 2000. Note that this group has always had a relatively high institutionalization rate, as evidenced by the fact that the short-dashed line lies everywhere above the other two time series. This series exhibits a sharp increase between 1950 and 2000. Relative to the peak year of 1960, the institutionalization risk for this group increased nearly 80 percent, from 2,521 per 100,000 to 4,512 per 100,000. In conjunction, the series in figure 5.2 suggest real declines in the institutionalization risks for those who would have been institutionalized in the past (both absolutely and relative to overall trends) and real, particularly large increases in institutionalization risks for those who were most likely to be institutionalized in 2000.

Figures 5.3 and 5.4 reproduce the analysis by gender. For women, institutionalization rates have declined quite sharply overall. For women who were likely to be institutionalized in mental hospitals in 1950, the decline exceeded the declines for women overall. Even among women who disproportionately comprised the institutionalized in 2000, the overall institutionalization risk declined over the period depicted. However, the risk for this latter group increased somewhat between 1980 and 2000.

The results for men are comparable to the results for all adults presented in figure 5.2, with some slight difference. We still see that the institutionalization rate for those likely to have been in a mental hospital in 1950 exceeded the overall risk for males in 1950 and 1960, but fell below the overall risk after 1970. For these men, however, the overall institutionalization risk did increase somewhat from the 1960 peak (from 1,701 per 100,000 in 1960 to 1,924 per

Figure 5.3   Institutionalization Rates for Women Age Eighteen to Sixty-Four Between 1950 and 2000, Actual Rates, Rates for Women Who Resemble 1950s Female Mental Hospital Patients, and Rates for Women Who Resemble Incarcerated Females in 2000

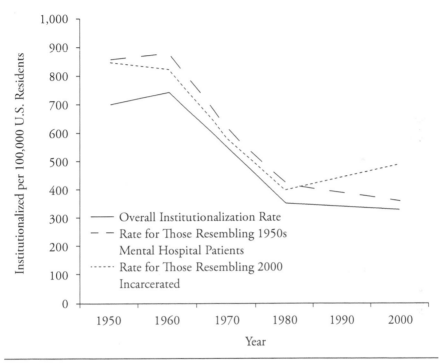

Source: Authors' tabulations are based on data from the U.S Census Bureau Integrated Public Use Microdata Samples of the U.S. Census of Population and Housing for census years 1950–2000.

100,000 in 2000). Among men from demographic groups reflecting the 2000 incarcerated population, the institutionalization risk increased sharply.

The dissimilarities between those in mental hospitals and those in prisons and jails, as well as the limits of the potential contribution of deinstitutionalization to prison growth, become particularly salient when we take a close look at the period between 1980 and 2000. Note that nearly 92 percent of the growth in U.S. incarceration rates between 1950 and 2000 occurred between 1980 and 2000, with most of the remaining 8 percent occurring during the latter half of the 1970s. Hence, a focused analysis on this time period is cen-

Figure 5.4   Institutionalization Rates for Men Age Eighteen to Sixty-
                 Four Between 1950 and 2000, Actual Rates, Rates for
                 Men Who Resemble 1950s Male Mental Hospital
                 Patients, and Rates for Men Who Resemble
                 Incarcerated Males in 2000

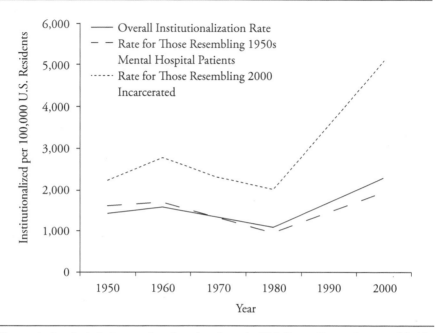

Source: Authors' tabulations are based on data from the U.S Census Bureau Integrated Public Use Microdata Samples of the U.S. Census of Population and Housing for census years 1950–2000.

tral to evaluating the potential importance of deinstitutionalization in explaining prison growth.

Figures 5.5 through 5.8 present comparisons of mental hospitalization rates in 1980 to change in incarceration rates between 1980 and 2000 for white and black males (figures 5.5 and 5.6) and white and black females (figures 5.7 and 5.8). Each figure provides comparisons for eight age groups between eighteen and sixty-four. Note that we would ideally wish to compare the change in mental hospital institutionalization rates over this period to the corresponding changes in incarceration rates. However, the census does not distinguish the incarcerated from mental hospital inpatients in publicly available data beyond 1980. Nonetheless, we know that by 2000 the overall population of state and county mental hospitals had declined to very low numbers

Figure 5.5   Comparison of the Change in Institutionalization Rates (2000 Institutionalization Minus 1980 Incarceration) to the Mental Hospital Inpatient Rate as of 1980: White Males

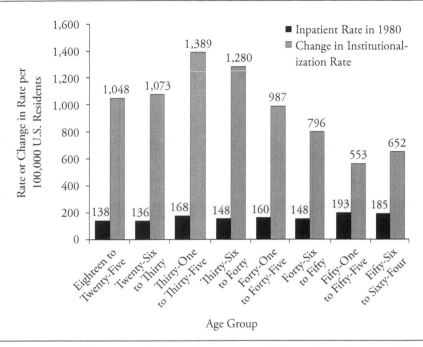

Source: Authors' tabulations are based on data from the U.S Census Bureau Integrated Public Use Microdata Samples of the U.S. Census of Population and Housing for census years 1980 and 2000.

in all states. Thus, if we assume for the sake of argument that the mental hospital population zeroed out by 2000, the mental hospital inpatient rate in 1980 equaled (in absolute value) the extent of deinstitutionalization between 1980 and 2000.

For white males, the mental hospital inpatient rate in 1980 was 12 to 17 percent of the change in incarceration rates between 1980 and 2000, with larger-percentage figures for older groups of males (those least likely to be incarcerated in 2000). This implies that deinstitutionalization over this period can explain at most 12 to 17 percent of the growth in incarceration for white males (assuming a one-to-one shift from mental hospitals to prisons among this population). The comparable figures for black males are considerably smaller. For relatively young black males (under age forty), the base mental

Figure 5.6   Comparison of the Change in Institutionalization Rates
(2000 Institutionalization Minus 1980 Incarceration) to
the Mental Hospital Inpatient Rate as of 1980: Black
Males

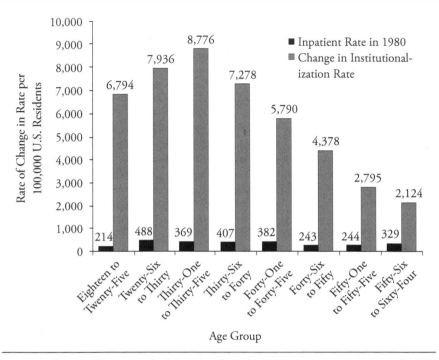

Source: Authors' tabulations are based on data from the U.S Census Bureau Integrated Public
Use Microdata Samples of the U.S. Census of Population and Housing for census years 1980
and 2000.

hospital inpatient rates ranged from 3 to 6 percent of the change in incarceration over the subsequent two decades. Similar to white males, the comparable
figures for older groups of black males were higher, though never exceeding
20 percent of the actual change. For white women, 1980 mental hospitalization rates constituted relatively larger proportions of the subsequent change
in incarceration (40 to 60 percent), while for black females the comparable
figures ranged from 10 to 30 percent across age groups.

These comparisons can be used to calculate a maximum potential contribution of deinstitutionalization to incarceration growth as well as several estimates of the impact of deinstitutionalization under alternative assumptions
regarding the rate at which deinstitutionalized mental patients are transferred
into prisons and jails. To do so, we first tabulate what the incarceration rate

Figure 5.7   Comparison of the Change in Institutionalization Rates (2000 Institutionalization Minus 1980 Incarceration) to the Mental Hospital Inpatient Rate as of 1980: White Females

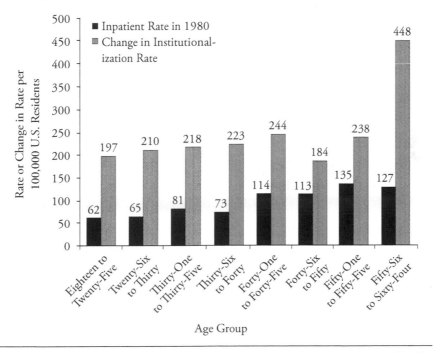

Source: Authors' tabulations are based on data from the U.S Census Bureau Integrated Public Use Microdata Samples of the U.S. Census of Population and Housing for census years 1980 and 2000.

would have been in 2000 for demographic groups defined by gender, race-ethnicity, and age assuming (1) that the mental hospitalization rate did not decline from the 1980 value, and (2) that each one-person decline in the mental hospitalization rate causes a one-person increase in the incarceration rate. For example, the mental hospitalization rate for white males age eighteen to twenty-five in 1980 was 138 per 100,000, while the change in the incarceration rate for this group was 1,048 per 100,000 between 1980 and 2000. Hence, the most that the deinstitutionalization of the mentally ill could have contributed to incarceration growth for this group was 13 percent (138/1,048 × 100). We then use these estimates for each demographic group to estimate what the overall incarceration rate would have been in 2000 taking into account the relative size of each demographic group in the U.S.

Figure 5.8   Comparison of the Change in Institutionalization Rates
                (2000 Institutionalization Minus 1980 Incarceration) to
                the Mental Hospital Inpatient Rate as of 1980: Black
                Females

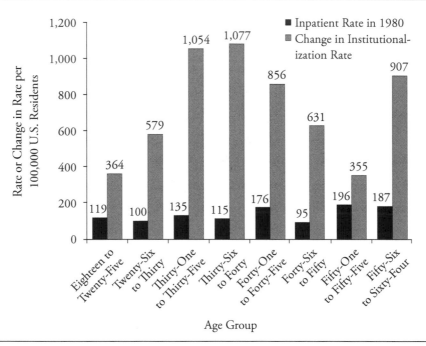

Age Group

Source: Authors' tabulations are based on data from the U.S Census Bureau Integrated Public
Use Microdata Samples of the U.S. Census of Population and Housing for census years 1980
and 2000.

population. The extent to which this hypothetical incarceration rate is lower
than the actual incarceration rate in 2000 provides a measure of the potential
contribution of deinstitutionalization to prison growth.

Table 5.6 provides some of the intermediate inputs for this tabulation. (To
conserve space we do not provide the age-specific tabulations.) The first two
columns of figures present the actual incarceration rates in 1980 and 2000 by
gender and race-ethnicity. The third column presents the hypothetical 2000
incarceration rate for each group assuming one-for-one transinstitutionalization and no deinstitutionalization since 1980. The fourth and fifth columns
provide alternative hypothetical estimates assuming transinstitutionalization
rates of one-half and one-quarter.

Table 5.6 Institutionalization and Incarceration Rates per 100,000 U.S. Residents by Race-Ethnicity and Gender, Actual (1980 and 2000) and Hypothetical, Assuming Complete Mental Hospital Deinstitutionalization Since 1980 and Alternative Transinstitutionalization Rates Between Mental Hospitals and Prisons

	1980 Actual Incarceration Rate	2000 Actual Institutionalization Rate	2000 Hypothetical Rate Assuming a Transinstitutionalization Rate of 1	2000 Hypothetical Rate Assuming a Transinstitutionalization Rate of 0.5	2000 Hypothetical Rate Assuming a Transinstitutionalization Rate of 0.25
White males	356	1,285	1,127	1,206	1,246
Black males	2,625	8,467	8,136	8,301	8,384
Other males	980	1,398	1,250	1,324	1,361
Hispanic males	1,000	2,919	2,833	2,876	2,897
White females	18	265	169	217	241
Black females	144	852	716	784	818
Other females	54	217	191	204	211
Hispanic females	60	265	212	239	252

Source: Authors' tabulations from the U.S Census Bureau 1980 and 2000 One Percent Public Use Microdata Samples from the U.S. Census of Population and Housing.

Note: Hypothetical institutionalization rates assume a contribution of deinstitutionalization to the overall 2000 institutionalization rate equal to the mental hospital inpatient rate in 1980 multiplied by the assumed transinstitutionalization parameter. Average institutionalization rates within gender and race groups are calculated by averaging the age-specific estimates using the 2000 population shares within gender and race groups as weights. The hypothetical tabulations assume complete deinstitutionalization between 1980 and 2000—that is, the simulations assume no mental hospital inpatients in 2000.

The results of this exercise reveal what is likely to be a modest contribution of deinstitutionalization to incarceration growth. Starting with black males (the group that is most overrepresented among the incarcerated and that has experienced the largest growth in incarceration), these tabulations indicate that at most deinstitutionalization contributed 331 persons per 100,000 to the 5,842 persons per 100,000 change in the incarceration rate experienced by black males (less than 6 percent of growth). For white males, the tabulations suggest that deinstitutionalization could be culpable for at most 17 percent of incarceration growth. The comparable figure for Hispanic males is 4 percent. Among women, the upper-bound estimates suggest that deinstitutionalization is a proportionally more important contributor to incarceration growth (39 percent for white women, 19 percent for black women, 16 percent for other women, and 26 percent for Hispanic women). Naturally, when we assume lower transinstitutionalization rates, the tabulated contribution of deinstitutionalization to prison growth falls.

Of course, the overall contribution of deinstitutionalization to prison growth will more closely reflect the estimates for demographic groups that constitute disproportionate shares of the prison population. That is to say, the overall impact will be closer to that of males, and in particular, to that of black and Hispanic males. Figure 5.9 graphically displays the actual jail and prison incarceration rates for 1980 and 2000 and several hypothetical overall incarceration rates in 2000: a hypothetical rate assuming no deinstitutionalization between 1980 and 2000 and one-for-one transinstitutionalization, a comparable rate assuming transinstitutionalization of one-half for one, and a comparable incarceration rate assuming transinstitutionalization of one-quarter for one. The hypothetical 2000 incarceration rate assuming a one-for-one transfer rate is roughly 90 percent of the actual rate for that year. Growth between 1980 and this hypothetical rate amounts to 87 percent of the actual growth in incarceration rates between 1980 and 2000. In other words, these tabulations indicate that deinstitutionalization over this period can account for no more than 13 percent of the corresponding growth in incarceration. To be sure, the estimated contributions to incarceration growth are smaller when we assume lower transinstitutionalization rates (7 percent assuming a transfer rate of one-half for one and 3 percent assuming a transfer rate of one-quarter for one).

While the potential contribution of deinstitutionalization to overall incarceration growth is relatively modest, its potential contribution to growth in

Figure 5.9   Actual Incarceration and Institutionalization Rates in
                1980 and 2000 and Hypothetical Institutionalization
                Rates for 2000 Assuming Alternative
                Transinstitutionalization Parameters

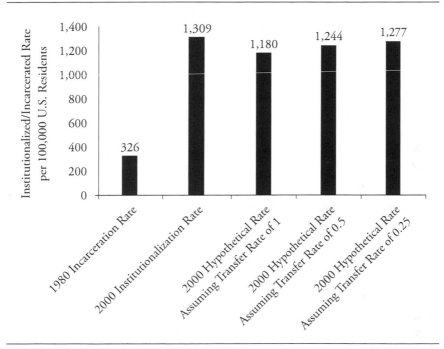

Source: Authors' tabulations are based on data from the U.S Census Bureau Integrated Public
Use Microdata Samples of the U.S. Census of Population and Housing for census years 1980
and 2000.

the incarceration levels of the mentally ill is much larger. Earlier we presented
estimates from inmate surveys finding that 14.3 percent of state prison inmates, 6.1 percent of federal prison inmates, and 14.7 percent of local jail
inmates have a prior diagnosis of severe mental illness. Combining these lifetime prevalence rates with 2000 corrections population totals suggests that in
2000 there were 277,000 severely mentally ill individuals who were incarcerated (66 percent of whom were in state or federal prison). The hypothetical
estimate in figure 5.9 assuming a one-for-one transfer rate suggests that deinstitutionalization contributed a maximum of 129 per 100,000 to the adult
incarceration rate in 2000. With approximately 108 million adults between
the ages of eighteen and sixty-four in 2000, this contribution translates into

140,000 additional prisoners (roughly half of the population of incarcerated persons with severe mental illness).

Moving beyond upper-bound estimates requires that we generate more precise estimates of the rate at which the deinstitutionalized from mental hospitals become reinstitutionalized in prisons and jails. We now turn to this challenge.

ESTIMATING THE TRANSFER RATE FROM MENTAL HOSPITALIZATION TO INCARCERATION

Our accounting exercise in the previous section illustrates how the contribution of deinstitutionalization to prison growth depends on the rate at which declining mental hospitalization rates lead to transinstitutionalization of the mentally ill into prisons and jail. In our simple tabulations, we assumed several alternative transfer rates, applied across the board to all demographic groups, and then crunched through to the implications for prison growth. However, there are a number of reasons to suspect that this transfer rate is different at different points in time and perhaps for different demographic groups.

For example, given the differences between the impetus to early deinstitutionalization (the introduction of pharmacological therapies and the incentives created by Medicare to transfer the elderly to nursing homes) and the forces driving declines in the mental hospital inpatient population from 1970 onward (legal challenges to involuntary commitment and state legal reforms making such commitments relatively more difficult), it is likely that deinstitutionalization followed a chronologically selective path, with the least ill and perhaps the least prone to felonious behavior deinstitutionalized the earliest. This alone suggests that the impact of declining inpatient populations on prison growth was larger during the last decades of the twentieth century.

Beyond selective deinstitutionalization, the impact of declining hospitalization rates on prison counts should interact with the degree of stringency in sentencing policy.[14] Specifically, a one-person decline in the mental hospitalization rate will have a larger impact on the incarceration rate when society is more likely to incarcerate a criminal offender and more likely to hand down longer effective prison sentences. We demonstrated in chapter 2 that the likelihood of being sent to prison conditional on the crime committed has increased, as has the time served for specific crimes. Hence, declining mental hospitalization rates should have a larger effect on prison populations in the later decades of the twentieth century relative to the earlier decades.

We might also expect differential transfer rates by gender and perhaps by race and the interaction of race with gender. For example, men may be generally more criminally prone than women, leading to a relatively larger transinstitutionalization rate for deinstitutionalized men. Moreover, to the extent that African American men are treated differentially and relatively harshly by the criminal justice system, we may also observe racial disparities in the rate of transfer between mental hospitals and prisons.

In this section, we present estimates of the rates at which those deinstitutionalized from mental hospitals have been transinstitutionalized in prisons and jails. We present separate estimates for the early phase of deinstitutionalization (1950 to 1980) and the later phase (1980 to 2000) and explore whether this rate varied by gender and race. For the early period, we use census microdata for each census year between 1950 and 1980 to estimate the proportion in mental hospitals and the proportion incarcerated for each demographic subgroup defined by state of residence, gender, broad age groupings, and race-ethnicity. Our estimates assess the degree to which those groups that experienced the largest declines in mental hospitalization rates also experienced the largest increases in incarceration rates, accounting for common state-level time trends as well as state-specific trends in institutionalization rates by age and race.[15]

Figure 5.10 presents these transinstitutionalization estimates for 1950 through 1980 for all men, for all women, and for each gender by race and ethnicity. The figures should be interpreted as the effect of a one-person decline in the mental hospital inpatient rate on the prison incarceration rate for the group in question. The figure reveals estimates that are near-zero for all men combined and for all women combined. When we look at estimates for specific race-gender groups, we also see very small numbers, several of which are the wrong sign. In all of the models that we estimate for this earlier period, we fail to find statistically significant relationships between changes in the mental hospital inpatient rate and changes in the prison incarceration rate— that is to say, all of the estimates presented in figure 5.10 are statistically indistinguishable from zero. Hence, this analysis finds no evidence of transinstitutionalization of the mentally ill from mental hospitals to prisons prior to 1980.[16]

Beginning with the 1990 census, the census data stopped separately identifying mental hospital inpatients from prison and jail inmates among those flagged as residing in institutional group quarters. Hence, the exact methods

Figure 5.10   Estimates of Transinstitutionalization Rates Between
                Mental Hospitals and Prisons and Jails, 1950 to 1980,
                by Gender and Race

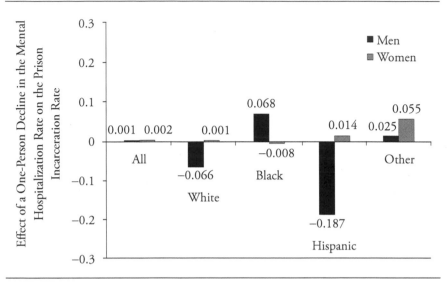

Source: Authors' estimates are based on data from the U.S Census Bureau Integrated Public Use Microdata Samples of the U.S. Census of Population and Housing for census years 1950–1980.

that we employ for the earlier phase of deinstitutionalization cannot be used for the later phase. However, the ability to separately identify mental hospital inpatients in 1980, coupled with the fact that the mental hospital population had declined to very low levels by 2000 (despite substantial population growth over this time period), does allow us to construct a proxy for the actual change in hospitalization rates within demographic groups.

Specifically, we gauged the change in hospitalization rates between 1980 and 2000 by negative one (–1) multiplied by the base hospitalization level in 1980. This approximation would be exact if the mental hospital population had declined to zero by 2000. Since this is not the case, however, we sought corroborating evidence on the suitability of our proxy using state-level data on state and county mental hospital populations for this time period. Figure 5.11 presents a state-level scatter plot of the change in mental hospital inpatients per 100,000 between 1980 and 2000 against the mental hospital inpatient rate in 1980. Note that our proposed proxy measure is basically the variable plotted on the horizontal axis (but measured at the level of each de-

Figure 5.11   Scatter Plot of the 1980 to 2000 Change in the Mental Hospital Inpatient Rate Against the 1980 Level of the Mental Hospital Inpatient Rate, by State

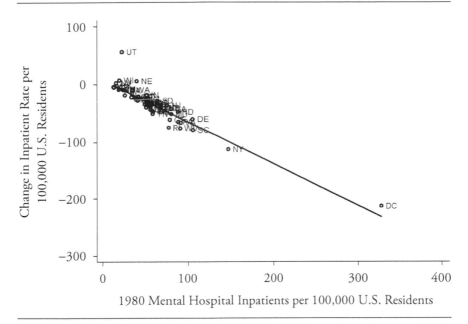

Source: Authors' tabulations are based on data from the U.S Census Bureau Integrated Public Use Microdata Samples of the U.S. Census of Population and Housing for census years 1980 and 2000. Mental hospital data by state come from Raphael (2000).

mographic subgroup rather than for the state overall, as in the figure). As is evident in the graph, the base level in 1980 was a very strong predictor of the overall change in hospitalization rates over the subsequent two decades. Hence, the 1980 hospitalization value provides a strong proxy for the subsequent change in this variable through 2000.[17]

Thus, to estimate the rate at which the deinstitutionalized mentally ill are being transinstitutionalized into prisons and jails for this later period, we use census data from 1980 and 2000 to estimate the increase in incarceration rates for detailed demographic groups (by state, age, and race) and assess whether those groups with higher mental hospital inpatient rates in 1980 experienced larger increases in incarceration rates. With the inpatient population at very low levels in 2000, this relationship provides the best available proxy for the transinstitutionalization rate over this time period.[18]

Figure 5.12   Estimates of the Transinstitutionalization Rates
                 Between Mental Hospitals and Prisons and Jails, 1980
                 to 2000, by Gender and Race

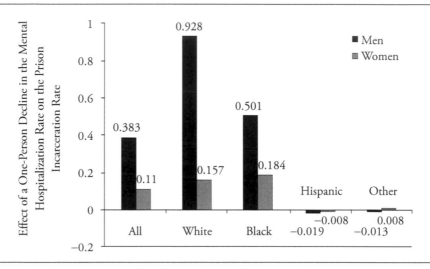

Source: Authors' estimates are based on data from the U.S Census Bureau Integrated Public Use Microdata Samples of the U.S. Census of Population and Housing for census years 1980 and 2000.

Figure 5.12 presents the results from this analysis. Again, we present results separately for men and women overall, as well as within gender by race and ethnicity. Each figure is interpreted as the effect of a one-unit decrease in the inpatient rate on the group's incarceration rate. There is considerably stronger evidence of transinstitutionalization during the 1980 to 2000 period, especially for men. For all men combined, our estimates suggest that each one-person change in the male hospitalization rate between 1980 and 2000 resulted in a 0.4 increase in the corresponding male incarceration rate. Moreover, this estimate is highly statistically significant.

The results for men by race and ethnicity reveal further differences in this relationship. The highly statistically significant estimate for white males suggests a near one-for-one transfer rate from mental hospitals to prisons over this time period. For black males, the estimate suggests a one-half-for-one transfer rate, though this effect is measured imprecisely.[19] For men in the "other" race category and Hispanic men, there is no evidence of transinstitutionalization.

The relationship between hospitalization and incarceration rates for women is substantially weaker than that observed for men. For women overall, the transfer rate estimate implies that a ten-unit decrease in the mental hospital inpatient rate leads to a one-person increase in the prison incarceration rate. This effect is only marginally significant. When we look at estimates by race and gender, we find larger effects for white women and African American women, and zero effect for other women and Hispanic women. We should note, however, that for each subgroup of women the estimates are statistically imprecise, and none are statistically distinguishable from zero.

Thus, we do find evidence of transinstitutionalization for the later phases of deinstitutionalization, but not for the first few decades of this process. This pattern is in line with expectations, since deinstitutionalization proceeded in a chronologically selective manner and those deinstitutionalized after 1980 (either literally through release or effectively by not being admitted to a mental hospital when in the past they would have been) were subject to increasingly harsh penalties for criminal activity.

There are at least three interpretations of the significant transinstitutionalization rates that we observe after 1980, each with its own policy implications. First, it may be the case that increases in incarceration are causing declines in the mental hospital population through the state budget rather than declines in mental hospital populations driving up incarceration rates via the transfer of the mentally ill into prisons and jails. This would be the case if prison spending has displaced mental health spending.[20] In other words, budgetary pressures caused by increasing prison populations may force states to pare back resources allocated to state mental hospitals. This interpretation would suggest that the mentally ill receive insufficient care owing to excessive spending on corrections but are not necessarily exposed to a higher incarceration risk. We believe that our empirical methodology rules out this particular issue by accounting for broad state-level trends in incarceration and the use of mental hospitals, and thus we will not discuss this line of reasoning further.

A second interpretation also involves a causal arrow that runs from prison populations to mental health populations, yet does indeed entail a higher risk of incarceration for the mentally ill.[21] Specifically, an elevated risk of incarceration may siphon the mentally ill out of mental health service systems and into corrections. Suppose that a mentally ill person faces several institutionalization risks—in particular, the risk of becoming incarcerated and the risk of being involuntarily committed to a mental hospital. An increase in the incarceration risk caused by tougher sentencing policy translates directly into a larger flow of mentally ill people into prisons and jails, precluding their inpatient admission into mental hospitals. The greater applicable scope of incarceration thus reduces the flow into mental hospitals and by extension the mental hospitalization rate. Note that in this explanation causality runs from the increased risk of incarceration to the decline in the mental hospital population. Rather than a reduction in services for the mentally ill leading to increased incarceration, stiffer sentencing essentially increases the competing risk that the mentally ill will be swept into corrections systems before ever being hospitalized for their ailments.

The final interpretation is the one commonly posited—namely, that the declining availability of inpatient beds increases the proportion of the mentally ill who go untreated, are at elevated risk of committing a violent act or some other crime, and thus are at an elevated risk of becoming incarcerated. Here the direction of causality runs directly from deinstitutionalization to prison growth: the declining public investment in the mental health infrastructure hoists responsibility for the severely mentally ill onto the criminal justice system.

The differences between these latter two interpretations of our empirical results are subtle and may appear to be splitting hairs. However, the importance of this distinction extends beyond mere semantics. If deinstitutionalization after 1980 drove the transinstitutionalization of predominantly white men, then it must necessarily be the case that the reduction in the likelihood of an inpatient mental health intervention has resulted in more crime and, by extension, more crime victims than the nation would have otherwise experienced. There have certainly been many high-profile instances of untreated mentally ill individuals committing horrific violent crimes. This interpretation of the evidence would suggest that the shuttering of mental hospitals over the past half-century is in part responsible for some of these events. On the other hand, if newly aggressive sentencing is driving the inverse relationship, then the criminal justice system is simply more likely to incarcerate (and perhaps incarcerate for longer periods) those among the mentally ill who commit felonies. Under such circumstances, crime may actually decrease owing to greater incapacitation. The treatment of the mentally ill is likely to suffer, however, when they are placed in prisons and jails rather than hospitals that are explicitly designed for and devoted to treating the mentally ill.

It is quite difficult to empirically disentangle and discriminate between these latter two interpretations of our findings. One way would be to find a third factor that affects mental hospitalization rates but affects prisons only indirectly through its impact on hospitalization and then exploit this factor to assess whether deinstitutionalization is driving prison growth or vice versa. For example, suppose that some states change their involuntary commitment laws to permit such commitment when an individual is found to be a danger to self or others, while other states change their laws to allow for involuntary commitment only when an individual is found to be a danger to others. Clearly, it will be easier to commit someone involuntarily in the former set of states than in the latter. Hence, if prison growth is slower in the states where it is easy to commit someone, then we would conclude that our empirical results are driven by a causal effect of mental hospital closings on prison growth rather than the other way around.

In practice, it is quite difficult to quantify differences across states, and especially over time, in involuntary commitment procedures. First, the language of state statutes is quite similar, and thus it is difficult to identify differences that in practice would result in differences in hospitalization rates. For example, *all* states allow for the involuntary civil commitment of those who, as a result of their illness, pose a danger to themselves or others. The primary existing differences pertain to whether someone who is "gravely ill" (unable to care for himself or herself) can be involuntarily committed and the evidentiary requirements stipulated in the legislation (Ross et al. 1996). In our own empirical work, we have been unable to find any relationship between state differences in statutory language pertaining to involuntary commitment and mental hospitalization rates.[22]

Second, the existing body of state case law plays an important role in determining how easy or hard it is to commit someone involuntarily (Brakel, Parry, and Winer 1985; La Fond and Durham 1992). Given that this case law is not necessarily reflected in the language of state statutes, and given the enormity of the task of categorizing the body of cases related to involuntary commitment proceedings, it does not appear that using variation in state precedents is a viable research strategy for discriminating between the alternative hypotheses.

What does this discussion mean for the interpretation of the findings in this chapter? Essentially, the evidence of transinstitutionalization that we observe for some demographic groups for the period 1980 to 2000 probably reflects both causal effects of deinstitutionalization on prison as well as stiffer sentencing policies increasing the likelihood that the competing risk of prison wins out over that of mental hospitals for the mentally ill. We have already discussed the alternative implications of these two causal pathways with regard to crime. Although a causal impact of deinstitutionalization must necessarily result in additional crime and victimization to generate a prison increase, a causal effect in the opposite direction is likely to prevent crime through the earlier and perhaps longer incapacitation of the criminally active mentally ill. That said, both causal stories imply that more mentally ill individuals serve time in prisons and jails rather than mental hospitals as a result of these policy shifts (whether driven by deinstitutionalization or by sentencing). Given the features of day-to-day life in American prisons, it is most likely that the mentally ill incarcerated suffer as a result.

CONCLUSION

Our findings can be used to estimate the proportion of prison growth attributable to the incarceration of those who in years past would more likely have been mental hospital inpatients. Using the gender-specific transinstitutionalization rates for the 1980 to 2000 period, our estimates suggest that such individuals account for 4 percent of incarceration growth during this period. Employing the transinstitutionalization parameters estimated separately by gender and race, our models suggest that the incarceration of those who would have formally been hospitalized in the past accounts for 7 percent of prison growth between 1980 and 2000. Thus, despite the impressions created by the juxtaposition of aggregate trends, deinstitutionalization, though a significant contributor, is not the smoking gun behind the tremendous growth in incarceration rates. Mental health policy is of second-order importance when compared to the contribution of shifts in sentencing policy that have taken place in most states.

Nonetheless, it is certainly the case that a relatively high proportion of the currently incarcerated mentally ill would not have been incarcerated in years past and would probably be receiving inpatient treatment in a mental facility. For the year 2000, our estimates indicate that between 40,000 and 72,000 incarcerated individuals would more likely have been mental hospital inpatients in years past. Relative to a stock of 277,000 severely mentally ill, this constitutes 14 to 26 percent of the mentally ill incarcerated population.

Certainly, it would be preferable from the viewpoint of the mentally ill, as well as from that of crime victims, to intervene prior to their commission of a felony. Some research has found evidence that mental health interventions have an impact on violent crime, suggesting that criminal activity associated with mental illness could be prevented outside of criminal justice channels. Perhaps most relevant to the discussion, Bernard Harcourt (2006) finds significant relationships between total institutionalization rates inclusive of mental hospital inpatients and state-level homicide, suggesting that withdrawing services by shuttering mental hospitals leads to more crime. David Marcotte and Sarah Markowitz (2009) have more positive findings: they demonstrate a negative association between increases in prescriptions for antidepressants and ADHD medication and violent crime. Both papers suggest that current criminal activity attributable to the mentally ill is not a necessary consequence of this particular human ailment.

In addition, interventions that prevent the incarceration of those with severe mental illness would certainly benefit them, considering that the regimented, often predatory environment common in U.S. prisons is not an ideal setting for treating mental illness. The mentally ill are likely to be at elevated risk for assault and victimization while incarcerated, and also likely to receive insufficient mental health services.

APPENDIX

Tabulating Hypothetical Institutionalization Rates for Those Most Likely to Be Institutionalized in 1950 and Those Most Likely to Be Institutionalized in 2000

Figures 5.2 to 5.4 present estimates of the institutionalization rates through time for those most likely to be institutionalized in 1950 and those most likely to be institutionalized in 2000 for each census year between 1950 and 2000. These time series are constructed by reweighting each census year's data to reflect the demographics of the institutional population in the reference years in question. Here we outline the specifics of these tabulations.

Let i index the eight age groups between eighteen and sixty-four listed in table 5.5, r index the four race-ethnicity groups, g index gender, and t index year. Furthermore, define w_{girt} as the proportion of the institutionalized population in year t that is of gender g, age group i, and race-ethnicity group r, and define I_{girt} as the corresponding institutionalization rate for this group. Taking the product of the group-specific institutionalization rate and the group institutionalization share and summing over all dimensions gives the institutionalization risk for someone with demographic characteristics that mirror those of the average institutionalized person. For example, this institutionalization risk in 2000 for those institutionalized in 2000 is

$$IR_{2000}^{2000} = \sum_{g} \sum_{i} \sum_{r} w_{gir2000} I_{gir2000} \tag{5A.1}$$

The institutionalization risk in equation 5A.1 will, of course, exceed the overall institutionalization rate, as it is a weighted average with higher weights placed on those demographic groups that disproportionately make up the institutionalized population.

To answer the two questions posed in the main text, we calculate the institutionalization risk for each analysis year for the institutionalized population from a specific year. For example, the institutionalization risk in 1950 for someone with demographic characteristics that resemble the institutionalized in 2000 is given by the equation

$$IR_{1950}^{2000} = \sum_{g} \sum_{i} \sum_{r} w_{gir2000} I_{gir1950} \tag{5A.2}$$

To the extent that we are institutionalizing the same people in 2000 as we did in 1950, the alternative risk measures in equations 5A.1 and 5A.2 should be of comparable magnitude. Calculating subsequent institutionalization risks for those who resemble the institutionalized in 1950 simply requires substituting the 1950 weights for the 2000 weights and the group-specific institutionalization rate for subsequent years.

A Steady-State Model of the Joint Determination of the Incarceration Rate and the Mental Hospital Inpatient Rate

Here we present a simple mechanical steady-state model of incarceration and mental hospital inpatient rates that highlights the various factors that may mediate the relationship between these two institutional populations and lead to the causal influence running in both directions. These issues are best demonstrated with a simple mechanical Markov model of steady-state incarceration and hospitalization rates. Define N as the proportion of the population that is not incarcerated and not in a mental hospital, M as the proportion in mental hospitals, and P as the proportion in prison. The vector $S' = [N,M,P]$

thus describes the distribution of the adult population across these three possible states of being. All three possible states are dynamic in the sense that individuals flow into and out of each state over defined time periods and in that the response to changes in the underlying determinants of each probability, the vector of population shares, adjusts over time toward a steady-state vector share.

Transitions between the three states are governed by the transition probability matrix

$$
T = \begin{bmatrix} 1 - T_{NM} - T_{NP} & T_{NM} & T_{NP} \\ T_{MN} & 1 - T_{MN} & 0 \\ T_{PN} & 0 & 1 - T_{PN} \end{bmatrix} \qquad (5A.3)
$$

where T_{ij} is the probability of transitioning from state i to state j in any given period (with $0 \le T_{ij} \le 1$), and where the transition probabilities in any given row must sum to one. For simplicity, we assume that the direct transition probabilities from mental hospitals to prison and from prison to mental hospitals are zero. While the elements of the matrix T are certainly determined in part by behavior (for example, higher offending levels should increase T_{NP}), they are also determined by the policy changes and innovations that drive deinstitutionalization as well as the sentencing and corrections policies implemented in most states during the last quarter of the twentieth century. For example, raising the evidentiary bar for involuntary commitment would lower the transition probability, T_{NM}. Expanding the scope of offenses punishable by incarceration would increase T_{NP}. Enhancing prison sentences would reduce the flow rate out of prison, T_{PN}.

The steady-state population share vector is implicitly defined by the condition

$$
TS = S \qquad (5A.4)
$$

in conjunction with the adding-up constraint, $N + M + P = 1$. Using these two conditions to solve for the steady-state population shares yields the solutions

$$
M = \frac{T_{PN}T_{NM}}{T_{PN}T_{MN} + T_{PN}T_{MN} + T_{MN}T_{NP}} \qquad (5A.5)
$$

$$P = \frac{T_{MN}T_{NP}}{T_{PN}T_{MN} + T_{PN}T_{MN} + T_{MN}T_{NP}} \qquad (5A.6)$$

$$N = 1 - M - N \qquad (5A.7)$$

Equations 5A.5 and 5A.6 can be used to illustrate how the relationship between deinstitutionalization and prison growth is likely to change over time. The steady-state solutions are also useful for uncovering a somewhat subtle identification problem that muddies our interpretation of the coefficient estimates in chapter 5. Beginning with the solution for M, we can characterize deinstitutionalization as reducing the admissions rate into mental hospitals, T_{NM}, and decreasing the length of stay for anyone committed to a mental hospital (with the reduction in spell length captured by an increase in the transition probability T_{MN}). It is simple to verify that $\frac{\partial M}{\partial T_{NM}} > 0$ and that $\frac{\partial M}{\partial T_{MN}} < 0$. Hence, both developments would lead to declines in the mental hospital inpatient rate.

The impact of these changes on the incarceration share can be analyzed by differentiating equation 5A.6 with respect to the transition rates into and out of mental hospitals. Doing so yields the result that the proportion incarcerated decreases when the admission rate into mental hospitals increases, while the incarceration rate increases with increases in the transition rate out of mental hospitals—that is, $\frac{\partial P}{\partial T_{NM}} < 0$ and $\frac{\partial P}{\partial T_{MN}} > 0$. In essence, these derivatives represent one of the central questions of this chapter: the transinstitutionalization effect of deinstitutionalization.

The suspicion that the values of these partial derivatives differ at different points in time is based on the fact that the transition parameters into and out of prison are not stable over time. In chapter 2, we documented that the admissions rates into U.S. prisons increased sharply, as did the expected value of time served, conditional on the conviction offense (increases in time served result in decreases in T_{PN}). The effects of these changes on our parameter of interest depend on the sign of specific cross-partial derivatives of the steady-state incarceration rate.

For example, suppose that prison admissions increase owing to enhanced resource allocation to police investigations and prosecutions. Such a change would lead to an increase in the transition probability T_{NP}.[23] This change has an impact on the marginal effect of transfer rates into and out of mental hospitals on the incarceration share, effectively enhancing the impact of changes that lead to further deinstitutionalization of the mentally ill. This follows from the fact that the cross-partial derivative, $\dfrac{\partial P}{\partial T_{NM} \partial T_{NP}}$, is negative. In other words, the negative effect on the incarceration rate of an increase in mental hospital admissions is larger (in absolute value) the larger the admissions rate to prison. Conversely, the positive impact on incarceration rates of decreasing mental hospital admissions is larger the higher the prison admissions rate. A similar argument can be made with respect to the cross-partial derivate $\dfrac{\partial P}{\partial T_{MN} \partial T_{NP}}$. Since this cross-partial derivative is positive, the effect on incarceration of increasing the release rate out of mental hospital is enhanced by a higher admissions rate into prison.[24]

The steady-state equation for the mental hospitalization rate is also useful for illustrating one of the several identification problems that we face in interpreting any correlation between incarceration and hospitalization rates. Specifically, differentiating equation 5A.5 with respect to the two incarceration transition probabilities, it is easy to show that $\dfrac{\partial M}{\partial T_{NP}} < 0$ and that $\dfrac{\partial M}{\partial T_{PN}} > 0$. In other words, policy choices that increase the prison admissions rate decrease the mental hospital population share, as do policy choices that increase sentence length. Hence, shifts toward tougher sentencing policies will induce a negative correlation between incarceration rates and mental hospitalization rates. Here, however, the interpretation is different. Rather than a reduction in services for the mentally ill leading to increased incarceration, stiffer sentencing essentially increases the competing risk that the mentally ill will be swept into corrections systems before ever being able to be hospitalized for their ailments.

CHAPTER 6

Demographic Change, the Economy, and the Crack Epidemic

As we have emphasized throughout this book, policy choices as well as criminal behavior ultimately determine a nation's incarceration rate. Specifically, the degree to which a nation decides to use prison as punishment and the intensiveness with which such punishment is employed determine who is sent to prison and for how long. Of course, except in the case of a wrongful conviction, a felony conviction and a prison sentence require a criminal act. The sanctions regime may affect the propensity of those who are not incarcerated to engage in crime through general deterrence and the long-term effects of incarceration on the offending of former inmates (the subject of chapter 7). However, other factors that are determined largely outside of the criminal justice policy domain also have an impact on behavior and ultimately crime and incarceration rates.

For instance, there are very strong relationships between the propensity to engage in illegal behavior, on the one hand, and age and gender, on the other. The state of the macroeconomy and the legitimate earnings prospects of the least-educated have an impact on crime rates, and on property crime rates in particular. And finally, innovations in illegal drug markets, such as the introduction of new products, can often affect the degree of violence surrounding the drug trade and may have psychopharmacological effects on users that influence the likelihood that they will engage in crime.

Over the past three decades, there have been important changes in these external determinants of crime (that is to say, factors determined outside of the criminal justice system) that are likely to have influenced criminal activity and by extension U.S. incarceration rates. Our analysis in chapters 2 and 3 suggests that collectively these factors play a minor role in explaining growth in U.S. incarceration rates. Nonetheless, several factors, in particular the introduction of crack cocaine to the drug market, are often cited as key driving forces.

In the present chapter, we discuss the contribution of three potential sources of behavioral change to the growth in U.S. incarceration rates. We begin with a discussion of the nation's changing sociodemographics. Over the past three decades, the United States has become older, more educated, and considerably more diverse. Nearly all of the observed compositional changes in the adult male population militate toward lower incarceration rates. We present tabulations of U.S. census data for 1980 and 2010 that strongly suggest that, absent any policy changes, our changing demographics in isolation would have led to fairly substantial declines in U.S. incarceration rates.

Next, we assess the role of the changing economy. It is indeed the case that legitimate employment prospects have eroded considerably for less-educated workers. Rising wage inequality has combined with absolute declines in real earnings at the bottom of the wage distribution to increase the likelihood of outright joblessness among the less-educated, especially among less-educated minority men. To assess the contribution of these changes to crime and incarceration growth, we draw on the empirical research literature on the relationship between earnings prospects and criminal activity to simulate what the U.S. incarceration rate for various groups would have been had the earnings distribution not changed as it did during the later decades of the twentieth century. Our conclusion is that declining employment prospects may explain a sizable, yet minority, share of incarceration growth for white males, but very little of the increases observed for black males. That being said, the alarming decrease in employment among less-educated minority men suggests that greater involvement in the criminal justice system may be reducing labor force participation. We discuss the possible avenues through which this may be occurring.

Finally, we discuss shocks to drug markets in the United States, in particular the introduction of crack cocaine. The crack epidemic is widely credited with causing a rash of violent crime, mostly driven by intergroup violence related to turf conflicts. We document the impact of crack cocaine on black male homicide rates and use these data to measure the arrival date of crack across U.S. states. Our analysis establishes several stylized facts. First, incarceration growth nationwide preceding the introduction of crack had already increased the nation's incarceration rate considerably. Second, although incarceration growth did accelerate somewhat following the onset of the crack epidemic, a continuation of the underlying incarceration trend that preceded the epidemic would explain a large share of incarceration growth during the late 1980s and beyond. Third, incarceration growth continued far beyond the observable waning of the crack epidemic. Finally, multivariate statistical analyses that explicitly control for the crack epidemic find little to no evidence that the introduction of crack cocaine explains the growth in state incarceration rates or prison admissions. In sum, the data do not support the hypothesis that a large increase in drug-related crime driven by the introduction of crack cocaine is responsible for the nation's high incarceration rates.

CHANGING DEMOGRAPHICS

In recent decades, we have observed several important demographic changes that bear directly on criminal offending and changes in incarceration rates. First, the foreign-born proportion of the population has increased substantially.[1] A growing body of research consistently finds that immigrants are less likely to engage in criminal activity compared to similar natives and considerably less likely to be incarcerated (Butcher and Piehl 1998, 2006; Wadsworth 2010). A recent study by Aaron Chalfin (2012) finds no effect of increased undocumented migration on a metropolitan area's crime rate, despite the lower levels of educational attainment and higher proportion of males among this segment of the U.S. immigrant population. Elizabeth Kneebone and Steven Raphael (2011) find that cities where relatively large increases in foreign-born populations occurred also experienced relatively large crime declines between 1990 and 2009. Given the findings of this research, we would expect the growing population of immigrants to lower U.S. crime and incarceration rates.

Second, the U.S. resident population has aged. Focusing specifically on the male population (the more criminally active half), between 1980 and 2010 the percentage of the male population under 18 years of age declined from 30 to 25 percent, while the percentage of those over 65 increased from 9 to 11 percent. Among those age 18 to 65, the average age increased over this time period from 37.5 to 40.5. Since the likelihood of committing a crime decreases with age, this demographic shift also should have decreased crime and incarceration.

Finally, American adults have become more educated. Average educational attainment has increased within all racial and ethnic groups. There is a strong negative association between education and the likelihood of committing a crime and being incarcerated. Moreover, there is strong evidence suggesting that additional years of education reduce the likelihood of serving time. The economists Lance Lochner and Enrico Moretti (2004) provide empirical evidence for the United States suggesting that those individuals who are constrained through the interaction of their birth quarter and the minimum compulsory attendance law from dropping out in their freshman and sophomore years of high school are less likely to be incarcerated as an adult than those who did not face such a constraint. Similarly, Randi Hjalmarsson, Helena Holmlund, and Matthew Lindquist (2011) present evidence for Sweden demonstrating that increases in the nation's compulsory school attendance age resulted in a decreased likelihood of serving time as an adult for those affected by the policy change.

The associations between these demographic factors and the likelihood of being incarcerated are evident in the tabulations in table 6.1. The table uses data from the 1980 Public Use Microdata Sample (PUMS) of the U.S. Census of Population and Housing and the 2010 American Community Survey (ACS) to calculate the proportion of men between eighteen and sixty-five years of age who were residing in institutionalized group quarters on the day of the census. From 1980 on, the lion's share of the non-elderly in such institutions were either in prison or in jail.[2] The table presents tabulations for both native-born men and foreign-born men for mutually exclusive race-ethnicity groups, and within each group by age and educational attainment. There are several notable patterns in the table. First, we observe increases in incarceration rates within nearly every demographic subgroup depicted in the table. Second, the table reproduces the large interracial and interethnic differences that we have already documented, with African Americans incarcerated at the highest rates, followed by Hispanics.

Table 6.1 also demonstrates the very large differences in incarceration rates between the foreign-born and native-born. For example, in 2010 incarceration rates for black immigrants were generally lower than those for white native-born men. Moreover, Hispanic immigrants were much less likely to be incarcerated at the time of the census relative to native-born Hispanic men. Finally, the table documents the strong negative relationship between educational attainment and incarceration rates within each of the demographic groups considered. We also see the highest incarceration rates among those who were sixteen to thirty years of age in each group.

Table 6.1   Institutionalized U.S. Males Age Eighteen to Sixty-Five, by Race-Ethnicity, Age, Education, and Nativity, 1980 and 2010

| | Non-Hispanic | | | | | | Hispanic | |
| | White | | Black | | Other | | | |
	1980	2010	1980	2010	1980	2010	1980	2010
Native-born men								
All	0.008	0.013	0.035	0.081	0.017	0.032	0.018	0.038
Age								
Eighteen to twenty-five	0.010	0.014	0.047	0.081	0.025	0.023	0.023	0.034
Twenty-six to thirty	0.009	0.020	0.053	0.123	0.020	0.034	0.023	0.051
Thirty-one to forty	0.007	0.017	0.035	0.104	0.015	0.045	0.018	0.050
Forty-one to fifty	0.006	0.013	0.018	0.078	0.011	0.042	0.010	0.036
Fifty-one to sixty-five	0.008	0.008	0.016	0.043	0.009	0.020	0.009	0.023
Education								
High school dropout	0.019	0.048	0.050	0.193	0.033	0.093	0.027	0.089
High school graduate	0.006	0.018	0.027	0.080	0.015	0.045	0.013	0.038
Some college	0.005	0.009	0.024	0.042	0.010	0.020	0.010	0.020
College graduate	0.002	0.002	0.011	0.011	0.004	0.003	0.004	0.004

Foreign-born men

All	0.005	0.004	0.012	0.012	0.003	0.004	0.007	0.018
Age								
Eighteen to twenty-five	0.009	0.003	0.019	0.025	0.005	0.004	0.010	0.022
Twenty-six to thirty	0.006	0.007	0.013	0.012	0.003	0.006	0.009	0.021
Thirty-one to forty	0.004	0.005	0.011	0.012	0.002	0.005	0.006	0.020
Forty-one to fifty	0.003	0.004	0.003	0.009	0.002	0.004	0.004	0.015
Fifty-one to sixty-five	0.006	0.003	0.012	0.010	0.003	0.003	0.003	0.011
Education								
High school dropout	0.008	0.014	0.019	0.035	0.006	0.016	0.008	0.022
High school graduate	0.006	0.006	0.012	0.015	0.005	0.008	0.008	0.016
Some college	0.004	0.004	0.007	0.009	0.002	0.001	0.005	0.013
College graduate	0.002	0.002	0.007	0.004	0.001	0.001	0.002	0.005

Source: Authors' tabulations from data from the U.S Census Bureau Five Percent Public Use Microdata Samples from the U.S. Census of Housing and Population (1980b) and the U.S Census Bureau *American Community Survey* (2010).

Table 6.2   The Adult Male U.S. Population in 1980 and 2010

	1980	2010
Age distribution		
Eighteen to twenty-five	0.249	0.184
Twenty-six to thirty	0.139	0.107
Thirty-one to forty	0.221	0.206
Forty-one to fifty	0.162	0.222
Fifty-one to sixty-five	0.229	0.281
Education distribution		
High school dropout	0.270	0.128
High school graduate	0.356	0.378
Some college	0.189	0.241
College graduate	0.185	0.254
Proportion foreign-born	0.067	0.166
Race-ethnicity distribution		
Non-Hispanic white	0.816	0.647
Non-Hispanic black	0.101	0.118
Non-Hispanic other	0.023	0.073
Hispanic	0.061	0.162

Source: Authors' tabulations from data from the U.S Census Bureau Five Percent Public Use Microdata Samples from the U.S. Census of Housing and Population (1980b) and the U.S Census Bureau *American Community Survey* (2010).

Table 6.2 documents shifts in the composition of the male population age eighteen to sixty-five over this time period. There are several quite stark changes. First, the population clearly aged. The percentage between eighteen and thirty years of age declined from 38.8 percent to 29.1 percent between 1980 and 2010, while the percentage over forty increased by 11.1 percent. There was a large decline in the percentage of adult men with less than a high school degree (from 27 percent to 12.8 percent) and a sizable increase in the percentage with at least some college. The proportion of foreign-born males increased discretely, and the racial-ethnic distribution became considerably more diverse.

What do these demographic changes imply for crime and incarceration in the United States? There are several ways in which we can address this question. A simple first pass would be to assess the degree to which these shifts have changed the relative representation of high-incarceration groups. We do so in the following manner. Using the four race-ethnicity groups, five age groupings, four educational attainment groupings, and two nativity groupings employed in table 6.1, we define 160 male demographic groups (4 race-ethnicity × 5 age × 4 educational attainment × 2 nativity = 160 race-age-education-nativity demographic groups). For each of these groups we calculate the proportion incarcerated from the 1980 census. We then rank the groups from lowest to highest in terms of their 1980 incarceration rates and use this ranking to compare and contrast the demographic distributions of adult non-elderly men in 1980 and 2010.

The results of this exercise are presented in figure 6.1. The figure shows the cumulative distribution of the adult male population across the ranked demographic groups in 1980 and 2010. The height of each line for a given group ranking shows the proportion of the population in a group with equal or lower rank. The 2010 cumulative distribution is generally above the 1980 distribution, indicating a decisive shift in the nation's demographics toward lower-incarceration groups. For example, 31 percent of the male population in 1980 was concentrated in the bottom 60 demographic groups, while the comparable figure for 2010 was 41 percent. Similarly, 78 percent of the 1980 male population was accounted for by 120 demographic groups with the lowest incarceration rates. The comparable figure for 2010 was 86 percent.

Alternatively, we can characterize the consequences of these demographic shifts by tabulating various hypothetical incarceration rates. For example, suppose that for each of our 160 demographic groups the proportion incarcerated did not change between 1980 and 2010. Since the distribution of the male population across these groups changed, we would still expect to observe a change in the proportion incarcerated under this hypothetical scenario owing to the demographic shifts alone. Calculating the average incarceration rate using the 1980 group incarceration rates and the 2010 population patterns provides an estimate of what would have happened due to demographic shifts alone. If the hypothetical rate increases relative to that observed for 1980, then demographic shifts contributed to incarceration growth. On the other hand, if the hypothetical rate decreases relative to the observed 1980 rate, then demographic change actually ran counter to the trend toward higher incarceration rates.

The first two columns of table 6.3 present these results. The first column shows the proportion incarcerated or institutionalized in 1980 for all males and for males in each race-ethnicity grouping. The second column shows what the incarceration would have been with the 2010 demographic distribution but under the assumption that the group-specific incarceration rates did not change. The results indicate that the proportion incarcerated would have

Figure 6.1   Comparison of the 1980 and 2010 Distributions of the
U.S. Male Population Age Eighteen to Sixty-Five Across
Demographic Groups Ranked by 1980
Institutionalization Rates

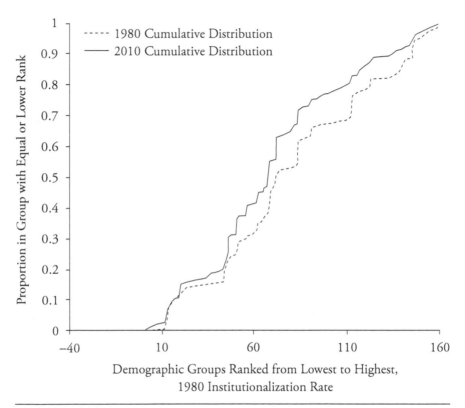

Demographic Groups Ranked from Lowest to Highest,
1980 Institutionalization Rate

Source: Authors' tabulations based on data from the U.S Census Bureau One Percent Public
Use Microdata Sample (PUMS) of the U.S. Census of Population and Housing (1980a) and
the U.S Census Bureau *American Community Survey* (2010).

declined by 18 percent among all men and by 30 percent among African
American men.

Alternatively, we could tabulate what the 2010 incarceration rate would
have been with 2010 group-specific incarceration rates and the 1980 demographic distribution of men. Given the patterns in the first two columns of
table 6.3, we would expect that had the nation's male demographics not
changed between 1980 and 2010, the incarceration rate would have been
higher. This is indeed the case. The third column in table 6.3 presents actual

Table 6.3 Actual Institutionalization Rates for Men Age Eighteen to Sixty-Five for 1980 and 2010 and Hypothetical Institutionalization Rates for Each Year Assuming the Demographic Distribution from the Other Year

	Actual 1980 Institutionalization Rate	1980 Institutionalization Rate with 2010 Population Shares	Actual 2010 Institutionalization Rate	2010 Institutionalization Rate with 1980 Population Shares
All males	0.011	0.009	0.031	0.039
Non-Hispanic white	0.008	0.006	0.015	0.023
Non-Hispanic black	0.034	0.024	0.109	0.165
Non-Hispanic other	0.010	0.007	0.020	0.032
Hispanic	0.014	0.010	0.043	0.064

Source: Authors' tabulations from data from the U.S Census Bureau Five Percent Public Use Microdata Samples from the U.S. Census of Housing and Population (1980b) and the U.S Census Bureau *American Community Survey* (2010).

Note: The figures represent the proportion of each group institutionalized in a given year. Hypothetical institutionalization rates in the second and fourth columns are weighted averages of the institutionalization rates for demographic groups applying the population share from the other year as weights. Demographic groups are defined by the interaction of the five age categories, the four race-ethnicity categories, the four educational attainment categories, and a nativity category indicating whether each individual is foreign-born. These dimensions define 160 demographic groups for each year.

proportions of males incarcerated or institutionalized in 2010. The final column tabulates what these proportions would have been had male demographics not changed since 1980. For all men, the percentage incarcerated in 2010 would have been 26 percent higher with 1980 demographics. The comparable figure for African American incarceration rates is 34 percent.

To summarize, the nation's demographics have changed considerably during the time period that is the focus of this book. The population has become older, more likely to be foreign-born, and more educated. The new demographics tend toward lower offending and toward a demographic composition with lower incarceration rates. In fact, our tabulations suggest that the nation's incarceration rate would have increased by a substantially greater amount had these changes not occurred.

THE EFFECTS OF INCREASING EARNINGS INEQUALITY

The increase in U.S. incarceration rates over the past three decades coincides with profound changes in the distribution of earnings and income. Beginning in the mid-1970s, wage inequality increased greatly, with real absolute declines in the earnings of the least-skilled workers and stagnating wages for workers at the center of the wage distribution (Autor and Katz 1999). Moreover, inequality in the upper half of the income distribution has also increased steadily since 1980, with earnings at the ninetieth percentile of the distribution steadily pulling away from those of the median earner (Autor, Katz, and Kearney 2008). Coincident with these changes in the earnings distribution are pronounced declines in the labor force participation rates of less-skilled men (Juhn and Potter 2006). In particular, the labor force participation and employment rates of relatively less-educated black men have dropped precipitously (Raphael 2005).

The potential connection between these labor market changes and the increase in incarceration is relatively straightforward. The wage that one's time can command in the legitimate labor market represents the opportunity cost of allocating time toward other pursuits, such as participating in crime, taking leisure, engaging in home production, and so on. The lower one's potential earnings, the more attractive are criminal opportunities with income-generating potential. Whether individuals who are amoral and not averse to risk commit a crime depends on whether the expected return to devoting a small amount of time to crime (which includes both the payoff and the expected punishment) exceeds both the value placed on their free time (their reservation wage) and potential legitimate earnings should this time be supplied to the labor market. For those who are morally averse to criminal activity and averse to risk, participating in criminal activity requires that the difference between the expected returns to crime and the returns to legitimate work exceeds a threshold that is increasing in the degree of moral as well as risk aversion.[3] Regardless, the likelihood of engaging in criminal activity (or stated in the language of modern microeconomics, supplying one's time to criminal pursuits) should increase as potential earnings in legitimate employment decline.

Declining wages for the least-skilled workers induce a greater proportion to participate in crime as the least risk-averse and those with the lowest moral aversion to committing crime among those who have not been criminally active are peeled out of the legitimate labor market and enter the pool of those who commit crime. This relatively larger criminally active pool increases the proportion at risk for incarceration and, holding the incarceration risk constant, increases the incarceration rate.

There is now considerable evidence that economically motivated crime increases with unemployment and decreases with average wages, especially the average wages of low-skilled workers. For example, Steven Raphael and Rudolf Winter-Ebmer (2001) find consistently positive effects of higher unemployment rates on property crime in an analysis of state-level panel data covering roughly the last quarter of the twentieth century. Using similar data, Eric Gould, Bruce Weinberg, and David Mustard (2002) find that property crime decreases with increasing wages. Jeff Grogger (1998) models the decision to participate in crime as a function of the wages an individual could earn in the labor market and finds that higher earnings potential reduces the likelihood of engaging in crime. Richard Freeman (1987) finds that those youth who believe that they could earn more on the streets than in legitimate employment are more likely to engage in criminal activity.[4] Finally, Raphael (2011) simulates where incarcerated offenders would be in the national wage distribution if they were non-institutionalized and working. This exercise reveals that nearly all would be concentrated in the bottom of the earnings distribution, a fact driven mostly by their low levels of formal education. The absence in the prison population of those with strong earnings potential suggests that low earnings may be one driver toward criminal activity.

It is possible to formally characterize the chain of effects linking wage declines to incarceration and then use this framework to provide a rough assessment of the potential importance of increasing earnings inequality. To see this framework, we employ a simplified version of the model laid out in chapter 3 to perform some back-of-the-envelope calculations regarding the potential contribution of increasing earnings inequality to prison growth. Recall from our previous discussion that the steady-state incarceration rate increases with the crime rate, increases with the likelihood of being caught and sent to prison, and increases with the effective sentence length handed down to convicted offenders. If we make the simplifying assumptions that only one type of crime is committed, that the likelihood of being caught and sent to prison is constant for all offenders, and that a uniform sentence is handed down for those sent to prison, we can approximate the steady-state incarceration rate by the following equation[5]:

$$Incarceration = Crime(wage) \times Incarceration\ Risk \times Sentence\ Length \quad (6.1)$$

Equation 6.1 explicitly notes that the crime rate depends on legitimate earnings in the labor market—that is to say, *Crime(wage)* literally reads the crime rate as a function of the wage. This theoretical reasoning suggests that higher legitimate earnings result in lower crime. Hence, higher wages also result in a lower steady-state incarceration rate. To be explicit, a change in legitimate earnings potential affects the incarceration rate according to the following equation:

$$\frac{\Delta Incarceration}{\Delta Wage} = \frac{\Delta Crime}{\Delta Wage} \times Incarceration\ Risk \times Sentence\ Length \quad (6.2)$$

Equation 6.2 tells us that the change in the steady-state incarceration rate caused by a change in wages (indicated by the ratio $\frac{\Delta Incarceration}{\Delta Wage}$ on the left-hand side of the equation) depends on three factors. First, a change in wages affects the proportion of the population engaging in crime (the factor denoted by $\frac{\Delta Crime}{\Delta Wage}$). We expect that a decline in wages will increase the crime rates, and thus the sign of the ratio given by the first term on the right-hand side of equation 6.2 is negative (i.e., an increase in wages causes a decrease in crime).

Second, the higher crime rate increases prison admissions through the risk of being apprehended, convicted, and sentenced to prison. Thus, the effect of a wage change on the incarceration rate is larger the higher the likelihood of being sent to prison conditional on committing a crime (what we denote as the "incarceration risk" in equations 6.1 and 6.2). Finally, the change in incarceration rate caused by a change in wages depends on the effective sentence length imposed on those convicted and incarcerated. The longer the sentence length, the larger is the effect of any wage-driven change in offending on the steady-state incarceration rate.

It is worth noting that the consequences of a change in any determinant of crime for the nation's incarceration rate depend on the key criminal justice policy parameters. That is to say, if we are more likely to punish an offender with prison and to hand out longer sentences, the impact of a change in offending driven by the economy, demographics, changes in education policy, and so forth, on the size of the prison population is larger. Hence, the effect of a change in wages is mediated by the sentencing regime, with tougher sentencing parameters resulting in a stronger relationship between the health of the low-wage labor market and the incarceration rate.

We use a slightly more complex version of equation 6.2 to provide a rough approximation of the potential impact of changes in the national wage structure on the overall incarceration rate.[6] In particular, based on the results from empirical research on the responsiveness of criminal behavior to potential earnings, empirically observed changes in earnings potential, and various estimates of the likelihood of being caught and sent to prison and of sentence length, we simulate the predicted effect of changes in the wage distribution over the last two decades of the twentieth century on incarceration growth. We focus on this two-decade period because most of the erosion in the earnings for the least-skilled occurred at that time (Autor, Katz, and Kearney 2008). Moreover, this period accounts for the lion's share of incarceration growth over the past thirty years.

Various empirical estimates have provided the key inputs to these calculations. Beginning with empirical research on the responsiveness of criminal participation to wages, Grogger (1998) provided the key estimate of this relationship often cited in the literature: a 10 percent decline in earnings potential increases the likelihood of committing a crime by two and a half percentage points. This estimate is based on an analysis of data from the 1979 National Longitudinal Survey of Youth (NLSY79) for the survey year 1980. The research sample consists of males between fifteen and twenty-two years of age who were not enrolled in school and not in the military. Disadvantaged minority men, the demographic group most likely to be predisposed toward criminal activity, are oversampled, and thus the estimated responsiveness is certainly on the high side when applied to older and more-educated men.

To estimate the likelihood of being caught and incarcerated conditional on having committed a crime, we could pursue a number of potential strategies. Here we look to those who admit to engaging in criminal activity and assess the likelihood that they will serve time during a given period. The 1980 survey question on which Grogger (1998) gauges criminal participation asks about the extent to which the respondent's income over the previous year came from illegal activity. Taking those who indicated any income from crime as the base population, the proportion interviewed in prison or jail at the time of the 1980 survey provides an indicator of the likelihood of being caught and incarcerated. Figure 6.2 presents the proportion of NLSY79 male respondents interviewed in prison or jail by their self-reported relative proportion of income derived from criminal activity. The figure clearly reveals that those more engaged in crime were more likely to end up incarcerated. However, the average incarceration probability across all those engaging in crime is relatively low (0.02), since the majority of respondents (75 percent) who reported income from crime reported very little such income.

We take 0.02 as an estimate of the incarceration risk for those who committed income-generating crimes in 1980.[7] Since the ratio of prison admissions to crimes committed roughly tripled between 1980 and the present (Raphael and Stoll 2009), we assume that the risk of incarceration in 2000 for those engaged in income-generating crimes was 0.06.[8] Note that since we are using a ballpark estimate of the incarceration risk for the latest year of the time period analyzed, our tabulations are akin to estimates of how much lower the incarceration rate would be under current sentencing practices if the earnings distribution had not changed over the period under study.

We must also discuss our choice for average time served. Roughly half of all prison inmates are released in any given year. This implies that the typical spell in prison is two years, since the expected value of spell duration can be approximated by the reciprocal of the release rate (as we discussed in chapter

Figure 6.2 **Proportion of NLSY79 Male Respondents Interviewed in Prison or Jail in 1980**

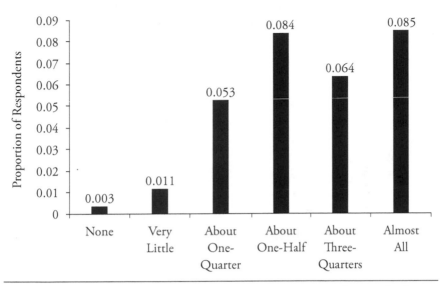

Source: Authors' tabulations from the Bureau of Labor Statistics, *National Longitudinal Survey of Youth 1979* (2002).

2). However, the marginal offenders coaxed into criminal activity by declining wages are likely to commit fewer and less serious crimes relative to those who would be committing crime regardless. Thus, we assume that such marginal offenders would serve no more than one and a half years on average.

Finally, we employ the wage change estimates presented in the research of Chinhui Juhn (2003) to gauge changes in average wages by race and educational attainment. Juhn presents estimated changes in the legal opportunity cost of crime for white men and black men by educational attainment.[9] For Hispanic men and other men, we assume that the changes in the wage structure experienced by black men with similar levels of education attainment apply.

The results of this exercise are presented in table 6.4. The first column presents estimates of the change in log wages between 1979 and 1998 for men by race and ethnicity (approximately equal to the proportional change in wages over this period). The numbers document the well-known erosion of the legal earnings prospects of the least-skilled men. The second column presents group-specific estimates of the effects of these wage changes on each group's incarceration rates based on the reasoning developed earlier. For each racial-ethnic group, we also estimate an overall change by taking the average of the effects by educational attainment and accounting for the proportion of the group's men in each education level. These overall figures suggest that changes in the wage structure increased the 2000 incarceration rate by 0.001 for white males, 0.002 for black males, 0.003 for Hispanic males, and 0.001 for other males.

Column 3 presents estimates from the 1980 and 2000 censuses of the actual change in the proportion of males institutionalized by race-ethnicity and by race-ethnicity and education. These figures capture men in either jail or prison. The final column presents the ratio of the predicted wage effects on incarceration to the actual changes. The results suggest that changes in the wage structure holding all else constant would account for 23 percent of the increase in incarceration among white men, 4 percent of the increase among black men, 21 percent of the increase among Hispanic men, and 33 percent of the increase among other men. For all men, combining the tabulations suggests that changes in the wage structure account for roughly 13 percent of the increase in incarceration. The disproportionate contribution of black male incarceration to overall growth pulls this estimate disproportionately toward the lower number for blacks.

To be sure, the results in table 6.4 are likely to overstate the role of wages. First, we are applying an estimate of the sensitivity of criminal participation to changes in wages estimated for a sample of disproportionately disadvantaged male youth to all men. We might expect that the generally high criminality of younger men would make them more sensitive to the relative returns of criminal as opposed to legitimate work opportunities. Second, we use an estimate of the likelihood of being caught for those just on the margin between offending and not offending that is comparable in magnitude to the likelihood of being sent to prison for engaging in the amount of crime that the average inmate would commit were he not incarcerated. The marginal offender propelled into crime by poor economic opportunities is unlikely to commit as much crime as those firmly committed to a life of crime. Finally, we have implicitly assumed that wages decline, as shown in table 6.4, for reasons that are independent of the increase in incarceration rates. If wage declines reflect in part a negative effect of having a criminal record on earnings and employment, these estimates will be biased upward.

An alternative yet related question is whether the increases in incarceration

Table 6.4　Estimates of the Effect of Changes in Earnings Opportunities on Male Incarceration (Jail and Prison Combined) Rates

	Δln Wage Offers, 1979 to 1998[a]	Predicted Effect of Wages on Percentage Incarcerated[b]	Actual Change in Incarceration Observed in the Census	Proportion of Increase Attributable to Change in ln(Wages)
White men				
Less than high school	−0.26	0.006	0.021	0.28
High school	−0.14	0.003	0.011	0.28
Some college	−0.04	0.001	0.004	0.21
College plus	0.13	−0.003	0.001	−2.95
All white men	—	0.001[c]	0.005	0.23
Black men				
Less than high school	−0.24	0.005	0.138	0.04
High school	−0.11	0.002	0.053	0.05
Some college	−0.04	0.001	0.024	0.04
College plus	0.04	−0.001	0.007	−0.12
All black men	—	0.002[c]	0.051	0.04
Hispanic men				
Less than high school	−0.24	0.005	0.016	0.34
High school	−0.11	0.002	0.024	0.10
Some college	−0.04	0.001	0.010	0.09
College plus	0.04	−0.001	0.004	−0.21
All Hispanic men	—	0.003[c]	0.015	0.21
Other men				
Less than high school	−0.24	0.005	0.021	0.26
High school	−0.11	0.002	0.007	0.34
Some college	−0.04	0.001	0.005	0.18
College plus	0.04	−0.001	0.000	0.00
All other men	—	0.001[c]	0.004	0.33

Source: Actual incarceration changes tabulated from the One Percent Public Use Microdata Samples (U.S. Census Bureau 1980a, 2000).

[a]Figures are estimates of changes in wage opportunity costs accounting for labor market dropouts presented in Juhn (2003). We assume that the changes in wage offers by education for black men apply to these other two race-ethnicity groups.

[b]The predicted effect of changes in wages on incarceration is calculated by multiplying the likelihood of being sent to prison conditional on engaging in criminal activity (we assume 0.06), the magnification factor (1.5), the effect of a change in ln wages on criminal participation (estimate of −0.25 from Grogger 1998), the actual change in the natural log of wages, and −1.

[c]The change in incarceration figure is the sum across education groups of the product of the proportion of males in the group of the given education level multiplied by the predicted change in incarceration for the race-education group.

that we have shown to be driven in large part by policy choices are in part responsible for the abysmally low employment rates of low-skilled minority men. Table 6.5 documents this development. Using data from all decennial censuses between 1950 and 2000 and data from the 2008 American Community Survey, the table presents employment-to-population ratios for whites and blacks by level of educational attainment for those eighteen to fifty-four years of age.[10] The table presents estimates for men and comparable estimates for women. The declining employment rates for relatively less-educated black men are stunning. In 1950, 82 percent of prime-age black men with less than a high school degree were employed. By 2008, this figure had declined to 35 percent. For black men with a high school degree, the comparable figures are 78 percent for 1950 and 61 percent for 2008. There are also declines in employment rates among less-skilled white men, but nowhere near the magnitudes observed for black men. It is also noteworthy that we see no such trends among women. In fact, for most groups of women, labor force participation increased considerably over this time period.

To be sure, part of the decline in employment is due to the mechanical removal of men from the non-institutionalized population. One cannot be employed in the conventional sense while incarcerated. Between 1980 and 2008, the employment rate of black men with a high school degree or less declined by fourteen percentage points. Candace Hamilton, Chris Meyer, and Steven Raphael (forthcoming) estimate that 34 percent of this decline was attributable to higher institutionalization rates that physically removed black men from the labor market.[11]

Aside from this mechanical effect, however, there are many reasons to believe that incarceration growth is permanently lowering labor force participation rates among the affected demographic groups and thus driving the trends we see in table 6.5. Robert Apel and Gary Sweeten (2010) find that following conviction for a crime, the postrelease labor force participation rates of young men punished with incarceration are discretely lower than the labor force participation rates of comparable young men convicted of felonies yet receiving alternative sentences. Because these men are less likely to be looking for work, Apel and Sweeten conclude, there is something about the incarceration experience that simply causes men to withdraw from the formal labor force on a larger scale. Charles Loeffler (2010) demonstrates that the pre-incarceration dip in employment commonly observed in the months leading up to a prison admission is largely attributable to pretrial detention, court

Table 6.5 Proportion of Black and White Adults Age Eighteen to Fifty-Four, Employed at the Time of the Census, by Race, Gender, and Educational Attainment, 1950 to 2008

	1950	1960	1970	1980	1990	2000	2008
Men							
Less than high school							
White	0.887	0.862	0.840	0.749	0.707	0.651	0.596
Black	0.820	0.772	0.737	0.589	0.488	0.394	0.353
High school							
White	0.915	0.943	0.932	0.890	0.866	0.824	0.789
Black	0.782	0.836	0.847	0.759	0.700	0.612	0.618
Some college							
White	0.718	0.869	0.824	0.851	0.854	0.842	0.824
Black	0.611	0.799	0.754	0.722	0.745	0.709	0.734
College plus							
White	0.916	0.948	0.941	0.942	0.941	0.931	0.932
Black	0.906	0.929	0.907	0.887	0.886	0.856	0.889
Women							
Less than high school							
White	0.307	0.339	0.400	0.444	0.493	0.493	0.450
Black	0.401	0.431	0.456	0.425	0.413	0.408	0.411
High school							
White	0.433	0.414	0.498	0.606	0.687	0.689	0.680
Black	0.485	0.510	0.589	0.621	0.632	0.604	0.644
Some college							
White	0.465	0.442	0.507	0.653	0.742	0.745	0.743
Black	0.549	0.587	0.628	0.660	0.726	0.717	0.738
College plus							
White	0.701	0.681	0.726	0.798	0.824	0.816	0.821
Black	0.728	0.849	0.856	0.866	0.885	0.848	0.873

Source: Authors' tabulations from the U.S. Census Bureau One Percent Public Use Microdata Samples (1950, 1960, 1970, 1980a, 1990, 2000) and the U.S. Census Bureau *American Community Survey* (2008a).

proceedings, and other time-consuming and incapacitating procedures associated with a criminal conviction. Harry Holzer, Paul Offner, and Elaine Sorensen (2005) find evidence that higher incarceration rates, accruing child support arrears, and the interaction between these two factors predict declines in employment rates among less-skilled African American men. There is also ample evidence of extreme employer reluctance to hire those with prior felony convictions, as well as evidence that many employers are legally proscribed from hiring convicted felons (Raphael 2011).

To summarize, our tabulations suggest that increasing earnings inequality contributed somewhat to incarceration growth, especially among white men. For all men, our tabulations suggest that earnings trends explain a relatively small share of growth—and very little among African American men, for whom incarceration rates increased tremendously. There is reason to believe that the worsening labor market outcomes observed for the least-skilled men in the United States are being driven in part by the increasing role of the criminal justice system in their lives. Although our principal motivation in this book is to understand what has caused unprecedented growth in U.S. incarceration rates, it is important to not lose sight of the many social domains that experience a collateral impact from this momentous change.

CRACK COCAINE

The last half of the twentieth century witnessed the rise and fall of several illicit drug epidemics. Each of these epidemics entails separate subcultures of use and sales, idiosyncratic economic relationships and market organizations, and particular pathways by which drug use and sales are likely to have an impact on crime and incarceration. During the 1960s and 1970s, intravenously injected heroin was the hard drug of choice among urban users in American inner cities. During the late 1970 and 1980s, recreational use of powder cocaine, consumed through inhaling or freebasing, became popular and widespread. The introduction of crack cocaine in the mid-1980s greatly increased cocaine use in relatively poor minority neighborhoods and is commonly cited as a key determinant of the spike in violent crime between the mid-1980s and the early 1990s. With the waning of the crack epidemic, marijuana use among criminally active youth increased substantially during the 1990s (Johnson, Golub, and Dunlap 2000). Finally, the 1990s witnessed the increasing use of crystal methamphetamine across the county (Dobkin and Nicosia 2009).

Individual drug epidemics primarily affect incarceration growth through their impact on crime. Moreover, the introduction of a new drug can be thought of as a behavioral shock to the criminality of a nation's residents. Bruce Johnson, Andrew Golub, and Eloise Dunlap (2000) lay out three avenues by which specific drug epidemics are likely to affect criminality, and these provide a useful framework for thinking about the consequences of recent drug epidemics for crime and incarceration. First, each drug has unique psychopharmacological effects on users that may have an impact on aggression, heighten a sense of paranoia, or alter other psychological factors that may predispose an individual toward violence. Second, users may turn to income-generating crime to support their habits. Such "economic-compulsive" criminal behavior may take the form of drug dealing, robbery, burglary, or larceny theft. Finally, since drug transactions are not governed by the legal system—that is to say, there are no formal mechanisms for contract enforcement and the protection of property rights—violent crime is likely to arise to settle disputes, protect market share, or collect payments.

The timing of the crack epidemic, along with the particular connections between violence and the market for crack, suggests that this particular behavioral shock was an important behavioral contributor to the growth in incarceration. First, while the exact timing of the start of the epidemic is uncertain, two careful studies of this question date the introduction of crack to 1984 at the earliest, with sales and use spreading throughout the country by the early 1990s at the latest (Grogger and Willis 2000; Fryer et al. 2005).[12] These years correspond to a time period when prison admissions for drug-related crimes increased absolutely, proportionally to the population, and proportionally to all prison admissions.

Second, the psychopharmacological effects of crack cocaine—or, more accurately, cocaine in general—are more likely, relative to other drugs, to predispose the user toward violence. In contrast with heroin and marijuana, which are depressants, cocaine is a stimulant that induces hyperactive states.

Third, the number of transactions per user is particularly high for crack cocaine, reflecting its sale in small, relatively inexpensive quantities.[13] A higher frequency of contact between dealers and users increases the number of opportunities for violence. Each contact carries a risk of the user victimizing the dealer, the dealer victimizing the user, or a third party bent on robbery victimizing the user, the dealer, or both.

Finally, the structure of the crack cocaine market was such that many young men were effectively employed by drug-selling operations in various capacities (MacCoun and Reuter 2001), with competing organizations often engaging in violent confrontations with one another over market share. At least one author (Grogger 2000) has hypothesized that the waning of violent crime during the 1990s was driven in part by a greater level of cooperation among drug-selling gangs and a greater propensity to rely on nonviolent means for settling turf conflicts.

A number of studies have attempted to estimate the effect of the crack cocaine epidemic on crime rates. For example, the criminologist Alfred Blumstein (1995) attributes the sharp increases in homicide among minority youth to the introduction of crack cocaine, the widespread availability of handguns, and the ensuing violence between rival suppliers of the drug. Grogger and Willis (2000) exploit differences in the timing of the introduction of crack cocaine across cities to estimate the effect of the drug on various aggregate crime rates. They conclude that had crack cocaine not been introduced, the peak in urban crime rates in 1991 would have been roughly 10 percent lower than that actually observed, and it would have been below the earlier 1981 peak (which it actually exceeded by 6 percent). Fryer and his colleagues (2005) have developed an index of crack cocaine usage that varies by city and state based on several indicators of the intensity of use, including cocaine-related emergency room visits, cocaine-related deaths, arrests, and drug busts, and the relative frequency of newspaper articles that mention crack cocaine. In a series of panel data regressions of various outcomes on the constructed crack index, they find that the introduction of crack cocaine predicted a sizable portion of the increase in black male youth homicide rates, changes in the proportion of black babies born at low birth weight, and changes in the proportion of births to unwed black mothers. Estimates of the effect of crack on overall crime rates in this study, however, are rather imprecise and, with a few exceptions, statistically insignificant.

Despite the timing of the epidemic and the clear connections between crack and violent crime, there are reasons to believe that the potential direct role of crack cocaine in explaining the explosion in incarceration growth is limited. To start, our decomposition of the increase in the incarceration rate indicated that even under relatively extreme assumptions about what the crime rate would have been in the absence of the incarceration increase, changes in criminal behavior can explain only a relatively small portion of the increase in incarceration. Moreover, the reviewed research on the effects of crack on crime suggest that at most the epidemic increased violent crime at the early 1990s peak by around 10 percent, with much lower effects on property crime. Clearly, an effect on crime of this order of magnitude cannot explain the near-quadrupling of the incarceration rate since 1985.[14]

In addition, the crack epidemic has diminished since 1990 while the incarceration rate has continued to grow. In fact, incarceration growth during the 1990s was of a similar order of magnitude as the absolute growth in the incarceration rate during the 1980s. Moreover, as we documented in chapter 4, during the 1990s several key changes were made to sentencing policy—including the passage in several states of stiff repeat-offender sentencing enhancements and the introduction of truth-in-sentencing laws throughout the country—that provide a clear alternative explanation for prison growth that coincides with declining crime rates.

The waning of the crack epidemic is readily observable in available gauges of the incidence of drug use. Figure 6.3 presents time series from the Monitoring the Future drug use survey (Johnston et al. 2012), covering the period from 1987 to 2011. For several age groups, the survey gauges the percentage of those with at least a high school degree who indicated that they used crack cocaine at some point over the previous year. The figure reveals pronounced declines from the late 1980s and a relatively low level of the use of crack cocaine overall.

Additional evidence of the waning crack epidemic comes from urinalysis tests administered to arrestees during the late 1980s and early 1990s in twenty-four locations under the guise of the Drug Use Forecasting program. Andrew Lang-Golub and Bruce Johnson (1997) present tabulations of the proportion of arrestees by age who tested positive for cocaine or crack for the period 1988 to 1996. These data are reproduced graphically in figure 6.4 for those nineteen, twenty-three, and twenty-seven years of age. The table reveals notable declines in the proportion who tested positive for crack, especially among younger arrestees. In subsequent work focused on New York City, Johnson, Golub, and Dunlap (2000) document a sharp decline in the proportion of young men arrested who had ever used crack relative to older arrestees. Moreover, through their ethnographic work these authors document a cultural shift away from crack cocaine driven in large part by the negative experiences with the drug of the older generation. To the extent that crack cocaine drove the growth in incarceration during the 1980s, the waning of the epidemic should have given rise to a decline during the 1990s (with both fewer

Figure 6.3   Percentage of High School Graduates Who Self-Report Having Used Crack over the Previous Year

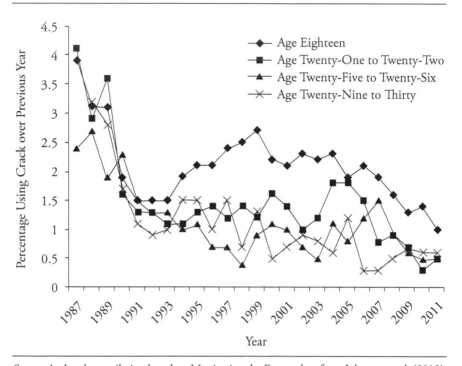

Source: Authors' compilation based on Monitoring the Future data from Johnston et al. (2012).

prison admissions for crack cocaine violations and the release of earlier offenders).

The rapid incarceration growth preceding the onset of the crack epidemic casts further doubt on the hypothesis that crack cocaine is a key driver. The effects of crack cocaine on crime rates across the nation appear to surface around 1984 at the earliest, but as late as the early 1990s in some states. A careful analysis of state-level incarceration rates reveals that in many states incarceration growth was well on its way before the onset of crack-related violence.

To illustrate this fact, we use microlevel data from the Federal Bureau of Investigation Supplemental Homicide Reports (SHRs) to estimate black male homicide rates for the period 1977 to 2007. Blumstein (1995) documents the unprecedented spikes in black male homicide rates, and many have come to characterize this particular crime as a key gauge of the crime wave unleashed by the introduction of crack cocaine. Not all states provided data in all years.

Figure 6.4   Percentage of Arrestees in the Twenty-Four Drug Use
Forecasting Program Locations Who Tested Positive for
Cocaine or Crack at the Time of Arrest, 1988 to 1996

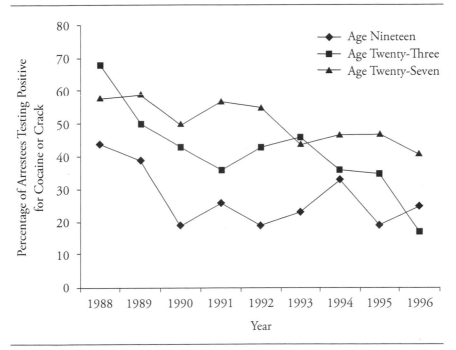

Source: Authors' compilation based on data from Lang-Golub and Johnson (1997).

Hence, we restrict our analysis to those that provided data to the SHR for all years from 1977 to 1996. This leaves us with thirty-two states and Washington, D.C.[15]

For each of these states, we identify surges in black male homicide rates during the mid to late 1980s and early 1990s and use the starting year of the surge to date the introduction of crack cocaine to the state.[16] We then use this dating scheme to compare incarceration growth before and after the onset of crack-related violence.[17] Figures 6.5, 6.6, and 6.7 present black male homicide rates as well as prison incarceration rates for the period 1976 to 1996 for eleven states with particularly pronounced spikes in those rates during the time period under study. In each figure, black male homicide is measured along the left vertical axis while the state's incarceration rate is measured along the right vertical axis. The homicide rate is marked with diamonds, while the incarceration rate is marked with squares. In each figure,

Figure 6.5   Incarceration Rates and Black Male Homicide Rates
                Surrounding the Onset of Crack-Related Violence in
                Washington, D.C., Illinois, Maryland, and
                Massachusetts

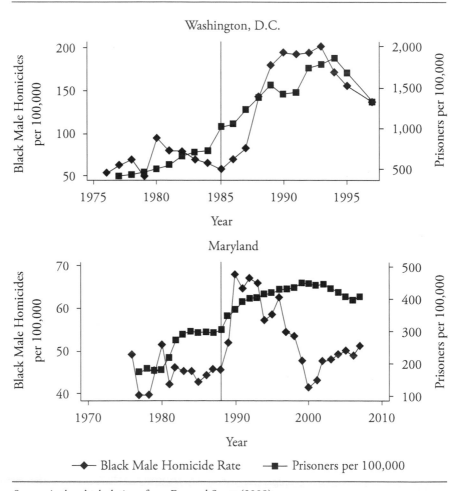

Source: Authors' tabulations from Fox and Swatt (2009).

we draw a vertical line at the year we deem as marking the onset of crack-related violence.

Figure 6.5 shows four places where considerable incarceration growth preceded the spike in black male homicide rates. In each location, there is little visible evidence that incarceration growth following the onset of the black male homicide spike accelerated relative to what had come before. For ex-

Figure 6.5   (Continued)

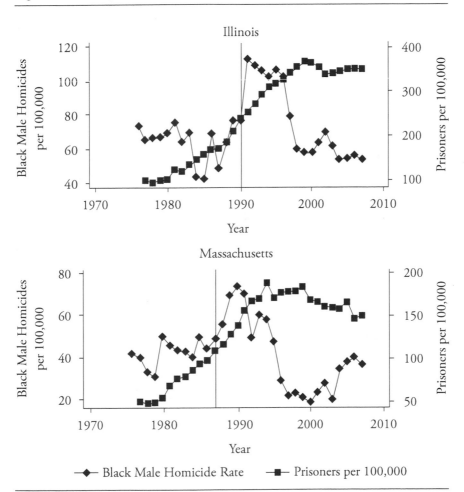

ample, in Illinois the incarceration rate increased from 99 per 100,000 to 241 per 100,000 in 1990 (a change of 142 per 100,000), the year preceding the sustained spike in black male homicide rates. Over the subsequent thirteen years, the Illinois incarceration rate increased to 343 per 100,000. In other words, incarceration growth following the black male homicide spike actually fell short of the growth preceding the spike. Comparable patterns are observed for Maryland, Washington, D.C., and Massachusetts.

Figure 6.6   Incarceration Rates and Black Male Homicide Rates
Surrounding the Onset of Crack-Related Violence in
Michigan, Minnesota, Texas, and Virginia

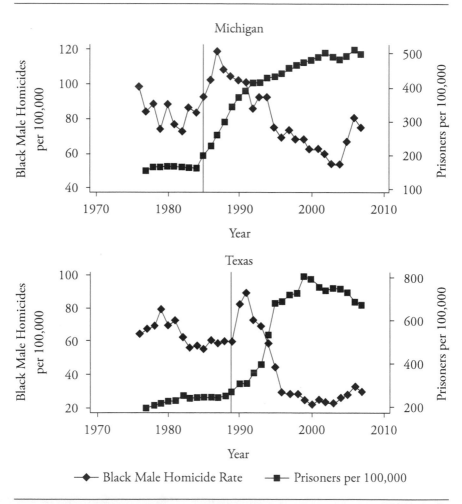

Source: Authors' tabulations from Fox and Swatt (2009).

In figure 6.6, there are several states where incarceration growth appears to
align with the spike in black male homicide rates, though imperfectly in most
instances. For example, we date the onset of crack-related violence in Michigan to 1985, the first year of many sustained increases in incarceration rates
for the state. The Texas incarceration rate increased sharply beginning in

Figure 6.6   **(Continued)**

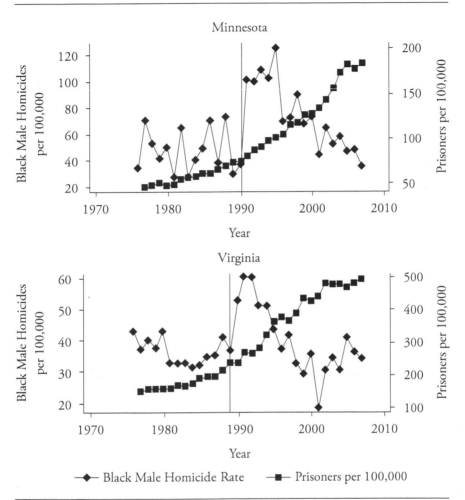

1993, while black homicide rates spiked in 1990 and 1991. Minnesota and Virginia, however, both exhibit appreciable growth in their incarceration rates before the observable spike in black male homicide and show little evidence of accelerated growth as a result of the homicide spike.

Figure 6.7 presents a particularly interesting contrast. Black male homicide rates increased sharply in the late 1980s in both North and South Carolina. In North Carolina, incarceration rates started to grow a few years later, although from a relatively high base level of over 250 per 100,000. In South Carolina, on the other hand, the incarceration rate increased from 229 per 100,000 to 424 per 100,000 between 1977 and 1989, the latter year being the last year of relatively low black male homicide rates. Hence, most of the incarceration growth in South Carolina over the past three decades preceded the onset of crack-related violence. Missouri resembles many of the other states, with high incarceration growth preceding the onset of crack-related violence and little evidence of accelerated growth following the onset.

On the whole, these eleven state-specific comparisons suggest a fair degree of incarceration growth prior to the much-noted spike in black male homicide rates. We can provide a summary comparison that makes use of data from all thirty-two states plus D.C. To do so we first define an alternative time scale for each state where the scale is set to zero in the year we designate as the start of the crack epidemic. The years following the crack epidemic are denoted as year 1, year 2, year 3, and so on. The years preceding the crack epidemic are denoted by year –1, year –2, and so on. Aligning all states on this scale permits us to characterize the average state incarceration rate in the years leading up to the crack epidemic and the average incarceration rates following for all states in our data.[18] Figure 6.8 presents these average state incarceration rates and black male homicide rates for the nine years preceding and following the onset of crack-related violence.

The figure reveals the very large spike in black male homicide rates from roughly 50 per 100,000 in year 0 to a peak of 75 per 100,000 in year 5. In the nine years preceding this spike, however, black male homicide rates were declining. During this pre-crack period, the average state incarceration rate increased from 136 per 100,000 to 223 per 100,000, a change of 87 per 100,000. During the nine post-crack years, the incarceration rate increased further, to 408 per 100,000, a change of 185 per 100,000. Thus, over the entire eighteen-year period, the average state incarceration rate increased by 272 per 100,000. If the underlying trend in incarceration growth had continued in the absence of the crack epidemic (that is to say, if the incarceration rate had increased by another 87 inmates per 100,000 residents between years 0 and 9), the state incarceration rate by the end of this period would have stood at 310 per 100,000. In other words, the existing trend alone would explain 64 percent of overall incarceration growth in the period depicted in figure 6.8.

Figure 6.7   Incarceration Rates and Black Male Homicide Rates
Surrounding the Onset of Crack-Related Violence in
North Carolina, South Carolina, and Missouri

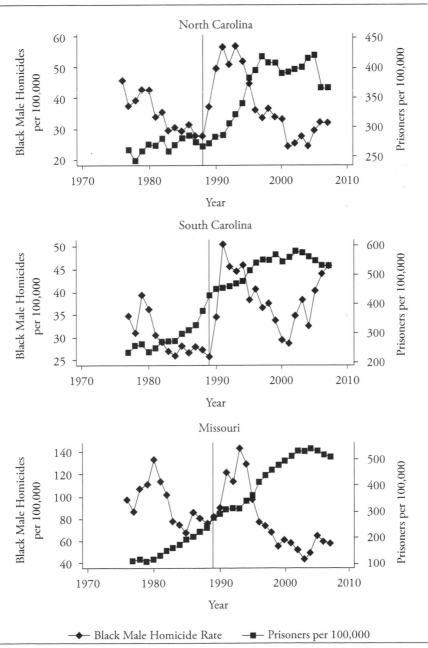

Source: Authors' tabulations from Fox and Swatt (2009).

Figure 6.8   **Average Black Male Homicide Rates and Incarceration Rates for the Years Preceding and Following the Onset of Crack-Related Violence**

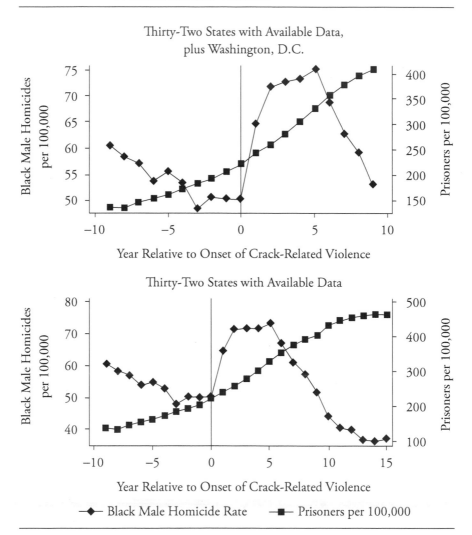

Source: Authors' tabulations from Fox and Swatt (2009).

Does this then mean that the increase in crime caused by the emergence of crack cocaine explains 36 percent of the rise in U.S. incarceration rates? Certainly not. We noted in chapter 4 that the 1990s was a decade of sentencing reforms characterized by stiff sentence enhancement for habitual offenders and the widespread adoption of policies designed to ensure that convicted offenders served large proportions of their sentences. Moreover, the War on Drugs, announced in 1982 several years before the onset of the crack epidemic, certainly enhanced the resources devoted to combating drug crime, and the series of sentencing reforms to follow greatly enhanced criminal penalties for drug crimes (in particular those involving crack cocaine). Such policy changes most certainly explain some of the acceleration in incarceration growth observed in the post-crack era. That being said, it would be very helpful to our deliberation to have direct empirical tests of the net effect of the crack cocaine epidemic on state prison incarceration growth that would permit us to distinguish the effects of the crack cocaine epidemic from the underlying year-to-year changes driven by other factors.

We propose the following as such a test. First, we use state-level incarceration rates for the states for which we have data on black male homicide rates to estimate the average incarceration rate for each year across our set of states. Next, we use statistical methods to estimate the trend in incarceration after accounting for interstate differences at a point in time and differences over time in black male homicide rates. The trend in overall averages should basically chart the overall growth in incarceration rates. To the extent that crack-related violence explains incarceration growth, our estimated trends that net out the contribution of black male homicide should show less growth by comparison, especially during the post-crack period. We control for the contribution of black male homicide rates in two different ways: first, we net out the effect of contemporary male homicide rates, and second, we estimate trends that account for the potential lagged effects of black male homicide rates on incarceration rates that extend back five years.[19]

The results from this exercise are graphically presented in figure 6.9. The top graph charts the estimated time trends not adjusting for black male homicide rates, time trends after netting out the contemporary contribution of black male homicide rates, and time trends after netting out the contemporary and lagged contributions of black male homicide rates. In estimating these underlying models, we use all states that report data in the SRF even if they do not report data in all years. Hence, the composition of states varies from year to year. The figure reveals three incarceration time paths that are nearly identical. In other words, controlling for black homicide rates does not explain any of the growth in incarceration rates between 1977 and 2009.[20] The lower graph in figure 6.9 depicts the time effect estimates adjusting for the year-to-year changes in the composition of states providing data in the SHR.[21] The results are nearly identical.

Figure 6.9   Estimated Incarceration Rate Time Series With and
Without Statistical Adjustments to Net Out the Impacts
of Changes in Black Male Homicide Rates, 1977 to
2009

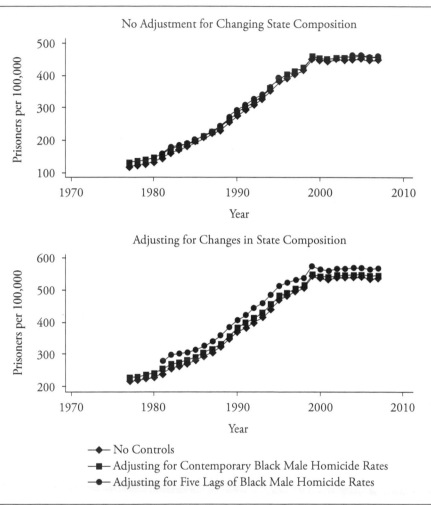

Source: Authors' analysis based on data from Fox and Swatt (2009).

It might be argued that our gauge of the effect of the crack epidemic is
incomplete and that changes in drug use, economic-compulsive-related
crime, and so on, may have preceded the spike in black male homicide rates
associated with drug turf wars. Moreover, our analysis focuses on overall
growth in incarceration rates; perhaps we should be focusing instead on new

admissions to prison, since they are most closely linked with contemporary and perhaps recent lags in drug-related crime and violence. Fortunately, there is one study that produces a relatively comprehensive index of the onset and intensity of the crack epidemic based on multiple social indicators.[22] Fryer and his colleagues (2005) test for an effect of crack cocaine usage on prison admissions and find no evidence of an impact. We reproduce their basic finding here.

Specifically, we match the crack cocaine index measured at the state level from Fryer et al. (2005) to state-level data on overall prison admissions per 100,000, new commitments per 100,000, and admissions due to returns-to-custody per 100,000. We restrict the data to the period from 1985 to 2000 because Fryer and his colleagues have little confidence in their index prior to 1985. We then use these data to estimate a series of linear regression models where the key dependent variable is the state-level prison admissions rate and the key explanatory variable is the crack index.

Table 6.6 presents these results. The first row of numbers provides the coefficient on the crack index from a simple regression of the specific prison admissions rate on the index. The next row presents the same coefficient estimates after statistically controlling for average differences across states in other factors that determined prison admissions. The final set of results is perhaps the most important, since the underlying statistical model removes from the two variables of interest all year-to-year changes in incarceration and crack usage that are common across states. In essence, this final set of results estimates the effect of the introduction of crack by assessing whether admissions rates increased earlier in states where crack appeared first (these results also correspond to the models estimated in Fryer et al. 2005).

Beginning with the total admissions rates, there is a significant positive association between admissions and the crack index and a somewhat larger positive estimate when we use only variation within states, but a significant negative effect when time effects are included in the specification. The largest estimate of the effect of crack on prison admissions (the coefficient of 14.71 in the model with state fixed effects only) predicts that the change in the crack index increased prison admissions between 1985 and 2000 by approximately 14 admissions per 100,000. Since the actual rate increased by 114 over this period, the largest estimate in the first column of table 6.6 suggests that crack explained no more than 12 percent of the growth in prison admissions over this time period.[23]

This is certainly, however, an overestimate. The fact that the marginal effect

Table 6.6   Estimated Marginal Effects of Variation in the State-Level Crack Index on Prison Admissions per 100,000 State Residents, Based on State-Level Panel Data, 1985 to 2000

	Total Admissions Rate	New Commitment Rate	Returns to Custody per 100,000
No state or year effects	11.83	6.22	7.63
	(2.59)	(1.59)	(1.79)
State effects only	14.71	10.49	4.65
	(2.40)	(1.51)	(1.35)
State and year fixed effects	−6.24	−0.57	−7.81
	(2.32)	(1.62)	(1.38)

Source: Authors' compilation. Figures in the table are the coefficient on the crack index taken from Fryer et al. (2005).
Note: Standard errors are in parentheses.

of the intensity of crack usage does not survive adjusting for common year-to-year shifts casts serious doubt on this estimate. The results in the final row indicate that states where the intensity of crack use increased above and beyond the average increase for the nation experienced declines in the prison admissions rate. Although this result may be biased by a reverse causal effect of prison on the crack epidemic (the explanation offered in Fryer et al. 2005), the large disparity between the estimated impact of crack omitting year effects and the impact including these effects suggests that crack cocaine has played a minor role.

To summarize, we conclude that there is little evidence that criminal behavior associated with the onset of the crack epidemic explains much of the increase in incarceration rates over the past three decades. Much of the incarceration growth precedes the onset of crack-related violence, and incarceration growth continued despite the waning of the crack epidemic. Moreover, there are many identifiable policy trends in the aftermath of the crack epidemic that militate toward longer sentences and higher incarceration, factors that on their own would explain the acceleration of incarceration growth during the 1990s. Finally, direct empirical tests for an impact of crack-related crime on an index of the intensity of the crack epidemic fail to explain the growth in either incarceration rates or prison admissions rates.

CONCLUSION

In this chapter, we have investigated three potential sources of behavioral change that may explain the growth in incarceration rates in the United States over the past three decades. From the outset we noted that the role of these factors was likely to be limited, since our decomposition analysis in chapters 1, 2, and 3 highlighted the overpowering impacts of sentencing policy reform on incarceration growth. Nonetheless, the analysis in this chapter, in conjunction with the analysis of deinstitutionalization in chapter 5, does suggest that some developments outside of the realm of criminal justice policy have had an impact on the nation's incarceration rate. We found evidence in chapter 5 of a modest contribution of the deinstitutionalization of the mentally ill, especially after 1980. Although this change in mental health policy does not explain a large portion of overall incarceration growth, it does explain a fair proportion of growth in the population of mentally ill inmates in the nation's prisons and jails.

Demographic change and the health of the low-wage labor market also have probably exerted significant yet offsetting effects on incarceration growth. The aging of the population, higher levels of educational attainment, and growth in the immigrant population have all acted to reduce our incarceration rate below what it otherwise would have been. Although we do not present direct estimates of the effects of the diminished employment prospects of low-skilled men, the findings from existing research, combined with data on earnings trends, suggest that diminished labor market prospects have in isolation increased offending and incarceration. On net, these two effects cancel one another out, with the magnitude of the impact of demographic change being somewhat larger than the simulated effects of the changing labor market.

What is likely to be the most surprising finding of this chapter to a lay reader concerns the relative contribution of the crack epidemic. Despite the common attribution of our high incarceration rate to crack cocaine, the evidence favoring such an inference is surprisingly thin. Substantial incarceration growth preceded the crack epidemic, incarceration growth continued well beyond the waning of the epidemic, and there is little evidence of a direct effect of crack-related crime on incarceration rates or prison admissions rates. In light of the analytical model in chapters 2 and 3 and the finding from empirical work of a modest effect of the crack epidemic on crime rates, perhaps this result is not too surprising. Frankly, it is impossible for a factor that causes a temporary 10 percent increase in crime to cause a quadrupling in the incarceration rate, problems of inconsistent timing aside.

To be sure, the crack epidemic certainly had substantial indirect effects on incarceration rates through policy. A fair amount of public hysteria surrounded the onset of the crack epidemic and resulted in sentencing reforms at the federal and state levels that contributed greatly to incarceration growth. The death due to a cocaine overdose of college basketball star Len Bias one day after signing with the Boston Celtics in 1986 is often cited as the trigger that ushered in the 1986 federal legislation establishing the notorious "100-to-1" rule—namely, the mandatory minimum handed down for a crack cocaine violation was of an order of magnitude equivalent to the punishment for one hundred times the amount of powder cocaine. This was followed by federal legislation creating enhanced minimum sentences for small amounts of crack cocaine in 1988 (Vagins and McCurdy 2006). However, the War on Drugs and the attendant mobilization of federal resources predate the emergence of crack cocaine by several years. As our discussion in chapter 4 illustrated, the political conditions were ripe for major legislation targeted at drug crime, and the emergence of crack cocaine and the media attention it attracted may have simply served as the proverbial straw that broke the camel's back. To the extent that states took their cue from Congress, that local prosecutors saw their bargaining position enhanced by the threat of tougher sentences should an offender be diverted into federal court, or that federal activity and frequent media coverage created a tough-on-crime legislative environment that eased the way for state-level sentence enhancements, the impact of crack cocaine on incarceration growth extended beyond its direct effect on crime.

CHAPTER 7

Incarceration and Crime

On July 31, 2006, the Italian Parliament passed legislation that reduced the sentences of most Italian prison inmates by three years, effective August 1, 2006. The clemency applied only to inmates convicted of a subset of felonies committed prior to May of that year. The passage of the "collective clemency" bill followed a six-year debate surrounding Italian prison conditions, spurred in large part by the activism of the Catholic Church and the personal involvement of Pope John Paul II. With Italian prisons filled to 130 percent of capacity, the onetime pardon was principally motivated by the need to address prison overcrowding.

Figure 7.1 displays a scatter plot of Italian monthly incarceration rates (measured as inmates per 100,000 residents) for the period from January 2004 to December 2008. The month of August 2006 is set to zero along the horizontal axis, with all months preceding and following measured relative to that month. The incarceration rate is relatively stable between January 2004 and August 2006. Between August and September 2006, however, the collective pardon induces a sharp decline. Over this one-month period, the prison population declined by 21,863 individuals, equivalent to a 36 percent decrease, with a corresponding decrease in the national incarceration rate from 103 to 66 inmates per 100,000.

Figure 7.2 displays corresponding monthly total crimes per 100,000 Italian residents. The national crime rate increased slightly during the pre-pardon

Figure 7.1   Scatter Plot of Monthly Incarceration Rate Against Month Measured Relative to August 2006

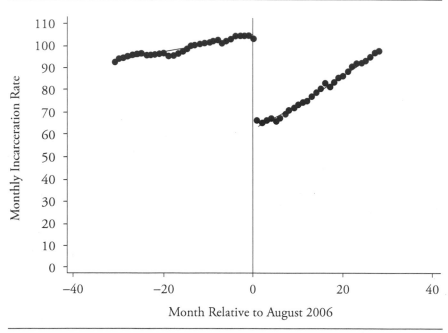

Source: Authors' compilation based on Italian Ministry of Interior (2009b), Ministero della Giustizia, Italy.

period, increased sharply between August 2006 and September 2006, and then steadily declined back to pre-pardon levels. The magnitude of the increase in crime coinciding with the mass prisoner release suggests that on average each released inmate generated fourteen felony crime reports to the police per year. Looking at variation within the country, we also note that Italian provinces that received more released inmates as a result of the pardon experienced relatively larger increases in crime. Although most of the increase in Italian crime associated with the collective clemency was attributable to theft, there was also a notable and statistically significant increase in robbery, a crime classified in most nations as a violent felony (Buonanno and Raphael, forthcoming).

Italy's experience with the 2006 collective clemency bill contrasts sharply with the recent experience of California. In April 2011, the state of California enacted broad correctional reform legislation under the banner of corrections realignment. The legislation eliminates the practice of returning parolees to

Figure 7.2   Scatter Plot of Total Monthly Crimes per 100,000 Italian
Residents Against Month Measured Relative to August
2006

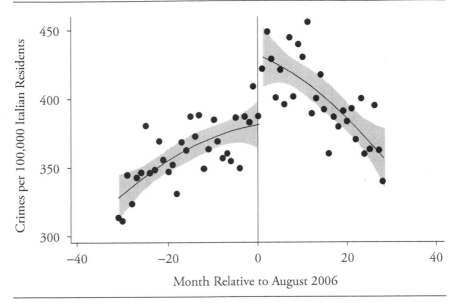

Month Relative to August 2006

Source: Authors' compilation based on Italian Ministry of Interior (2009a), Ministero dell'Interno, Italy.

state prison custody for technical parole violation for all but a small set of the most serious and mentally ill offenders. The legislation also defines a group of nonserious, nonsexual, nonviolent offenders who upon conviction will serve their sentences in county jails. These offenders will earn good time credits more quickly than they would within the state prison system and can be given split sentences that involve alternative monitoring within the community. More generally, judges are now afforded greater discretion to devise alternatives to confinement in the sentencing of these offenders.

The legislation was prompted by an order by a federal three-judge court impanelled as a result of legal decisions in two lawsuits against the state filed on behalf of California prison inmates. In Plata v. Brown, it was alleged that California was providing inadequate health care services to its prison population. In Coleman v. Brown, it was alleged that the system was providing inadequate mental health services. These cases were consolidated and appealed to the U.S. Supreme Court. The Supreme Court affirmed the three-judge court ruling that prison overcrowding led to inadequate health and mental health care in violation of the Eighth Amendment prohibition against cruel and unusual punishment. The three-judge court ordered the California Department of Corrections and Rehabilitation (CDCR) to reduce its prison population from roughly 200 percent of design capacity to less than 137.5 percent of design capacity. Assembly Bill 109 (AB 109, referred to in the state as "corrections realignment") was passed and implemented to achieve this goal.

These reforms did not affect the California prison population as suddenly as was observed in Italy. However, realignment did result in a relatively quick reduction in the California prison population that was larger in magnitude than that experienced in Italy. Moreover, while Italy authorized a onetime release with an impact on the prison population that would be reversed by subsequent business-as-usual, California permanently altered sentencing and parole practices in a way that will lead to long-term sustained declines in its incarceration rate. Within a few weeks of the legislation's implementation on October 1, 2011, admissions to the state prison declined from roughly 2,100 per week to 1,000. Six months following the legislation, weekly admissions had settled at roughly 600 per week.

These admissions declines had immediate impacts on the state's incarceration rate. Figure 7.3 shows the California incarceration rate by week from January 2011 to the middle of October 2012. Along the horizontal axis of the graph, the week of the first post-realignment population count (the week ending October 5, 2011) is set to zero, and all other weeks are measured relative to this date. During the pre-reform period, the figure reveals a relatively stable incarceration rate that exhibited a slight downward trend. With the passage of realignment, we observe a sharp decline in the state's incarceration rate. By the end of 2011 (three months into the implementation of reforms), the incarceration rate had declined to 392 per 100,000—a decline per 100,000 relative to the last pre-reform week of 34 inmates per 100,000 (similar in magnitude to the immediate decline caused by the Italian pardon). By the end of June 2012, the state's incarceration rate had declined further, to 359 per 100,000, a level not experienced since 1992 (which predates the passage of California's "three strikes" ballot amendment). By October 2012, the incarceration rate had declined to 354 per 100,000 and appeared to have stabilized. In total, the permanent decline in California's incarceration rate by 72 per 100,000 over the first year of the reform period is nearly twice the temporary decline experienced by Italy as a result of the collective clemency bill.

Figure 7.3   California Incarceration Rates by Week, January 2011 to October 2012

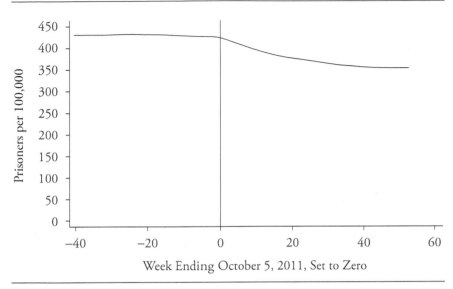

Source: Authors' compilation based on California Department of Corrections and Rehabilitation Weekly Population Reports (2011/2012).
Note: Weeks are expressed relative to first full post-realignment week.

And what has been the impact on California crime rates? Figure 7.4 displays monthly violent crime rates for the period January 2010 to June 2012. These are the most recent data available and provide coverage for nine postreform months.[1] During these months, violent crime declined relative to the months immediately preceding the reform. Crime appeared to be trending downward, however, over this time period. A better comparison is between violent crime for the period October 2011 to June 2012 and comparable crime rates a year earlier (that is to say, for the period October 2010 to June 2011). These two periods are highlighted on the figure. With the exception of February 2012, violent crime in each post-realignment month was lower than the comparable crime rate one year earlier. For February, the ratio of the violent crime rate in 2012 to the violent crime rate in 2011 is 1.006.

Figure 7.5 displays comparable data for property crime. Here we see higher property crime rates relative to one year earlier in seven of the nine postreform months for which we have data. However, we also see crime rising relative to one year previous in the two months prior to the implementation of AB 109, suggesting that property crime was trending upward for reasons other than the

Figure 7.4   California Monthly Violent Crime Rates, January 2010
              to June 2012

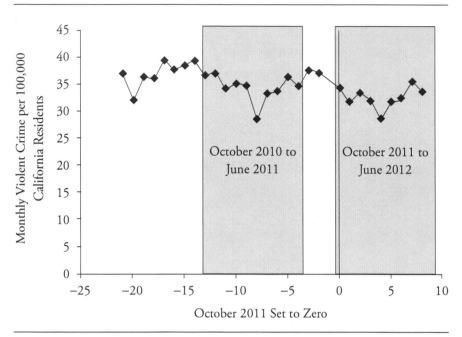

Source: Authors' compilation based on unpublished data from the California Department of Justice, Criminal Justice Information Services Division.

declining prison population. Relative to the difference in incarceration rates, the higher post-realignment crime rate suggests modest effects on crime relative to what was observed in Italy. For example, the monthly felony property crime rate in December 2011 was higher than the comparable rate in December 2010 by 5.8 incidents per 100,000. Meanwhile, the difference in incarceration rates between these two months was 39 inmates per 100,000, suggesting that each realigned inmate generated 0.14 new property offenses per month, or roughly 1.78 new offenses per year. If we account for the increase in the state's jail population equivalent to roughly 35 percent of the decline in the prison population, the figure would increase to 2.7 new offenses per year. This estimated impact on property crime is considerably smaller than the Italian estimate.

Raphael (2013) analyzes the effects of the realignment reforms on the California crime rate exploiting the fact that the effect of realignment has varied considerably across California's fifty-eight counties. Prior to realignment, there were large differences across counties in the propensity to use the state

Figure 7.5   California Monthly Property Crime Rates, January 2010 to June 2012

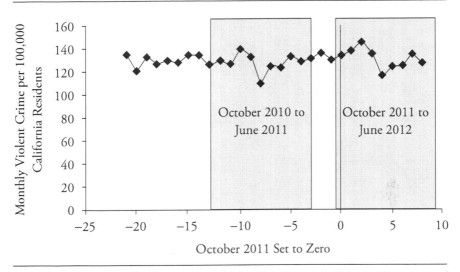

Source: Authors' compilation based on unpublished data from the California Department of Justice, Criminal Justice Information Services Division.

prison system to punish lower-level offenders. As a consequence, the number of inmates "realigned" to counties has tended to be larger in those counties that used the system relatively intensively prior to the reform. There is no evidence that those counties that received more realigned inmates experienced relatively greater changes in violent crime from the pre-reform period to the postreform period. Moreover, there is also no evidence in this cross-county analysis of an impact of realignment on burglary or larceny theft, though there is some evidence of a small effect on auto theft. Note that this analysis statistically accounts for the fact that some realigned offenders were being incarcerated in county jails.

What explains the difference between the experiences of Italy and California? For one, these are two very different places, with different demographics and systems of policing and criminal sentencing. Hence, the disparity may be due in part to differences in institutional and cultural factors. However, there are other key differences between the two case studies that are probably key to understanding the difference in outcomes. First, the pre-pardon incarceration rate in Italy stood at roughly 103 per 100,000 residents, which is quite close to the U.S. incarceration rates that existed prior to 1980. In California the pre-reform incarceration rate was between 425 and 430 per 100,000, more than four times that of Italy. If we add California's 75,000 jail inmates (which makes for a more appropriate comparison to Italy since Italy has a unified prison and jail system), this rate increases to 625 per 100,000. Our earlier analysis demonstrated that most of the growth in the U.S. incarceration rate in recent decades was driven by policy choices that have increased the likelihood of being sent to prison conditional on the crime committed as well as the amount of time that a person can expect to serve. Hence, one possible explanation is that California casts a much wider net in terms of who is sent to prison and for how long. Consequently, the average pre-reform inmate in California was perhaps less criminally prone than the average inmate in Italy, where prison is used more sparingly.

Second, Italy's collective pardon was broadly applied to all inmates with three years or less left on their sentence, with exceptions for inmates who had been convicted of offenses involving organized crime, felony sex offenders, and those convicted of terrorism, kidnapping, or exploitation of prostitution. California reduced its prison population more selectively, largely by discontinuing the policy of returning to custody parole violators who had not been convicted of a new felony. Hence, California's policy experiment may have been more effective at selectively reducing the prison population in a way that increased the street time of the least-serious offenders.

All of these factors are suggestive of great heterogeneity among those serving time in their propensity to offend when they are on the street. Moreover, in situations where policy choices increase the scope and scale of incarceration, this heterogeneity will increase as individuals who pose relatively little threat to society become more likely to be caught up in the criminal justice system alongside more dangerous convicted felons. Of course, it can be argued that a high incarceration rate has an impact on crime through other avenues, with deterrence of potential offenders a key consideration. To the extent that stiff sentences prevent crime through such deterrence, incarcerating someone who is convicted of a crime but poses little future threat to society may still be justified on utilitarian grounds.

In this chapter, we analyze the relationship between the use of incarceration and crime rates. We begin with a conceptual discussion of the various avenues through which crime and incarceration are linked and discuss the current state of knowledge regarding each mechanism. We then present estimates of the net effect of incarceration on crime in the United States and discuss how this relationship has changed with the growing prison population.

INCARCERATION, INCAPACITATION, AND DETERRENCE

Incarcerating a criminal offender may affect crime through several channels. First, placing a criminally active person in custody curtails that person's ability to commit crimes in non-institutional society. This "incapacitation effect" for a specific individual essentially equals the crimes that the person would have committed had he or she been free rather than in prison. There is little reason to believe that this incapacitation effect is constant for all those sent to prison. Some prison inmates are generally more criminally prone than others, an issue that we discuss at great length shortly.

Second, some potential offenders may be deterred from committing crime by the threat of a prison spell. To the extent that potential criminals consider the costs and benefits of their actions, stiffer sentences in the form of a higher likelihood of being sent to prison or receiving a longer sentence may increase costs above benefits and tip the decision-making scales in favor of behaving. Of course, such "general deterrence" requires that potential offenders accurately assess the likely consequences of their actions and that such individuals be sufficiently future-oriented to be deterred by changes in sentencing policy.

Finally, the experience of serving time in prison may alter the future offending trajectories of former prison inmates. It is important to note that for a given incarceration rate, an associated proportion of the non-institutional population has served prison time in the past. Higher incarceration rates generally correspond to a larger population of former prisoners, and their criminal offending may be affected by their experiences in prison. A prison spell may reduce offending if the experience itself deters (a factor often referred to as "specific deterrence," since the experience deters a specific person). Alternatively, education and treatment services while incarcerated may have rehabilitative effects on those who pass through prison and thus reduce future offending.

Of course, there are several ways in which a prison spell could increase an inmate's future offending. For example, he or she might adopt the behavioral norms of prison pertaining to the use of violence and approaches to conflict that are not acceptable in non-institutionalized society. Inmates may learn from other inmates, and they may pursue outside of prison the contacts they made with highly criminally active individuals while they were in prison. Finally, the stigma of having served time may limit an individual's legitimate opportunities once released and increase the relative returns to crime. When prison enhances future criminal offending, criminologists refer to prison as having a "criminogenic" effect on former inmates.

The effectiveness of prison as a crime control device depends on these three causal channels linking incarceration and crime. Prison certainly incapacitates people. However, the amount of crime incapacitated by a year in prison most certainly varies from person to person and is likely to be very low, if not negligible, for older inmates and for many inmates convicted of less serious offenses. In a high-incarceration-rate regime, we might expect particularly low average incapacitation effects to the extent that the broad applicability of prison as punishment nets the less criminally prone individuals along with the high-risk offenders. To the extent that many are deterred by the threat of prison, however, the costs of incarcerating these low-risk individuals may be outweighed by the deterrence benefits derived from making examples of them. The long-term effects on crime of having more people funnel through prisons can go in either direction. We discuss each of these avenues in turn and offer our summary of the current state of knowledge.

Prison and Incapacitation

Individuals differ considerably in their propensity to criminally offend. Moreover, there are clear average lifetime trajectories in the propensity to engage in crime that are observed throughout the world. In general, a small number of individuals commit the lion's share of felony offenses. Moreover, the likelihood of engaging in criminal activity tends to decline sharply with age beyond the age of eighteen.

This cross-person heterogeneity in the propensity to offend is central to understanding how the magnitude of the average incapacitation effect of prison changes with policy-induced increases in incarceration. In a world where incarceration is reserved for only the most serious offenders and sentences are relatively short, the criminal justice system prosecutes and incarcerates those offenders who commit the most serious offenses, and for periods of time that will span their younger, most criminally active years. As a consequence, the average amount of crime prevented per prisoner-year served should be relatively high. By contrast, in a world where incarceration is applied liberally and long sentences are the norm, the average number of crimes prevented per prison-year served is relatively low, owing to the fact that the criminal justice system is dipping further into the criminally active population for incarcerations (and netting less serious offenders as a result) and incarcerating people who are older.

There is ample empirical evidence of incapacitation effects that are often quite substantial at low incarceration rates yet quickly diminish as the incarceration rate increases. For example, in their thorough analysis of the 2006 Italian collective clemency bill, Buonanno and Raphael (forthcoming) produced several findings consistent with diminishing incapacitation effects. First, they demonstrate that Italian provinces with high pre-pardon incarceration rates suffered smaller increases in crime per released offender than Italian provinces with relatively low pre-pardon incarceration rates, holding pre-pardon crime rates constant. In other words, those provinces that were incarcerating their residents at a relatively high rate given their crime rate appeared to be incarcerating less dangerous people—strong evidence of diminishing crime-fighting returns to scale. Second, the incapacitation effect associated with early returns to custody following the pardon was considerably larger than the incapacitation effect associated with later returns to custody. In other words, those pardoned inmates who fail the soonest are the most criminally active and pose the greatest risk to society.

Ben Vollaard (2013) presents additional evidence of decreasing returns to scale, albeit in an institutional context very different from and less punitive than that of the United States. Vollaard analyzes the impact of a sentence enhancement in the Netherlands targeted at repeat offenders defined as those with more than ten prior felony convictions. In 2001 the Netherlands enacted an enhanced sentence of two years for such offenders, first allowing a small number of municipalities to experiment with the enhancement before applying it nationwide in 2004. Vollaard finds very large annual incapacitation effects of this policy change, on the order of fifty to sixty reported thefts prevented per year of incarceration. He also finds, however, that those municipalities that dipped further into the repeat-offender pool when they applied the sentencing enhancement experienced significantly smaller crime reductions per additional prison-year served. This latter finding is particularly interesting since the Dutch incarceration rate as of 2004, inclusive of pretrial detainees, was 124 per 100,000, or less than one-fifth the comparable incarceration rate for the United States.[2]

Empirical research for the United States strongly suggests that the crime-preventing effects of incarceration have declined as the incarceration rate has increased. Rucker Johnson and Steven Raphael (2012) provide estimates of the effects of a one-person increase in incarceration on felony property and violent crime for the United States for two different periods of time, 1978 to 1990 and 1991 to 2004. The former period was characterized by a relatively low number of prisoners (186 per 100,000 U.S. residents), while the latter period was characterized by a much higher incarceration rate (396 per 100,000). For the early period, an additional prison-year served prevented roughly 2.5 felony violent offenses and 11.4 felony property offenses.[3] Note that the figure for total crimes prevented is quite close to the implied annual reverse incapacitation effects caused by the 2006 Italian pardon. This is particularly striking since the U.S. incarceration rate during this earlier period was much closer to that of Italy at the time of the pardon. The figures for comparable crimes prevented per prison-year served for the period 1991 to 2004 were much lower (0.3 violent felony offenses and 2.7 felony property offenses). These findings are consistent with the evidence of diminishing returns to scale reported in a study by Raymond Liedke, Anne Morrison Piehl, and Bert Useem (2006).

Emily Owens (2009) provides further evidence of relatively small incapacitation effects for recent years for one U.S. state. Owens analyzes the criminal activity of convicted felons who served less time as the result of a change in Maryland sentencing policy that eliminated the practice of considering juvenile records when sentencing adult offenders. Owens finds that these former prison inmates indeed committed additional crimes during the time period when they would have been incarcerated had they been sentenced in years past. The implied incapacitation effects are quite small, however, on the order of one-fifth the size of the incapacitation effects from earlier research conducted during the 1970s base on inmate self-reports.

The recent experience of California documented earlier provides perhaps some of the strongest evidence of the crime-preventing effects of incarceration diminishing with increases in the incarceration rate. Despite a shock to the state incarceration rate that was nearly double in magnitude that of the Italian pardon, the immediate impact on crime rates was very slight. This observation suggests that many of the inmates who would have otherwise been sent to state prison in California have generated very little in the way of crime reported to the police.

Although this may seem hard to believe, it is interesting to note that even among those doing time in California's prisons there is a great deal of heterogeneity in the propensity to offend behind bars and that the majority of the state's inmates are relatively well behaved while incarcerated. There is strong empirical evidence that the propensity to offend behind bars (especially the propensity to engage in violence) correlates with the propensity to offend when on the street.[4] In fact, recent behavior while incarcerated was a commonly used indicator of rehabilitation by parole boards under indeterminate sentencing in the past. Hence, heterogeneity in offending while incarcerated is likely to be indicative of heterogeneity in the incapacitation effects associated with incarcerating the current stock of prison inmates.

Fortunately, we have access to data that allow us to characterize such heterogeneity among the incarcerated population in California. Similar to other state prison systems, California periodically reviews the within-prison behavior of inmates for the purpose of classifying them according to security levels and then assigning them to specific institutions accordingly. Such reclassification hearings occur every six to twelve months and often result in inmate transfers between institutions with varying levels of security and inmate liberty. Some of the inmates' rules violations are quite serious, such as those involving violent assaults on other inmates and staff, while others are less serious (trafficking in contraband, possession of controlled substances, consensual sex, and so on).

We have administrative records pertaining to all serious rules violations by state inmates who served for a complete review period at any point in 2008 (that is to say, all inmates for whom we can observe two consecutive reclassification hearings).[5] We observe whether each inmate acquired an A violation (use of force or violence against another person), a B, C, or D violation (a breach or hazard to facility security; a serious disruption of facility operations; the introduction, distribution, possession, or use of controlled substances, alcohol, or dangerous contraband) or an E or F violation (an attempt or threat to commit any of the A through D violations or being under the influence or use of alcoholic beverages, controlled substances, unauthorized drugs, or intoxicants in an institution, community correctional facility, or camp).[6]

Before describing the incidence of these rules violations, we would note that the behavior of 80 percent of inmates between classification reviews was such that CDCR officially lowered their security classification score. In other words, 80 percent of the inmates were deemed to be more or less behaving between reviews. This general compliance is certainly evident in the low proportions of those who obtained official rules violation reports. Figure 7.6 shows the percentage of inmates who committed various rules violations. Roughly one-quarter of all inmates committed one serious rules violation over the course of the review period, meaning that three-quarters did not. Fewer than 2 percent committed a violent act that was met with an official

Figure 7.6   Percentage of Inmates Serving an Entire Review Period in a California State Prison in 2008 Who Acquired a Rules Violation Report Between Classification Hearings

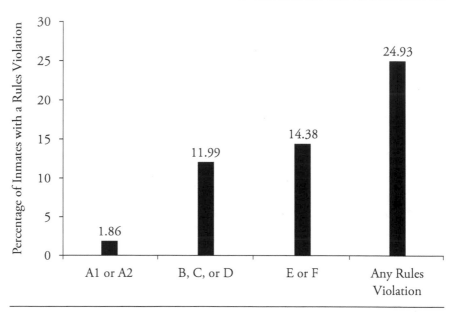

Source: Authors' tabulations of California Department of Corrections and Rehabilitation administrative records.

report and sanction. The incidence was higher for nonviolent infractions. Although these incidences were certainly high, it is notable that the majority of inmates were not engaging in these types of behaviors.[7] Figure 7.7 shows the relationship between the likelihood of committing a rules violation and age.[8] For all violations there is a very clear inverse relationship between the likelihood of committing an infraction and age, highlighting one very strong predictor of the likelihood that an individual will offend.

Hence, prison certainly incapacitates. However, the degree to which incapacitation results in lower crime varies from inmate to inmate. In general, the average incapacitation effect is lower when prison sentences are long and are applied with relative liberty. Moreover, even among those we send to prison, it is easy to document large disparities in criminal behavior and, most importantly for policy purposes, the power of at least one obvious predictor. This empirical research suggests that the United States has greater latitude for the

Figure 7.7 The Relationship Between the Likelihood of Acquiring a Rules Violation and Age Within California State Prisons, 2008

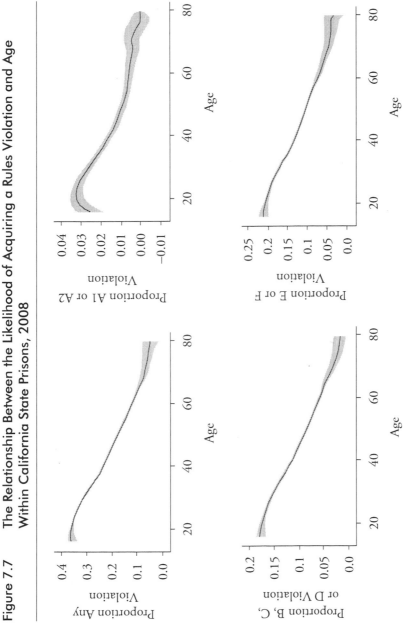

Source: Authors' tabulations of California Department of Corrections and Rehabilitation administrative data.

selective use of prison to incapacitate those who pose the greatest risk to society. To the extent that such selective incapacitation could be achieved, we could lower incarceration rates and the attendant fiscal and social costs with little impact on crime.

To be sure, even if more selective incapacitation does not necessarily increase crime by convicted offenders, it may lead to crime increases as a result of less general deterrence. We turn now to this issue.

The Threat of Prison and General Deterrence

A large and growing body of empirical research is attempting to measure general deterrence. The basic premise motivating this empirical work is that the threat of severe punishment will deter some potential offenders from committing crime. Some of the more high-profile and influential research in this domain focuses on the deterrent effect of capital punishment. Since the 1970s, several research teams have claimed to demonstrate that each execution saves numerous lives via general deterrence (Ehrlich 1975; Dezhbakhsh and Shepherd 2006). However, two reports by the National Academy of Sciences (Blumstein, Cohen, and Nagin 1978; Nagin and Pepper 2012), as well as four thorough reviews of this body of work (Donohue and Wolfers 2005, 2009; Chalfin, Haviland, and Raphael 2012; Charles and Durlauf 2012), conclude that nearly all of the research in this field is fraught with basic methodological problems that preclude any such inference.

Certainly punishment via confinement is a less drastic sanction than capital punishment. Nonetheless, prison sentences create very real personal costs for the punished offender, and thus it is theoretically plausible that the threat of a prison sentence deters crime. For example, being denied basic liberties, losing control over one's time, and having others control one's daily activities are very tangible costs of incarceration, as is the heightened risk of victimization by fellow inmates. State prisoners, and especially federal prisoners, are often housed very far from their home communities and have limited contacts with family and friends. Hence, any policy that increases either the likelihood of doing time or the effective sentence length could potentially deter.

General deterrence requires that those at risk of committing an offense be cognizant of the likelihood of being caught and the punishment that awaits them. Moreover, the extent to which one factors in the potential costs of incarceration certainly depends on the weight that one places on the costs that will be borne in the distant future (and for a long prison sentence, far into the future). In other words, a lengthy prison sentence will deter criminal activity only insofar as potential offenders take into account future costs and benefits when deciding whether to offend. Such considerations probably have little influence in determining levels of unpremeditated violent offenses that occur in emotionally charged settings. Even for premeditated offenses, the effectiveness of incarceration as a deterrent may be neutralized for those who have little knowledge of the likelihood of being caught and are extremely oriented toward the present.

There are many empirical studies of the deterrent effects of incarceration. On balance, our reading of this research is that the evidence suggestive of large general deterrence is relatively weak. Some studies find convincing evidence of general deterrence when the targeted offenders (usually repeat offenders facing very severe sanctions for subsequent crimes) are well informed regarding the consequences of their actions. The magnitudes of these effects, however, tend to be small relative to the effects of incarceration on crime operating through incapacitation. (Note that these conclusions accord with a recent review of this research presented in Nagin, 2013.)

A key challenge faced by empirical studies of general deterrence is to disentangle general deterrence effects from the effects of physically incapacitating a prison inmate. The research on general deterrence falls into broad groupings based on the methodological strategy pursued toward this end. One common strategy is to identify sentence enhancements that apply to offenses that nearly always result in a prison sentence. Since such enhancements rarely result in increased admissions to prison, any decline in crime associated with a sentencing policy change may be attributed to enhanced general deterrence caused by the longer expected sentence. The analysis of California's 1982 Proposition 8 by Daniel Kessler and Steven Levitt (1999) pursues such a strategy. The California ballot initiative enhanced sentences for a subset of violent felonies that nearly always result in a prison sentence. Hence, we would not expect any immediate impact of the proposition on crime operating through incapacitation.[9] The authors show a pre-post decline in serious violent crime in California. They also find that the targeted crimes declined relative to less serious felony offenses that were not targeted by the proposition, and that this relative decline departed from contemporaneous and comparable crime trends in the rest of the United States.

The conclusions in Kessler and Levitt (1999) have not gone uncontested. Cheryl Webster, Anthony Doob, and Franklin Zimring (2006) take issue with Kessler and Levitt's omission of even-numbered years from their descriptive crime statistics tables. Focusing on the odd-numbered years surrounding the passage of Proposition 8 shows a discrete and sustained drop in crime rates between 1981 and 1983. Adding the even-numbered years to the analysis reveals, however, that the decline in crime preceded the ballot measure's passage. Webster and her colleagues also take issue with Kessler and Levitt's choice of comparison groups, arguing that property offenses do not provide a sound benchmark against which to compare trends in violent crime.

The apparent ineffectiveness of this particular California proposition in the immediate aftermath of its implementation may have been due to poor knowledge among potential violent offenders of the provisions of the ballot initiative. All such propositions certainly receive a fair amount of press coverage, but it may be unlikely that potential violent offenders are following state electoral politics. Certain sentence enhancements have been better publicized, however, and in such a way that the specific offenders targeted by these enhancements are likely to be aware of the consequences should they reoffend. Moreover, many of these enhancements have been empirically evaluated.

Steven Raphael and Jens Ludwig (2003) analyze the general deterrence effects of a 1990s effort in Richmond, Virginia, to combat homicide by enhancing the sentences faced by felons found to be in possession of a firearm, a program called Project Exile. The central goal of Project Exile, through the coordinated efforts of Richmond law enforcement and the regional U.S. attorney's office, was to prosecute in federal courts all felon-in-possession of a firearm (FIP) cases, drug and gun cases, and domestic violence and gun cases, regardless of the number. Exile also included a massive advertising campaign intended to send the clear message of zero tolerance for gun offenses and to inform potential offenders of the swift and certain federal sentence.

Project Exile effectively enhanced sentences because the federal penalties for these firearm offenses were more severe than those in effect in Virginia at the time. Exile was announced in 1997. The disparity between the federal and state systems may have been particularly dramatic for FIP convictions for which the federal penalty was five years with no chance of early release. In addition to the differences in prison terms, gun offenders diverted into the federal system were denied bail at a higher rate than those handled in state courts. Moreover, they served time in a federal penitentiary that was likely to be located out of state. Both aspects of the program are thought to have imposed additional costs on offenders.

In their examination of the impact of Richmond's Project Exile on homicide and other crimes, Raphael and Ludwig (2003) conclude that the claims of dramatic declines in homicide rates made by supporters of the program were unfounded. Although Richmond's gun homicide rate did indeed decline during the implementation of Project Exile, the decline was in line with what was occurring across the country in comparable localities with no such programs. To be specific, cities with the largest increases in homicide rates during the 1980s and early 1990s also experienced the largest decreases during the late 1990s. Richmond happened to be among the handful of cities that had experienced unusually large increases in homicide rates during the 1980s. Consequently, nearly all of the reduction in murder rates experienced by Richmond following Project Exile may be attributed to the large increase in gun homicides that occurred prior to Exile's implementation. In other words, none of the decline in gun homicide rates in Richmond could be attributed to general deterrence.

One set of sentence enhancements for which the targeted offenders are generally made well aware of the tougher sentences they face should they reoffend are those passed through state repeat offender laws, often referred to as "three strikes" laws (see chapter 4). Such laws enhance the sentences of offenders with prior serious or violent felony convictions. California was one of the first states in the nation to adopt a "three strikes" law in 1994. The California law doubles the required sentence for any new offense for offenders with a prior conviction for one serious or violent felony (often referred to as a "second striker"). For offenders with two serious or violent felonies (potential "third strikers"), the sentence for a subsequent felony offense is an automatic life term, with a minimum sentence of twenty-five years. Prior prison inmates in the state of California with strike offenses on their criminal history records are certainly aware of the sentence enhancements they face if convicted of subsequent felonies.

Eric Helland and Alexander Tabarrok (2007) provide a quite convincing empirical assessment suggesting that general deterrence has been enhanced by the California law. For individuals released from California state prisons, they analyze postrelease arrest outcomes that vary in terms of the number of prior strikes on their criminal history records and thus the sentences they face should they reoffend. The study compares those with two prior strikes to those who had one prior strike, were charged and tried for a second-strike offense, but were convicted of a less serious felony the second time around that did not result in an increase in their strike count. Helland and Tabarrok find that within three years of release 40 percent of those with two strikes on their criminal history record were rearrested, compared with 48 percent of those in the comparison group. This eight-percentage-point differential is highly statistically significant.

Although this is pretty clear evidence of a general deterrence effect, it is noteworthy that even when facing a sentence of twenty-five years to life for any felony (even for less serious offenses such as drug felonies, receiving stolen property, larceny, and so on), 40 percent of second strikers in this study were still rearrested within three years. Moreover, this re-arrest rate is only 17 percent lower than that for offenders facing much less severe punishment for future offenses. Although the evidence certainly suggests responsiveness to incentives, managing the offending of this particular population requires interventions that extend beyond the credible threat of stiff punishment.

Francesco Drago, Roberto Galbiati, and Pietro Vertova (2009) present a similar analysis of sentence enhancements targeted at repeat offenders. These authors exploit a unique feature of the 2006 Italian mass pardon discussed earlier. To reiterate, the Italian collective clemency bill released most inmates with three years or less remaining on their sentence. Those who reoffended after release faced an enhanced sentence through the addition of the remainder of their unserved time to whatever new sentence was meted out for the new offense. Drago and his colleagues find that those inmates who faced a longer sentence enhancement (conditional on observables) were less likely to reoffend after being released. This added general deterrence effect was small, however, relative to the pure reverse incapacitation effect caused by the release of these inmates (Buonanno and Raphael, forthcoming). Moreover, as Daniel Nagin (2013) has noted, those pardoned inmates who faced longer sentence enhancements as a result of a longer unserved sentence also served less time in prison than those who faced shorter sentence enhancement. Hence, an alternative and equally plausible interpretation of the results in this study is that the more time one serves the more likely one is to commit crime in the future.

Several scholars have exploited the discontinuity in the severity of criminal sentencing upon reaching the age of majority to test for general deterrence. Since the severity of punishment increases discretely in most states at the age of eighteen, general deterrence should give rise to a corresponding discontinuous drop in criminal offending. Steven Levitt (1998) compares the change in offending between single years of age in states where the enhancement associated with being tried as an adult is relatively large and in states where the differences between juvenile and adult sentencing practices are more modest.

He finds larger declines in offending at the age of eighteen in the former states relative to the latter.

David Lee and Justin McCrary (2009), on the other hand, find no such evidence. Analyzing high-frequency arrest data with more granular informa-tion on the age of the arrestees, they find no evidence of a decline in offending associated with turning eighteen. They calibrate a dynamic model of criminal participation to forecast the expected declines in offending under various as-sumptions regarding the degree to which youth are present-oriented and as-suming rational responses to enhanced adult sentences. The predicted de-clines from this model far exceed what is observed in the data, leading the authors to conclude that youthful offenders either are extremely myopic, are uninformed as to the consequences of being tried as an adult, or are making decisions to participate in crime that are not well characterized by rational choice modeling.

The findings in Lee and McCrary (2009) raise the important question of whether the extent of general deterrence depends only on the expected value of the offender's sentence (that is to say, the expected value of time served equal to the likelihood of being caught and convicted times the expected de facto sentence length). Certainly, criminal offenders' time preferences—and perhaps their time-inconsistent preferences—mediate the general deterrence effects created by enhancement of already long sentences.

Randi Hjalmarsson (2009) digs deeper into the offending behavior of youth as they pass through the age of majority. Using a nationally representa-tive longitudinal data set, Hjalmarsson first assesses whether youth, and young men in particular, are aware of the harsher punishments that await them should they commit and be convicted of a felony offense as an adult. She documents this relatively harsher punishment using several data sources that clearly establish that offenders tried in adult criminal courts are much more likely to be punished with confinement than those tried in juvenile courts for comparable crimes. Next, Hjalmarsson shows that youth do indeed perceive a discretely higher likelihood of prison or jail time when they reach the age of majority in their respective states of residence. Interestingly, she finds surprisingly little evidence that youth criminal activity is deterred by this change in risk perceptions and only modest evidence of an effect of the threat of stiffer sanctions on the likelihood of committing larceny theft of less than $50. Hjalmarsson finds no measurable impacts on any other property, violent, or drug crimes.

In his recent treatise on crime control policy, Mark Kleiman (2009) argues for a shift toward sentencing practices that deemphasize sentencing severity yet increase the certainty of punishment. The thinking behind this proposition rests largely on the abundant empirical research (some of which we discussed earlier in the chapter) demonstrating the relative insensitivity of the behavior of the criminally active to enhanced sentences. Kleiman argues that this is to be expected given the profile of the average person who commits felonies. Kleiman also presents evidence of much greater responsiveness to sanctions that occur with great certainty. We discuss this work in more detail in the concluding chapter.

On balance, recent research on the general deterrence effects of the threat of incarceration yields evidence of modest effects in some instances and no deterrence in many others. General deterrence appears to be stronger when targeted offenders are well aware of the potential enhancements and punishments are meted out with a fair degree of certainty. There is very little evidence of an impact of extremely harsh punishment (that is, longer sentences, capital punishment) on the levels of the crimes they are intended to deter. This may reflect a tendency toward extreme present-orientation among those most likely to commit crime, poor information regarding likely sentencing outcomes, or both. Finally, in terms of overall crime control, general deterrence effects, when detectable, tend to be small relative to the effects of incarceration on crime operating through incapacitation.

The Experience of Prison and Future Offending After Release

The relatively high current incarceration rate in the United States translates directly into a larger pool of former prison inmates in non-institutional society. As we documented in chapter 1, roughly 5 percent of non-institutionalized adult males, and up to 17 percent of non-institutionalized African American males, have served time in a state or federal prison. A prison experience may either increase or decrease offending among former inmates relative to what their level of offending would otherwise have been. For example, a sufficiently harsh experience may deter future offending. Moreover, programming and services provided to inmates while incarcerated may rehabilitate them and reduce their offending.

On the negative side, prison inmates are exposed to a very criminally active peer set while institutionalized. To the extent that inmates adopt the norms and values of their peers, this may increase their criminal offending postrelease. Moreover, inmates may build stronger criminal ties behind bars and draw upon these social networks in non-institutional society. Former prison inmates also face substantial and real stigma upon release. To the extent that such stigma makes it difficult to achieve conventional markers of success (find legitimate employment, form lasting relationships), the relative attractiveness of participating in crime may be enhanced.

It is an inherently difficult task to empirically assess whether a prison term reduces future offending or increases it. Ideally we would compare the offending trajectory of a criminal offender who is sentenced to prison to that of a comparable individual who receives a noncustodial alternative sentence. We would need to carefully align the criminal histories of these two offenders to be sure to draw comparisons where both are of similar ages and not under some form of criminal justice custody, so as to not confound differential incapacitation or age with a long-term impact of a prior prison spell. Moreover, we would need to ensure comparability along all other possible determinants of criminal activity between those who are sentenced to prison and those who are not—a particularly difficult task given that prison sentences on average tend to be applied to more serious offenders.

An additional complicating factor faced by research on this question is that actual time served—and by extension, when and under what circumstances an inmate is released—can vary greatly for inmates with similar prison sentences. Through differential accumulation of good time credits, additional sentences for felonies committed while incarcerated, or the explicit decision-making of parole authorities in indeterminate sentencing states, those released from prison may be less likely to reoffend than inmates with similar offenses who are retained for longer periods. This consideration may create both heterogeneity in the effect of a prison sentence on future offending and a possible sample selection problem for empirical analyses of the long-term effects of incarceration on future offending. Regarding the first factor, states where release dates depend to a greater extent on good behavior and markers of rehabilitation may incentivize rehabilitation and lead to better postrelease outcomes.

Indeed, there is empirical evidence consistent with this line of reasoning. In an analysis of prison releases in the state of Georgia, Ilyana Kuziemko (2013) shows that when afforded discretion the state parole board manages to selectively release those inmates with a relatively low risk of offending. Moreover, Raphael and Stoll (2004) find evidence that the effect of prison releases on crime is lower in states with discretionary parole systems relative to states with mandatory parole systems.

Regarding the selection problem, the well-behaved may be disproportionately represented among releases. Studying the effect of prison on long-term offending must necessarily focus on those who are released. If the most criminally active are more likely to be retained, such research may overstate the salutary effects of a prison spell on future offending by focusing on those releases who managed to earn release. Moreover, if release dates are measured inaccurately (for example, if the research uses the date equal to the admissions date plus the minimum sentence as a proxy for release), the most criminally active among those sent to prison are likely to still be in custody and incapacitated. The apparent "good behavior" of those who are still in custody will artificially suppress average criminal activity among those sent to prison relative to a chosen comparison group.

A large body of research focuses on evaluating the net effect of these mechanisms on offending levels after release. Daniel Nagin, Frances Cullen, and Cheryl Lero-Johnson (2009) provide a very thorough review of this research. These authors review several groups of studies, including a handful of randomized control experiments in which the prison sentences are effectively randomly assigned; a set of studies that construct comparison samples for prison inmates using various matching techniques; and a series of studies that attempt to achieve comparability between those who have been sent to prison and those who have not by controlling for observable characteristics using multivariate regression modeling. Nagin and his colleagues also provide a review of research on the effects of time served on future offending behavior. Although the reviewed body of empirical work does not consistently point in one specific direction, the findings regarding the net effects of having served a prison sentence tend to point toward a slightly criminogenic impact of having served time on future offending.

Of course, given the multiple avenues linking serving time to future offending, the ultimate effect of a prison sentence is likely to vary greatly from one inmate to the next, since each will respond differently to the influences and incentives faced while incarcerated. For example, there is evidence that inmates held in harsher conditions become more hardened and criminally prone. Keith Chen and Jesse Shapiro (2007) analyze the effects of serving time in higher-security facilities relative to lower-security facilities in the federal prison system. Like many state systems, the federal prison system employs a numeric security classification score based on factors that predict behavioral risks and escape risk. (In many states, age, sentence length, prior misconduct, and gang affiliation are often key determinants.) When security scores rise above predetermined cutoffs, inmates are assigned to higher-security institutions, where there is considerably less freedom of movement and peer inmates are on average a more serious group of offenders. Chen and Shapiro find that inmates who just miss the cutoff to be assigned to lower-security institutions are more likely to recidivate after release than inmates placed in prisons that are less harsh. In a similar analysis, Steven Raphael and Sarah Tahamont (2012) find similar effects of high-security placement on the likelihood that inmates will commit serious behavioral infractions while incarcerated in a California state prison.

Further evidence of the effect of the conditions of confinement on within-prison behavior is presented by Sarah Tahamont (2012). Using a nationally representative survey of prison inmates, she assesses the impact of a connection to family and friends, operating through within-prison visits, on the likelihood of misconduct while incarcerated (much of which involves quite serious incidents, including assault on fellow inmates and corrections officers). Exploiting the fact that inmates housed very far from their home communities are considerably less likely to receive family visits, Tahamont finds very strong salutary effects of visits on inmate misconduct, although she also finds some evidence that the likelihood of a drug violation increases with family visits. To the extent that these behavior patterns extend beyond prison release, such variation in the conditions of confinement will cause variation in the long-term effects of incarceration on future offending trajectories.

A particularly novel demonstration of the heterogeneous impacts of incarceration on future offending behavior is presented by Patrick Bayer, Randi Hjalmarsson, and David Pozen (2009). Using administrative data on the Florida juvenile justice system, these authors assess whether the criminal histories of an inmate's fellow inmates have an impact on the likelihood that the inmate will offend in the future and on the types of future offenses committed. The study provides quite convincing evidence of adverse peer effects that tend to reinforce (or perhaps aggravate is a more appropriate word) the offending tendencies of incarcerated youth. For example, they find that youth who are serving time for burglary and whose peers are disproportionately made up of those convicted of burglary are more likely to commit a new burglary after being released. Bayer and his colleagues find similar patterns for youth convicted of larceny, drug offenses, aggravated assault, and felony sex offenses. Interestingly, peers are found to have a strong reinforcing effect on offending behavior (a burglar housed with other burglars is more likely to commit more burglary in the future), but not for youth with no history of committing a specific offense.

There is also evidence suggesting that the stigmatizing effect of incarceration may differ, with particularly serious effects for African American men. Stigma poses very real challenges for former inmates, especially when they seek legitimate employment. Employers often actively screen out those with prior convictions and prior time served for a number of reasons. First, employers may consider prior criminality a predictor of important unobservable traits, such as honesty or dependability. This may be particularly important to employers filling positions where monitoring by management is imperfect and where it may be difficult or costly to readily observe worker productivity.

Second, employers may fear being held liable for any criminal actions committed by their employees on the company's time. In negligent hiring and negligent retention cases, an employer may be sued for monetary damages caused by the criminal actions of any employee who the employer either knew or should have known had committed prior crimes that made the employee unsuitable for the position in question. Not surprisingly, research analyzing employer-stated preferences with regard to hiring those with criminal histories consistently finds that employers filling positions that require substantial contact with customers are among the most reluctant to hire former prison inmates (Holzer, Raphael, and Stoll 2006, 2007).

Finally, employers may be prohibited under local ordinances, state law, and sometimes federal law from hiring convicted felons into specific occupations. According to Shawn Bushway and Gary Sweeten (2007), ex-felons are barred from employment in roughly eight hundred occupations across the country, with the composition of these bans varying across states and in some instances localities. Occupations covered by such bans range from barber shop owners to emergency medical technicians to cosmetologists.

How important is prior criminal history to the screening and hiring practices of employers? Unfortunately, there are no national-level surveys of employer practices that can be used to answer this question. However, a handful of surveys of employers in various metropolitan areas and one state survey have queried respondents about their willingness to hire convicted felons. The most recent effort was carried out in 2003 by the Survey Research Center at the University of California at Berkeley. The sample includes California business and nonprofit establishments with at least five employees, excluding gov-

Table 7.1   Indicators of Employer Willingness to Hire Workers with Specific Characteristics into Nonprofessional, Nonmanagerial Jobs, 2003

Degree of Acceptability for the Most Recently Filled Position	Has a Criminal Record	Unemployed for a Year or More	Minimal Work Experience
Definitely accept	0.018	0.077	0.090
Probably accept	0.271	0.538	0.318
Probably not accept	0.339	0.368	0.454
Definitely not accept	0.371	0.018	0.137

Source: Authors' tabulations from Institute for Research on Labor and Employment (2003).

ernment agencies, public schools and universities, and establishments in the agricultural, forestry, or fisheries industries.[10] Table 7.1 presents tabulations regarding employer responses to queries about the acceptability of certain types of applicants for the most recently filled nonmanagerial, nonprofessional position. Employers were asked to think of the most recent position filled that met these criteria. They were then asked whether they would definitely accept, probably accept, probably not accept, or definitely not accept a specific type of applicant. The survey inquired about three applicant traits: an applicant with a criminal record, an applicant who had been unemployed for a year or more, and an applicant with minimal work experience.[11]

Fully 71 percent of employers indicated that they would probably not or definitely not hire a worker with a criminal record. The comparable figure for a worker who had been unemployed for a year is 38.6 percent, while the comparable figure for a worker with minimal experience is 59.1 percent. In prior research with Harry Holzer (Holzer, Raphael, and Stoll 2006), using data from an older establishment survey, we found a comparable reluctance to hire those with criminal records and much less reluctance to hire workers who had been unemployed, who were current welfare recipients, or who had little experience. The one category of applicants for whom employers exhibited a comparable (yet still less severe) reluctance to hire was applicants with gaps in their employment history. Certainly, prior criminal history and unaccounted-for gaps in one's résumé may be related in reality and in the minds of employers. In all, the California data and prior research clearly indicate a particular reluctance to hire workers with a criminal past.

The stigmatization associated with prior convictions and prison time most certainly inhibits a successful transition upon release to productive, law-abiding roles in non-institutional society. Although many former inmates overcome this challenge, employer inhibitions probably throw sand in the gears for many others. There is some evidence from audit studies that these barriers pose particular problems for African American men. Devah Pager (2003) provides evidence that employers have complicated perceptions of the relationship between race and criminality. Pager conducted an audit study in Milwaukee in which pairs of auditors of the same race were sent to apply for the same jobs, one with a spell in prison listed on his résumé and one with no such signal. Among the white auditors, 34 percent of the non-offenders received a callback, in contrast to 17 percent of ex-offenders. The comparable figures for blacks were 14 and 5 percent. Although all of the African American auditors experienced very low callback rates, the extremely low callback rate for African Americans with a criminal history (5 percent) on their résumé is particularly salient.

To summarize, in our reading of this body of research, we find little evidence that a prison spell reduces future offending below what it would otherwise be, and perhaps weak evidence that on average the incarceration experience makes former inmates more prone to commit crime. However, the mechanisms through which these effects operate certainly admit much heterogeneity, and thus the impact of the experience on specific individuals is likely to vary greatly. There is certainly evidence that prior convictions and incarceration create stigma and that the criminal propensities of some individuals are enhanced by their time behind bars. However, we can also imagine that, among others, access to drug treatment, education, vocational training, and consistent health care, as well as the experience itself, would reduce future offending. This is an area of inquiry greatly in need of further research.

EMPIRICAL ESTIMATES OF THE EFFECT OF PRISON ON CRIME

The three channels through which incarceration may affect crime rates—through incapacitation, general deterrence, and its long-term impact on offending—ultimately cumulate to a net effectiveness of incarceration as a crime control device. We have already discussed the evidence of diminishing incapacitation effects. We have said little about how the marginal effects through general deterrence and long-term effects on offending trajectories change with the scale of incarceration, as there is no empirical evidence specifically addressing this issue. There is, however, evidence on how the net effect on crime operating through the first two channels changes as the incarceration rate increases.[12]

Specifically, a number of studies estimate the net effectiveness of incarceration as a crime control device using state-level data (Levitt 1996; Liedke, Piehl, and Useem 2006; Johnson and Raphael 2012). This research analyzes the relationship between year-over-year changes in state incarceration rates and corresponding changes in crime. Ultimately, the research produces estimates of the effect of a one-person change in the incarceration rate on crime rates. The two studies that assess how these effects change over time estimate this relationship for time periods with different incarceration levels. To the extent that the net effects of incarceration on crime are lower during time periods when the incarceration rate is higher, the data suggest diminishing net effects of incarceration on crime.[13]

Here we present estimates of the net effects of incarceration on crime, making use of the methodological strategy presented in Johnson and Raphael (2012). Specifically, we assembled a data set that measured crime rates, incarceration rates, and a number of average socioeconomic characteristics for each state and each year for the period 1977 to 2010.[14] We then used these data to estimate the average effects of a one-person increase in a state's incarceration rate on crime rates using crime data from the FBI Uniform Crime Reports.

We estimate average effects for the entire thirty-three-year period. We also estimate average effects for three subperiods: 1977 to 1988, 1989 to 1999, and 2000 to 2010. Figure 7.8 displays the average state incarceration rate during these three periods. Clearly, the earliest has the lowest average incarceration rate (171 per 100,000) compared to the middle period (349 per 100,000) and the most recent period (449 per 100,000). To the extent that the average effectiveness of incarceration in controlling crime changes with scale, we should see different estimates for these three periods. The appendix to this chapter provides a more detailed description of data sources and estimation methodology.

Table 7.2 presents estimates of the average effect of incarceration on crime for the entire thirty-three-year period. We present estimates for overall violent crime rates (the sum of murder, rape, robbery, and aggravated assault) and overall property crime rates (the sum of burglary, larceny, and motor vehicle theft), as well as estimates for each individual felony offense. For each crime rate, the table presents results from four models that estimate the effect of a change in a state's incarceration rate on the change in the state's crime rate.

Figure 7.8   Average State Incarceration Rates for 1977 to 1988, 1989 to 1999, and 2000 to 2010

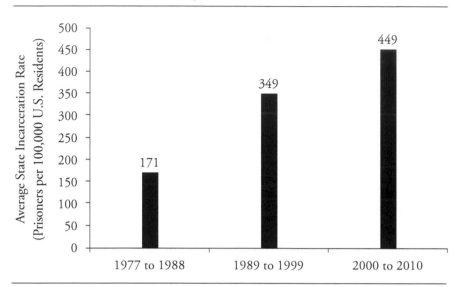

Source: Authors' tabulations from Bureau of Justice Statistics (various years), *National Prisoner Statistics* data series, BJ5.

Note: Averages are weighted by state population.

The first model does not control for any additional variables and the results simply reflect the relationship between year-over-year changes in incarceration and corresponding changes in crime rates. The second model adds controls for changes in state-level demographics and standard socioeconomic characteristics that are likely to have an impact on crime. The third model statistically adjusts for all factors that change from year to year for all states in a common manner. The final model adds a control for state linear time trends. We present this level of detail so that readers can gauge for themselves the sensitivity of the results to specification choices.

The results in table 7.2 yield fairly consistent evidence of sizable average effects of incarceration on crime for most of the crime categories analyzed in the table. For example, there is consistent evidence of a negative and statistically significant average effect of incarceration on the murder rate and the rate of sexual assault. There is also very strong evidence of significant negative effects on the overall property crime rate, the burglary rate, and the larceny rate.

How large are these effects? Some simple back-of-the-envelope calculations reveal the meaning of the magnitudes presented in table 7.2 The most de-

Table 7.2 Estimates of the Average Effect of a One-Person Increase in State Prison Incarceration Rates on Various Crime Rates, 1977 to 2010

	(1) No controls		(2) Controlling for State Demographics		(3) Controlling for State Demographics and Year Effects		(4) Controlling for State Demographics, Year Effects, and State Time Trends	
Violent crime	-0.299	(0.184)	-0.378	(0.199)***	-0.119	(0.171)	-0.195	(0.175)
Murder	-0.013	(0.004)*	-0.014	(0.005)*	-0.009	(0.005)***	-0.009	(0.005)***
Rape	-0.027	(0.007)*	-0.033	(0.009)*	-0.024	(0.011)**	-0.025	(0.013)***
Robbery	-0.299	(0.090)*	-0.300	(0.122)**	-0.177	(0.121)	-0.229	(0.140)
Assault	0.040	(0.152)	-0.030	(0.115)	0.089	(0.122)	0.068	(0.138)
Property crime	-3.4178	(0.899)*	-3.798	(1.302)*	-2.353	(0.731)*	-2.887	(0.905)*
Burglary	-1.884	(0.551)*	-1.806	(0.597)*	-0.970	(0.354)*	-1.159	(0.492)**
Larceny	-1.251	(0.417)*	-1.467	(0.649)**	-1.097	(0.332)*	-1.281	(0.357)*
Motor vehicle theft	-0.280	(0.197)	-0.524	(0.189)*	-0.286	(0.255)	-0.445	(0.289)

Source: Authors' tabulations from FBI Uniform Crime Reports (various years) and Bureau of Justice Statistics (various years), *National Prisoner Statistics* data series, BJS.

Note: Standard errors are in parentheses and account for clustering in the error term variance-covariance matrix within states. The coefficient estimates come from an instrumental variables regression of the year-to-year change in the given crime rate on the year-to-year change in the incarceration rate measured at the state level. The difference between the actual incarceration rate and the steady-state incarceration rate implied by the state's prison admissions and release rates forms the basis for the instrumental variable for the change in incarceration rates. This methodology is discussed in greater detail in the chapter 7 appendix. The regression models for the second column of results include controls for changes in per-capita income, state unemployment rates, state poverty rates, state age structure, and the proportion of the state population that is African American. The third column adds a complete set of year fixed effects, while the final column adds a complete set of state fixed effects. Since the regressions are based on changes in the dependent and explanatory variables rather than levels, the inclusion of state fixed effects in the specification is equivalent to adjusting each model for state-specific linear time trends.

*Statistically significant at the 1 percent level of confidence; **statistically significant at the 5 percent level of confidence; ***statistically significant at the 10 percent level of confidence tailed specification (the last column) for the murder rate model yields an aver-age effect of a one-person increase in the incarceration rate on the murder rate of –0.009 (statistically significant at the 10 percent level of confidence). With an average incarceration rate in the states over the period analyzed of 329.8 per 100,000, this implies that incarceration in general reduced the murder rate over this period by 2.97 (0.009 × 329.8). The average murder rate over this period was 7.43 homicides per 100,000. Hence, our estimates imply that if we were to have abolished prisons with no compensatory social investment, homicide rates would have been 40 percent higher over this period. Compa-rable back-of-the-envelope calculations for rape, robbery, and overall property crime suggest that these crime rates would be 23, 39, and 22 percent higher with a zero incarceration rate.

Although these effects may seem large and perhaps suggestive that reduc-ing the incarceration rate would result in large increases in crime, the logic behind such back-of-the-envelope calculations does not apply to partial re-ductions in the prison population and the manner in which a selective scaling back is likely to occur. First, we would expect that a deliberate policy choice to reduce the use of incarceration would also involve an expansion in the use of some other form of criminal justice intervention or crime-preventing social investments that would compensate. This is clearly what is unfolding in Cali-fornia, where the reduction in the state's incarceration rate is coinciding with expanded investment in community corrections.

Second, and more important for policy, these back-of-the-envelope calcu-lations applied the average effect of incarceration on crime to project the ef-fects of reducing the prison population. This would be appropriate if the policy under consideration was to abolish prisons. However, if the policy under consideration is to pare back but not eliminate prison populations, ap-plying the average effects would be inappropriate.

The reason why is shown in tables 7.3 and 7.4, which present comparable estimates of the effects of incarceration on crime rates for the three subperiods corresponding roughly with the 1980s, the 1990s, and the 2000s. Here we present results only for the first three model specifications used in table 7.2.[15] Beginning with the violent crime results in table 7.3, we observe clear differ-ences in the effects of incarceration on crime rates across the subperiods. Be-tween 1977 and 1988, the average effect of a one-person increase in the in-carceration rate on overall violent crime was a reduction of 1.3 to 2.1 incidents (depending on the model specification). Note that these estimated impacts on violent crime are substantially larger than the average effects for the entire period that we presented in table 7.2. All of these estimates are at least marginally statistically significant.

For the two latter time periods, however, the estimated effects are either the wrong sign (slightly positive for the period 1989 to 1999) or negative and very small (for the period 2000 to 2010). None of them are statistically significant, suggesting that growth in incarceration rates during these latter two time periods had no measurable effect on overall violent crime rates. We observe substantial and statistically significant effects of incarceration growth on rape and robbery crime rates for the earliest period, but very little evidence of an effect for the latter two periods. The results for murder are mixed, with significant coefficients during the 1990s and insignificant coefficients during the earliest and latest periods.

Table 7.4 reveals very similar results for property crime. For the earliest time period, the results suggest that each one-person increase in the incarceration rate reduced the overall felony property crime rate by between 9 and 19 incidents per 100,000 residents. Again, these estimates are much larger than average effects estimated in table 7.2 using data from all thirty-three years. During the last period, these estimates drop to between 2 and 3 incidents per 100,000 and are all statistically insignificant. Similar cross-period differences are observed for burglary and larceny theft.

These results are strongly suggestive of diminishing marginal returns to incarceration. Moreover, they provide a coherent explanation for the differences in the outcomes of the two case studies discussed at the beginning of this chapter. California, with its very high pre-reform incarceration rate and selective reduction in the incarceration rate through reduced admissions, saw very little impact of its prison reforms on crime rates, and any such impact was concentrated on less serious property crime. Italy, on the other hand, with its very low (by U.S. standards) pre-pardon incarceration rate and broadly applied pardon, released very criminally active people into non-institutionalized society and suffered a crime spike as a result.

CONCLUSION

The proposition that the use of incarceration reduces crime is not controversial. The high incidence of serious misconduct behind bars, the average socioeconomic and demographic characteristics of current prison inmates, and the criminal histories of inmates all suggest that prisons do indeed house many

Table 7.3 Estimates of the Effect of a One-Person Increase in the Prison Incarceration Rate on Violent Crime for 1977 to 1988, 1989 to 1999, and 2000 to 2010

	No Controls		Controlling for State Demographics		Controlling for State Demographics and Year Effects	
Violent crime						
1977 to 1988	−2.110	(1.079)***	−2.262	(1.044)**	−1.298	(0.724)***
1989 to 1999	0.061	(0.388)	0.106	(0.288)	0.034	(0.177)
2000 to 2010	−0.012	(0.304)	−0.069	(0.256)	−0.177	(0.309)
Murder						
1977 to 1988	−0.022	(0.037)	−0.021	(0.036)	−0.006	(0.037)
1989 to 1999	−0.011	(0.005)***	−0.012	(0.004)*	−0.010	(0.004)**
2000 to 2010	−0.009	(0.007)	−0.009	(0.007)	−0.009	(0.008)
Rape						
1977 to 1988	−0.158	(0.059)*	−0.151	(0.053)*	−0.104	(0.038)*
1989 to 1999	−0.016	(0.015)	−0.017	(0.012)	−0.019	(0.010)***
2000 to 2010	0.001	(0.021)	0.003	(0.019)	−0.004	(0.026)
Robbery						
1977 to 1988	−1.811	(0.784)**	−1.814	(0.758)**	−1.171	(0.545)**
1989 to 1999	−0.014	(0.166)	−0.001	(0.124)	−0.048	(0.087)
2000 to 2010	−0.012	(0.149)	−0.034	(0.129)	−0.151	(0.145)
Assault						
1977 to 1988	−0.119	(0.337)	−0.276	(0.288)	−0.016	(0.271)
1989 to 1999	0.102	(0.235)	0.135	(0.197)	0.112	(0.155)
2000 to 2010	0.008	(0.171)	−0.030	(0.147)	−0.020	(0.194)

Source: Authors' tabulations from FBI Uniform Crime Reports (various years) and Bureau of Justice Statistics (various years), *National Prisoner Statistics* data series, BJ5.

Note: Robust standard errors that cluster on states are reported in parentheses. The coefficient estimates come from an instrumental variables regression of the year-to-year change in the given crime rate on the year-to-year change in the incarceration rate measured at the state level for the indicated time periods. The difference between the actual incarceration rate and the steady-state incarceration rate implied by the state's prison admissions and release rates forms the basis for the instrumental variable for the change in incarceration rates. This methodology is discussed in greater detail in the chapter 7 appendix. The regression models for the second column of results include controls for changes in per-capita income, state unemployment rates, state poverty rates, state age structure, and the proportion of the state population that is African American. The third column adds a complete set of year effects.

*Statistically significant at the 1 percent level of confidence; **statistically significant at the 5 percent level of confidence; ***statistically significant at the 10 percent level of confidence

Table 7.4   Estimates of the Effect of a One-Person Increase in the Prison Incarceration Rate on Property Crime for 1977 to 1988, 1989 to 1999, and 2000 to 2010

	No Controls		Controlling for State Demographics		Controlling for State Demographics and Year Effects	
Property crime						
1977 to 1988	−18.096	(8.087)**	−19.267	(7.968)**	−8.640	(4.777)***
1989 to 1999	0.319	(0.943)	−0.245	(0.680)	−1.289	(0.654)***
2000 to 2010	−2.822	(1.696)	−2.134	(1.414)	−2.049	(1.527)
Burglary						
1977 to 1988	−8.694	(3.606)**	−9.176	(3.572)**	−4.437	(2.076)**
1989 to 1999	−0.277	(0.195)	−0.409	(0.284)	−0.477	(0.253)***
2000 to 2010	−0.390	(0.419)	−0.241	(0.387)	−0.342	(0.462)
Larceny						
1977 to 1988	−8.701	(4.182)**	−8.954	(4.161)**	−3.278	(2.437)
1989 to 1999	0.678	(0.629)	0.302	(0.424)	−0.526	(0.401)
2000 to 2010	−1.726	(0.994)***	−1.108	(0.822)	−1.178	(0.925)
Motor vehicle theft						
1977 to 1988	−0.702	(0.815)	−1.137	(0.747)	−0.924	(0.926)
1989 to 1999	−0.081	(0.318)	−0.139	(0.262)	−0.284	(0.202)
2000 to 2010	−0.703	(0.489)	−0.785	(0.428)***	−0.526	(0.444)

Source: Authors' tabulations from FBI Uniform Crime Reports (various years) and Bureau of Justice Statistics (various years), *National Prisoner Statistics* data series, BJ5.

Note: See table 7.3 note.

*Statistically significant at the 1 percent level of confidence; **statistically significant at the 5 percent level of confidence; ***statistically significant at the 10 percent level of confidence

highly criminally active individuals. That being said, prisons also house many older inmates, many inmates who have not been convicted of serious violent felonies, and many inmates who manage to do their time without getting into further trouble. Abolishing prisons would certainly increase the nation's crime rates. That might not be the outcome, however, of selectively scaling back the use of incarceration with an eye to reserving it for those who pose the greatest risk to society.

We have presented a detailed discussion of large bodies of research that suggest that the crime-preventing effects of incarceration vary quite a bit from inmate to inmate and that on average the effectiveness of prison in reducing crime rates diminishes as the incarceration rate increases. Evidence of such diminishing returns is clear in the United States, where the incarceration rate has grown to unprecedented levels, but it has also been documented in other nations with much lower incarceration rates. Our empirical research certainly suggests that there were large gains to be had in terms of crime control during the 1980s in increasing the size of the prison population. The same is not true today. In fact, a full accounting of the on-budget costs and off-budget social costs of incarceration is likely to reveal that today, with our much higher incarceration rate relative to the 1980s, we are in the mirror-opposite position.

An optimal crime control policy geared toward minimizing crime for a given level of public expenditures would invest further public resources in interventions for which the return per dollar spent is the highest. An optimal policy would also scale back any intervention that resulted in the returns per dollar spent falling short of comparable returns from alternative interventions. Are there alternative crime control policy tools that yield a larger bang for the buck than additional prison beds? Moreover, are there other policy tools that could enable us to use current prison capacity more efficiently while reducing the scale of incarceration? We turn to these questions in our final chapter.

APPENDIX

In this appendix, we describe our methodology for estimating the effects of a one-person change in a state's incarceration rate on crime rates. We apply a two-stage-least-squares estimator to a state-year-level panel data set. Our data set covers the period from 1977 to 2010. In all models, the explanatory and dependent variables are measured as year-over-year changes (that is, the state-year panel data are first-differenced).

A key methodological issue in panel data studies of the effects of incarceration on crime is the likely simultaneous relationship between incarceration and crime rates. To break the simultaneity and measure causal effects, we employ the instrumental variables strategy developed by Johnson and Raphael (2012), who developed an instrumental variable that can succinctly be described as a prediction of the change in a state's incarceration rate between two years, based on the disparity between the state's actual incarceration rate and the steady-state incarceration rate implied by the admissions and release rates in the base year. When the state's actual incarceration rate is below the implicit steady-state rate, the instrument predicts an increase. Conversely, when a state's incarceration rate is above the implicit steady-state rate of the state, the instrument predicts that the incarceration rate will decrease. The absolute value of the magnitude of the predicted change in the incarceration rate increases with the absolute value of the difference between the actual and implicit steady-state rates in the base year of the change. Johnson and Raphael derive the theoretical conditions under which the instrument identifies exogenous variation in incarceration usable for identifying the causal effects of an incarceration change on crime rates.

We obtained data on aggregate flows into and out of prison by state and year from the National Prison Statistics (NPS) database. These data provide the total admissions and total releases from prison within a calendar year. Data on the stock of prison inmates under each state's jurisdiction come from the Bureau of Justice Statistics; these data measure the stock of inmates as of December 31 of the stated calendar year. State-level population and demographic data as well as data on state-level poverty come from the U.S. Census Bureau. State-level unemployment rates come from the Bureau of Labor Statistics while state-level data on per-capita income are drawn from the Bureau of Economic Analysis.

In the original analysis, Johnson and Raphael (2012) construct the instrumental variable predicting changes in incarceration rates from annual estimates of prison admissions and release rates that were smoothed across years with a high-order, state-specific polynomial regression. The results were not sensitive to this smoothing of the underlying data. In the current application, we employ the unsmoothed transition probabilities as the instrument; using the unsmoothed data provides us with stronger first-stage relationships between the predicted change in incarceration and the actual change.

Our panel data set covers the period from 1977 to 2010 and the fifty states and Washington, D.C.[16] All models are weighted by state population. Table 7A.1 displays the first-stage relationship between the predicted change and actual changes in incarceration rates from several specifications when the model is fit to the entire time period. The first column presents the results from a bivariate regression. The second column adds demographic and socioeconomic covariates that vary at the state-year level. The third column adds a complete set of year fixed effects. Finally, the fourth column adds a complete set of state fixed effects. Note that since the models are estimated in first-difference form, state-level fixed effects are already differenced out of the data.

Table 7A.1   First-Stage Effect of the Predicted Change in Incarceration Rates Based on the Last Period Shock on the Current Change in Incarceration Rates

	(1)	(2)	(3)	(4)
Predicted Δ incarceration	0.670	0.637	0.542	0.519
	(0.125)	(0.134)	(0.139)	(0.157)
Δ percentage in population age zero to seventeen	—	−2.418	−0.426	−1.007
		(2.272)	(2.394)	(2.419)
Δ percentage in population age eighteen to twenty-four	—	−4.669	3.272	2.649
		(3.787)	(3.773)	(3.798)
Δ percentage in population age twenty-five to forty-four	—	−2.011	−1.194	−2.217
		(3.281)	(3.711)	(3.787)
Δ percentage in population age forty-five to sixty-four	—	−3.433	2.343	1.705
		(3.693)	(4.561)	(4.624)
Δ unemployment rate	—	−2.018	−1.759	−1.699
		(0.641)	(1.017)	(1.009)
Δ poverty rate	—	−0.966	0.347	0.376
		(0.518)	(0.598)	(0.607)
Δ percentage black	—	0.902	0.787	0.840
		(0.153)	(0.246)	(0.241)
Δ per-capita income	—	−0.002	−0.001	−0.001
		(0.0001)	(0.002)	(0.002)
Year effects	No	No	Yes	Yes
State effects	No	No	No	Yes
R^2	0.122	0.137	0.277	0.286
N	1,621	1,621	1,621	1,621
F-statistic[a]	28.54	22.34	15.25	10.84
(P-value)	(0.000)	(0.000)	(0.000)	(0.002)

Source: Authors' tabulations from FBI Uniform Crime Reports (various years) and Bureau of Justice Statistics (various years), *National Prisoner Statistics* data series, BJ5.

Note: Robust standard errors clustered by state are reported in parentheses. All models include constant terms and are weighted by the state-year populations. Dependent variable = ΔIncarceration Rate.

[a]F-test from a test of the significance of the instrumental variable.

Table 7A.2   Results from *F*-Tests of the Instrumental Variable from the First-Stage Regressions of the Two-Stage-Least-Squares Models of the Effects of Changes in Incarceration Rates on Crime for Three Subperiods

	1977 to 1988	1989 to 1999	2000 to 2010
No controls	18.50	11.74	13.91
	(0.000)	(0.001)	(0.001)
Demographic and	21.38	10.38	14.16
economic covariates	(0.000)	(0.002)	(0.000)
Covariates plus year	18.14	10.66	10.54
effects	(0.000)	(0.002)	(0.002)
Covariates plus year	1.13	5.21	1.06
effects and state effects	(0.292)	(0.27)	(0.309)

Source: Authors' tabulations from FBI Uniform Crime Reports (various years) and Bureau of Justice Statistics (various years), *National Prisoner Statistics* data series, BJ5.

Note: The figures in the table are *F*-statistics from a test of the statistical significance of the instrumental variable predictor of changes in incarceration rates from the first-stage regression of the change in incarceration rate on the instrument and other covariates. Associated *P*-values are presented in parentheses below each *F*-statistic.

The inclusion of the state fixed effects in the first-difference models is equivalent to controlling for state-specific linear time trends. These four specifications correspond to the model specifications of the two-stage-least-squares models underlying the main empirical results presented in the main text of the chapter. In all models, the predictive power of the instrumental variable is respectable, with the *F*-statistic on a test of the exclusion restriction in excess of 10 in all specifications.

Table 7A.2 presents the results from an *F*-test of the first-stage relationships for the same four specifications applied to the three subperiods that we analyze in chapter 7. The instrument performs well for all specifications except for the most detailed. When state fixed effects are added for the three subperiods, the explanatory power of the instrument is diminished considerably. In fact, the instrument is statistically insignificant for the earliest and latest subperiods for this specification. Hence, the estimation results for the three subperiods employ the first three model specifications only.

CHAPTER 8

What Now?

In this book, we have documented a tremendous shift in criminal justice policy in the United States that has rendered the nation first in the world in the number of its residents who are involuntarily confined in prisons and jails. Over three decades, our incarceration rate has more than quadrupled, with commensurate increases in the public resources devoted to maintaining our prisons and jails. There is very little evidence that this shift is the result of higher crime rates. In fact, U.S. crime rates are at all-time lows. On the other hand, there is overwhelming evidence that a constellation of federal and state legislation intended to allow law enforcement "to be tough on crime" has increased the propensity to punish offenders with a prison sentence and increased effective sentence lengths.

It is true that higher incarceration rates do to some degree buy us lower crime rates. There is a crucial and highly policy-relevant distinction, however, between the average impact of a change in the incarceration rate on crime and the marginal effect of a change in the incarceration rate on crime. That is to say, on average the increase in the incarceration rate from 100 to 500 per 100,000 lowered crime, and we could tabulate the average number of crimes prevented per inmate. However, the policy changes that marginally increased our incarceration rate from, say, 400 to 500 per 100,000 generated much smaller, perhaps negligible effects on crime. At higher incarceration levels, policy-induced increases in the incarceration rate come from adding to already lengthy sentences for inmates who are relatively old in terms of the age-offending profile or from incarcerating more marginal offenders who pose relatively low risk to society when not institutionalized. A key implication of this distinction between average and marginal effects is that further increasing an already high level of incarceration generates increasingly smaller benefits per inmates in terms of crime reduction. Conversely, lowering the incarceration rate from a high level does not necessarily increase crime rates.

Our analysis raises an important question: are we overusing prisons in the United States? We can think of several possible frameworks for thinking about this normative question. First, we could ask whether the benefits in terms of crime prevented of increasing the incarceration rate from, for example, 400 to 500 per 100,000 outweigh the budgetary and social costs associated with such an increase. In other words, holding constant all other efforts and social investments devoted to controlling crime, can we justify our policy of maintaining a high incarceration rate based on the crime effects alone?

Of course, framing the question in this manner ignores the fact that there are other options in the policy tool kit that can be used to address crime. The many possible interventions that have proven to be effective in reducing national crime rates include policing and specific policing strategies, drug treatment, early life human capital investments, remedial educational investments, and cognitive retraining for adults with criminal history records. Hence, a complete assessment of whether we overuse incarceration must consider the relative benefits of all possible policy interventions and the effects of reallocating resources from one intervention to another. In other words, can we come up with an alternative constellation of crime control policies and criminal sanctions that would reduce incarceration and the attendant collateral costs yet maintain crime rates at acceptably low levels?

We believe that the answer to this question is yes. However, affecting such a policy shift would require a proactive approach to crime control rather than a reactive set of institutions that address crime after the fact. Such a policy would require fundamental reforms to sentencing practices and the creation of a more balanced distribution of discretion in the criminal justice system between prosecutors, judges, and correctional authorities. Such a policy shift would also require that we acknowledge and accept that low crime rates today can be achieved from social investments made in the past and that lower crime rates in the future require that we maintain current levels of social investment today. Finally, such a policy shift would also require that we explicitly acknowledge the enormous social costs of the incarceration boom that extend way beyond the budgetary impact on states.

Here in our final chapter, we offer our thoughts on these questions. We begin by asking whether the net benefits of recent increases in incarceration are positive. We then couch this discussion in terms of alternative crime control strategies that are less invasive yet equally if not more effective at controlling crime. Finally, we discuss what it takes to reduce prison populations and draw on the experience of states that have done so.

HIGH INCARCERATION RATES: DO THE COSTS OUTWEIGH THE BENEFITS?

We have documented the diminishing effectiveness of further increases in incarceration as a crime control strategy. In fact, our empirical analysis in chapter 7 suggests that the large increases in incarceration since the early 1990s have shown little benefit in terms of lower crime. We have also documented the budgetary costs of incarceration. We have said less about the many collateral social consequences of the massive increase in the nation's incarceration rate. Although it is difficult to place a dollar value on these collateral consequences, they clearly contribute to the social costs of using incarceration to lower crime and effectively diminish the net benefits of this particular intervention.

To the extent that the total value of the on-budget and off-budget costs of our high incarceration rates exceeds the value of the benefits associated with lower crime, we might argue that reducing incarceration rates below current levels would be justified even if crime were to rise as a result. To be sure, scaling back incarceration does not necessarily result in higher crime, since compensatory social investments could be made with the associated savings from lower corrections spending (the subject of the next section). Even in the absence of such compensating investment, however, a reduction in incarceration rates that results in slightly higher crime could easily be justified based on the total social costs of incarceration.

This line of reasoning is not uncommon in other policy domains. For example, we could reduce speed limits across the nation to fifty-five miles per hour on all freeways. In fact, the federal government tied federal highway funding to such a policy during the 1970s in response to the oil crisis, and all states adopted this low speed limit as a result.[1] When subsequent federal legislation in 1995 eliminated the national speed limit, many states quickly raised speed limits on freeways and rural highways, a change that caused significant increases in traffic fatalities and injuries (Friedman, Hedeker, and Richter 2009).Certainly, states could opt to lower their speed limits back to fifty-five miles per hour but do not. This public choice reveals a willingness to accept a higher level of traffic fatalities in exchange for shorter commute times.

A more apt analogy is one commonly discussed in introductory economics classes: what is the optimal level of inventory loss from theft in a retail establishment? Certainly, retailers could reduce shoplifting to near-zero with sufficient investment in cameras, security guards, undercover personnel devoted to detecting shoplifting, and other such tools. At some point, however, the cost of preventing the marginal shoplifter exceeds the cost of the loss in inventory through theft. In other words, the optimal level of shoplifting from a benefit-cost framework is likely to be greater than zero.

A back-of-the-envelope calculation of the benefits of recent increases in incarceration in terms of impacts on serious felony offenses can be compared to these same benefits in terms of the on-budget costs of incarceration. The RAND Corporation has created a "Cost of Crime Calculator" based on a set of research studies that attempt to estimate the effects on society of specific criminal incidents.[2] Our analysis of the effects of incarceration on crime in chapter 7 revealed no evidence of an impact of incarceration growth since 2000 on violent crimes, but some evidence of effects on auto theft and larceny theft. Our estimates for this latter period, in conjunction with RAND's Cost of Crime Calculator, suggest that each additional prison-year served during the last decade generated benefits in terms of reduced crime equal to a bit less than $11,000.[3] If we account for the tendency to underreport crimes to the police, this benefit would rise to roughly $15,000.[4] Note that this figure is considerably lower than the average expenditures per inmate for many states (reported in chapter 1).

Of course, a fuller cost-benefit analysis would incorporate the social costs of incarceration growth that are not reflected in public budgets—what we refer to here as the collateral consequences of incarceration. Among the many

such collateral consequences, the following have received considerable research attention in the past several decades:

- *The adverse effects on the postrelease employment prospects of former prison
  inmates:* Harry Holzer, Steven Raphael, and Michael Stoll (2006) document an extreme reluctance among employers to hire former inmates. In
  addition, Raphael (2011) documents that a high proportion of employers
  of relatively less-skilled workers in California indicate that they are legally
  proscribed from employing convicted felons. In their audit research, Devah Pager (2003) and Pager, Bruce Western, and Bart Bonikowski (2009)
  document the translation of this stated employer reluctance into large
  differences in job offer rates, with particularly low job offer rates for African Americans with criminal records. Moreover, the evidence that employers use race and gender as a cheap screen to weed out applicants with
  criminal records suggests that race, crime, and interactions with the criminal justice system have become more tightly linked in the minds of key
  actors in society.

- *The aggravation of racial disparities in educational attainment:* During the
  1960s and 1970s, educational disparities between African American and
  white youth narrowed. In the 1980s and beyond, however, this progress
  came to a halt and disparities began to widen once again, especially
  among young men. William Evans, Craig Garthwaite, and Timothy
  Moore (2012) attribute this change to the crack epidemic and the higher
  likelihood that African American young men will serve time. There are
  many mediating pathways linking crack to poor educational attainment
  outcomes, including weaker family support and resources being diminished by drug addiction. The pathways mediating the effects of incarceration on educational attainment are likely to operate principally through
  expectations regarding the returns to education. If one expects to cycle in
  and out of prison, what is the point of staying in school? This is an area
  of crucial importance that is in need of much more research.

- *The health consequences for former inmates and their communities:* Jason
  Schnittker, Michael Massoglia, and Christopher Uggen (2011) review
  recent research linking mass incarceration to health outcomes and health
  disparities. Some of the research reviewed finds that a spell in prison actually improves access to health care, since many of those who are incarcerated lack health insurance and are likely to have underutilized the health

resources available to them. However, there are also key research studies that find evidence of within-prison transmission of infectious disease (hepatitis in particular) and transmission of infectious disease through various channels in the communities from which inmates disproportionately come. Rucker Johnson and Steven Raphael (2009) find evidence that racial disparities in incarceration rates and incarceration growth explain the lion's share of racial disparities in AIDS infection rates. Moreover, several studies reviewed by Schnittker and his colleagues find evidence of unusually high levels of disability and stress-related illness among former prison inmates. It is also certainly the case that the health effects of the massive increase in incarceration rates extend beyond the direct effects on current and former inmates. We have already mentioned research linking incarceration growth to the spread of AIDS in the black community. Christopher Wildeman (2012) finds discretely higher infant mortality rates among newborns with incarcerated fathers with no pre-incarceration history of domestic abuse. Moreover, the increased stress and reduced resources associated with having an incarcerated partner, son, or father may be a factor in the relatively poor cardiovascular health outcomes for African American women (Hedwig and Wildeman, 2011).

- *The negative repercussions for the children of the incarcerated:* Over half of male state prison inmates and 60 percent of female state prison inmates are the parents of children under the age of eighteen (Glaze and Maruschak 2009). Among the age groups that make up the bulk of the prison population (twenty-five- to thirty-four-year-olds and thirty-five- to forty-four-year-olds), the proportion of those who are parents is considerably higher, with the figure reaching 80 percent among female state prisoners between the ages of twenty-five and thirty-four. Wildeman (2009) provides the most authoritative assessment of the risk of experiencing a parental incarceration. Examining birth cohorts of children born in 1978 and children born in 1990, he finds that, among the 1990 cohort, one in four black children and one in twenty-five white children experienced a parental incarceration by the age of fourteen. Among black children born to high school dropout parents, half experienced a parental incarceration by this age. A parental incarceration certainly has an impact on the material well-being of children. Johnson (2009) analyzes the impact of paternal incarceration on the household incomes and poverty rates of children born between 1985 and 2000, using longitudinal data. In the year prior to a father's incarceration, average annual household income, in 1997 dollars, stood at \$38,960. During the period of incarceration, average annual household income dropped by nearly \$9,000. Concurrently, the proportion of these children living in households below the poverty line was 22 percent prior to the father's incarceration. During the father's incarceration, this poverty rate increased to nearly 31 percent. There is also evidence of increased behavioral problems among the children of the incarcerated. Analyzing the effect of parental incarceration on aggressive behavior among very young children, Wildeman (2010) finds that aggressive behavior increases among young boys with incarcerated fathers. Moreover, this increase in externalizing behavior is concentrated among the young children of men who have not committed violent acts and who are not abusive within their households.

- *Diminished political participation:* In many states, individuals with an active criminal justice status are denied the franchise. According to a report by the Sentencing Project (2012), forty-eight states and the District of Columbia prohibit voting while incarcerated. In addition, thirty-five of these states do not allow those on parole to vote, and thirty-two states prohibit voting among those on probation. Four states prohibit voting among all convicted felons, even after they have completed their sentence. The Sentencing Project estimates that one in forty adults is currently unable to vote owing to either current involvement with the criminal justice system or a lifetime ban for a prior felony conviction. Roughly 7 percent of adult African Americans are currently disenfranchised. At least one study (Uggen and Manza 2002) has found evidence that felon disenfranchisement may alter electoral outcomes in very close races.

- *Greater racial inequality:* As is evident in each of the domains discussed here, the disproportionate representation of African Americans in the nation's prisons and jails, and African American males in particular, translates directly into racial disparities in the collateral consequences of incarceration growth. Given the order of magnitude of incarceration growth over the past three decades, the criminal justice system has become a very important factor in aggravating racial inequality across multiple domains.

To be sure, this brief discussion of the collateral consequences of the high U.S. incarceration rate touches only the surface of the work on this topic and does not articulate all of the possible derivative social consequences of this massive change in U.S. policy. Several books could be written on the collateral consequences of incarceration, and in fact several authors have done so (see, for example, Pager 2007; Pettit 2012; Wakefield and Wildeman 2012; Western 2006). This list of collateral consequences does, however, convey the degree to which the tentacles of the prison boom stretch into the many social domains and sources of inequality that are of first-order importance in the United States. Moreover, this discussion goes beyond the budgetary costs to illustrate the many other costs of incarceration that diminish the true net benefits from further prison expansion.

Hence, given the relatively small effects of recent increases in the nation's incarceration rate, the fact that it is relatively less serious crimes that appear to be affected by these recent increases, the tendency of the monetary value of these benefits (in terms of spending per inmate) to fall short in most states, and the enormous and less easily measured social costs of incarceration, we believe that it is reasonable to conclude that we are overusing prisons in the United States. Our high incarceration rates cannot be justified, in isolation, by the number of crimes prevented. Moreover, when other options are available that can reduce crime at lower social cost, the current policy regime becomes even less defensible.

ALTERNATIVES TO HIGH INCARCERATION RATES: OTHER COST-EFFECTIVE PUBLIC INTERVENTIONS

Our thinking on optimal crime control strategies is guided by several basic insights from optimization theory. Suppose that society wishes to maintain crime rates at a specified level and has at its disposal several policy options for doing so—for example, hiring police, investing in early childhood education, and incarcerating people. Presumably, we would like to achieve our objective (a given low crime rate) in the most efficient manner possible. That is to say, we would like to employ that mix of policy interventions that delivers our desired low crime rate with the lowest possible costs, where costs are broadly defined to include both the budgetary outlays and the social costs of our policy choices. Let's assume that for each possible policy tool the marginal benefits of expanding its use diminishes with scale. For example, the benefits from hiring additional police officers decline as the police force grows, or, as we have empirically demonstrated, the crime-preventing benefits of increasing the prison population diminish as the incarceration rate increases.

The efficient, or lowest-cost, policy strategy would be that for which our various policy tools are employed to the point where the marginal benefit in terms of crimes prevented for each additional dollar spent is equal across all possible interventions. In other words, our policy mix is efficient when a dollar spent on policing generates the same benefit as an additional dollar spent on prisons or early childhood interventions. Why is this strategy efficient? Suppose that our current policy strategy is inefficient by our definition. Specifically, at our current mix of policing levels and incarceration expenditures, suppose that the benefit-cost ratio (the "bang for the buck") associated with additional spending on police is higher than the comparable benefit-cost ratio for additional prison expenditures. Under this scenario, if we were to reduce the prison population and reinvest the savings in more police, the crime reduction from the additional policing levels would exceed the crime increase caused by the reduction in the prison population. On net, crime would decline with the same level of expenditures. Of course, reallocating spending in this manner would push us further down the diminishing-returns path for policing and increase the benefits on the margin from additional prison spending (since, by reducing the incarceration rate, the benefits on the margin of additional incarceration spending would rise). In other words, the resource reallocation described here would narrow the difference in the benefit-cost ratios of these two interventions. Ideally, we would continue to reallocate resources in this manner until the benefits-per-dollar-spent is equalized across these two interventions.

A key implication of this line of reasoning is that if the bang for the buck is not equal across interventions, we could reallocate resources in a manner that would reduce crime without increasing expenditures. A further implication is that when the bang for the buck differs across our alternative intervention, we could achieve the same crime rates at lower social cost. The preceding discussion illustrates that we are currently at a point where the benefits on the margin derived from our current high incarceration rate in terms of crime reduction probably fall short of the costs in terms of explicit outlays and harder-to-price collateral consequences. Based on this reasoning, we argue that a move toward lower incarceration rates could probably be justified, even if crime were to increase as a result. However, there is no reason why our public choice should be framed in this manner. There are other arrows in our quiver besides state and federal prisons that could be used to address crime. To the extent that the bang for the buck of these alternatives is higher than that associated with recent increases in incarceration, we could reduce incarceration rates, reallocate the freed resources toward other, more effective interventions, and have lower incarceration rates without higher crime.

Perhaps the most obvious policy tool with the strongest research base confirming its impact on crime is expansion of local police forces. There is considerable empirical evidence of the general effectiveness of higher police staffing levels in lowering crime rates. Broad city-level analyses (Levitt 1997, 2002; Chalfin and McCrary 2012), a study that exploits temporary increases in policing (Di Tella and Schargrodsky 2004), a study that analyzes surges in hiring associated with federal policy (Evans and Owens 2007), and a high-frequency time series analysis (Corman and Mocan 2000) consistently find relatively large effects of expanding a city police forces on local crime rates. Paul Heaton (2010) estimates that in several cities the benefit in terms of reduced crime of hiring an additional police officer exceeds $300,000 per year—a figure that substantially exceeds the annual cost of the additional officer. Although one benefit from expanding police forces is most certainly the ability to apprehend and incapacitate highly criminally active individuals, a more consistent police presence is also likely to deter criminal activity, especially among those who may be passing through a high-offending age range but for whom a future life in crime is certainly not a preordained outcome. Hence, sentencing reforms geared toward reducing incarceration rates, coupled with expanded policing, could certainly lead to lower incarceration rates, either no increase or perhaps a decrease in crime, and no increase in public spending on crime control.

Aside from expanded policing, there is growing evidence that more targeted and moderate use of incarceration can be as effective in preventing crime as a policy regime that relies on long sentences, if not more so. In this vein, Mark Kleiman (2009) presents an ambitious and creative agenda for a national shift in crime control policy. A key component of this strategy is more effective management of those on probation and parole through careful monitoring, swift and certain penalties for rules violations, and moderate sanctions that graduate in severity as violations increase or become more serious.

Kleiman (2009) places great stock in the results from the HOPE (Hawaii's Opportunity Probation and Enforcement) demonstration. The program entailed the careful monitoring and frequent drug testing of those on probation. Those who tested positive for drugs or missed an appointment were immediately arrested and forced to serve very short jail sentences (a few days to a week). Expectations were clearly communicated to HOPE participants by a presiding judge, and the sanctions for violations were swift and certain. The predictability and certainty of the sanctions regime created a high level of compliance among those on HOPE, and the evaluation suggested that, relative to a matched comparison sample, HOPE participants were considerably less likely to violate their probation terms and be sent to jail.

To the extent that the HOPE program results can be replicated when similar programs are implemented in other jurisdictions and on a larger scale, this program offers an alternative to incarceration for managing less serious offenders that is likely to be fruitful. The program still makes use of incarceration, but in a targeted and graduated manner and in the form of local jail spells in lieu of incarceration terms in state prison. Even as more long-term incapacitation of incorrigible offenders remains possible, the program uses the graduated sanctioning regime to weed out those offenders with the highest chances of succeeding outside of state prisons. Kleiman's (2009) strategy essentially amounts to using existing prison and jail capacity in a smarter manner; this strategy would be likely to result in quicker desistance from crime by those less committed to such a life, as well as less incarceration and less crime.

To some degree, the key elements of the HOPE demonstration reflect the practices of specialized courts and "intermediate sanctions" strategies that are already in operation in many localities across the country. Specialized courts are designed to meet the criminal justice and treatment needs of offenders whose criminal behavior is driven in part by such factors as drug use, domestic violence, and mental illness. Intermediate sanctions (also referred to as "community sanctions") offer a continuum of non-confinement-based sentences, including but not limited to intensive community-based supervision, electronic monitoring of offenders, short "shock incarcerations" in local jails, house arrest, and community restitution requirements.

Drug courts provide one of the more salient examples of this approach. Drug court programs typically operate in one of two ways. Diversionary courts mandate that offenders attend drug treatment programs. Successful completion is met with the dropping of the original charges and thus no criminal conviction on the individual's criminal history record. Post-adjudication courts intervene after individuals have already been tried and convicted of a drug-related offense. Sentencing is deferred and eventually suspended once individuals graduate from their treatment program. Some courts use a combination of both diversionary and post-adjudication methods (Gottfredson and Exum 2002).

One of the key components of drug courts is their use of incentives and graduated sanctions to reward or punish participants. In addition to mandatory drug treatment, participants are subject to frequent drug testing and ongoing status hearings before a judge. Judges have the discretion to implement sanctions and case modifications based on case plan compliance. Examples include increasing an individual's level of treatment, the frequency of urine screenings and status hearings, and, in some cases, jail time (Gottfredson and Exum 2002).

Several high-quality evaluations of drug court programs have found significant increases in treatment program participation, significant decreases in future drug use, and significant decreases in recidivism (Deschenes, Turner, and Greenwood 1996; Marlowe, De Matteo, and Festinger 2003; Gottfredson and Exum 2002; Rossman et al. 2011). A recent multi-site evaluation carried out by the Urban Institute (Rossman et al. 2011) noted the particularly important role played by drug court judges and the important mediating effect of frequent interactions with the judge, perceptions of fair handling by those diverted to drug courts, and the ability of the participant to speak during the proceedings.

The HOPE demonstration project, the positive results from drug court evaluations, and other research on the potential effectiveness of non-incarceration-based alternatives suggest that there are indeed other ways of doing business for more marginal offenders. We believe that Kleiman's (2009) vision for an effective and expanded community corrections system tailored to the highly present-oriented decision-making that drives many criminal offenders should be heeded in particular. Sanctions that are communicated clearly and swiftly applied are likely to generate the greatest behavioral responses. Moreover, the call for moderation and substitution of certainty for severity is likely to engender greater deterrence at lower cost to taxpayers, to those who offend, and to those who care about those who offend.

Of course, we could also approach crime control more proactively and less reactively. In the current state of affairs, we identify the criminally active and then punish them harshly with lengthy prison spells. An alternative strategy would be to use selective policing practices that deter crime in the first place and ramped-up investments in early childhood through adolescence. Kleiman

(2009) offers several examples of innovative policing practices that target police enforcement efforts and resources on particular problem areas, in conjunction with clear communication to potential offenders of the enforcement
strategy, and have led to drastic local improvements in crime with few arrests.
This strategy has been applied to shutting down open-air drug markets and
addressing gang violence. In many ways, such efforts follow Kleiman's exhor-
tation to increase the certainty of sanctions rather than the severity; by lever-
aging the deterrent effect associated with a heightened likelihood of being
caught, they are highly effective. To the extent that we could deter criminal
activity while young men are in the age range where they are most criminally
active, we might alter entire lifetime offending trajectories and certainly lifetime trajectories of official involvement with the criminal justice system.

Regarding proactive investments in individuals as a crime control strategy,
there is evidence that small changes in educational attainment result in appreciable changes in the likelihood of serving time in prison. Solid empirical
evidence has revealed a sizable salutary effect of education on criminal offending based on increases in compulsory school attendance ages in the United
States (Lochner and Moretti 2004), the United Kingdom (Machin, Marie,
and Vujić 2010), and Sweden (Hjalmarsson, Holmlund, and Lindquist
2011). Interestingly, changes in compulsory schooling attendance ages are
likely to increase educational attainment for those most at risk of criminal
offending, since youth who attend school beyond the minimum compulsory
age tend to offend at relatively low rates. Hence, raising the compulsory
school attendances age to, say, eighteen across all states might be a particularly
well-targeted intervention that would lower crime, reduce incarceration, and
generate other tangible benefits for those who attend more school.

There is also some, though somewhat limited, evidence that very early
childhood human capital investments have long-run effects on offending,
during both the teenage and early adult years. In a thorough review of this
research, Lance Lochner (2011) discusses several well-known early childhood
interventions such as the Perry Preschool Project, the Abecedarian Project,
Head Start, and home nurse visits under the Infant Health and Development
Program. The effects of such early childhood interventions on criminal offending may operate through several mediators—including lifetime educational attainment, impacts on parenting practices, and early life skills acquisi-
tion—that aid in mediating conflict later in life. Although several of these

programs have demonstrable effects on arrests and self-reported criminal activity, some do not, and in some instances separate empirical evaluations of the same program (Head Start in particular) yield differing conclusions regarding crime effects. Regardless, the evidence of salutary effects, coupled with the very high social costs associated with felony criminal offending, suggests that the crime control benefits of such efforts deserve much greater attention.

Hence, there are certainly other compensatory investments that could be made to fight crime if states and the federal government altered sentencing policy with an eye to reducing prison populations. Several of these alternatives have been proven to generate benefits in excess of costs, and their bang for the buck generally exceeds that of additional prison time served for marginal offenders. Moreover, several of these interventions are proactive and prevent crimes from occurring in the first place rather than react to victimizations after the fact. There are many paths to the top of the mountain. Some clearly exert less of a toll on society than others.

REDUCING INCARCERATION RATES
THROUGH SENTENCING REFORM

Between 2010 and 2011, the U.S. prison population declined by 15,023. This was the second year in a row of decline in the state prison population, and the first two years of decline following decades of prison growth (Carson and Sabol 2012). The substantial decline overall has been driven primarily by the large decline in the prison population of California, though several other states have also experienced substantial decreases—most notably New York, Texas, Florida, Michigan, and New Jersey. We have shown that the lion's share of incarceration growth over the past three decades can be attributed to sentencing policy changes that have increased sentence length and the frequency with which we send people to prison. Not surprisingly, the slight reversal we are currently witnessing and the substantial declines in California are policy-driven as well.

The recent reforms in California illustrate how quickly a modest policy reform can draw down a prison population. California's realignment reform ends the practice of returning to state custody parole violators who do not commit a new felony. The reforms also divert to local jails felony offenders who are convicted of relatively nonserious offenses and have no serious of-

Figure 8.1   Total Weekly Admissions to the California Department of Corrections and Rehabilitation, October 1, 2010, to August 31, 2012

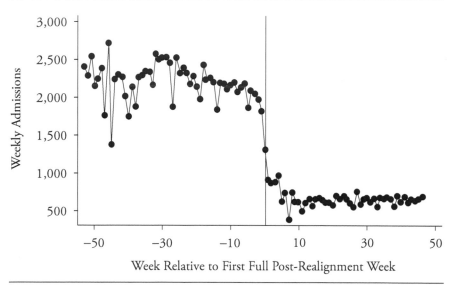

Source: Special tabulations provided to the authors by the California Department of Corrections and Rehabilitation.

fenses on their criminal history record. Not a single individual was released early. The population decrease was driven entirely by diverting these new admissions to alternative sanctions.

Figure 8.1 displays weekly admissions to the California prison system by week for the period from January 2011 to mid-October 2012. We observe a very large decline in weekly admissions with the implementation of the California reform, from roughly two thousand per week prior to the reform to approximately six hundred per week after. Table 8.1 shows how admissions have changed by the offense resulting in admission to prison. The lion's share of the decrease is driven by the discontinuation of the practice of returning parolees at a high rate. The remainder is essentially driven by the diversion of low-level property crime offenders and drug offenders to local jails.

It is interesting to note what has happened in California's county jails as a result of this reform. First, the total jail population has increased somewhat, by about one-third of the number of inmates realigned from state prisons to the counties. In other words, up to two-thirds of these realigned inmates are

Table 8.1 Total Prison Admissions and Average Weekly Prison Admissions, by Offense, Between October 2010 and August 2012

Offense Category	Total Admissions	Average Weekly Admissions			
		All Weeks	Pre-Realignment	Post-Realignment	Difference, Post- and Pre-Realignment
All offenses	148,180	1,481 (78.99)	2,196 (34.16)	675 (20.27)	−1,521 (41.00)*
Murder and manslaughter	2,753	27.53 (0.72)	29.51 (1.05)	25.29 (0.86)	−4.21 (1.38)*
Robbery	6,840	68.40 (1.22)	68.81 (1.55)	67.94 (1.93)	−0.88 (2.45)
Assault	15,667	156.67 (2.61)	161.98 (3.45)	150.68 (3.80)	−11.30 (5.12)**
Sex	5,456	54.56 (1.09)	57.66 (1.46)	51.06 (1.49)	−6.59 (2.09)*
Kidnapping	417	4.17 (0.20)	4.47 (0.28)	3.83 (0.28)	−0.65 (0.40)
Burglary, first	4,642	46.42 (1.02)	45.60 (1.17)	47.34 (1.73)	1.75 (2.05)
Burglary, second	5,872	58.72 (3.16)	86.55 (1.83)	27.34 (1.09)	−59.20 (2.20)*
Theft and fraud	14,029	140.29 (7.42)	205.81 (4.15)	66.40 (2.62)	−139.41 (5.04)*
Drugs	18,447	184.47 (9.44)	267.87 (4.67)	90.42 (4.26)	−177.44 (6.38)*
Escape	45	0.45 (0.06)	0.32 (0.07)	0.60 (0.10)	0.27 (0.13)**
DUI	2,541	25.47 (1.14)	33.94 (1.15)	15.91 (0.71)	−18.03 (1.40)*
Arson	312	3.12 (0.15)	3.04 (0.20)	3.21 (0.23)	0.18 (0.30)
Weapons	5,934	59.34 (1.47)	66.86 (1.52)	50.85 (2.03)	−16.02 (2.50)*
Other	3,620	36.20 (0.94)	41.51 (1.12)	30.21 (1.01)	−11.29 (1.52)*
Parole, return to custody	7,975	79.75 (7.75)	135.96 (8.77)	16.36 (3.55)	−119.60 (9.90)*
Parole, pending review	53,001	530.04 (49.58)	986.33 (16.56)	15.48 (7.03)	−970.85 (18.79)*

Source: Authors' tabulations based on a special tabulation of weekly admissions by offense generated by the California Department of Corrections and Rehabilitation.

Note: Standard errors are in parentheses.

*Statistically significant at the 1 percent level; **statistically significant at the 5 percent level.

not incarcerated in either county jail or prison. Second, the population of convicted inmates in county jail has increased while the population awaiting trial has declined (Raphael 2013). Hence, jail capacity at the county level has been reshuffled in what is likely to be a more efficient use of incarceration capacity—toward greater use for convicted offenders and less use for those awaiting trial.

California's experience is a stark illustration of what it takes to generate permanent reductions in the prison population. In particular, we see that sentencing and parole policies governing the flows into prison are clearly key determinants of prison populations and that reforms that reduce the inflow reduce the population overall.

In an annual review of developments in state prison populations, the Pew Center for the States (2010) provides further examples of state-led efforts to reduce state prison populations, identifying key policy reforms and efforts responsible for observed declines across the United States. For example, the study notes, investment in a community-based treatment and diversion program in Texas has relieved prison population pressure. Michigan reduced its prison population by over 10 percent in three years by reducing parole revocation rates and total time served. Mississippi rolled back its time served requirement for nonviolent felons from 85 percent to 25 percent of the sentence. Nevada increased the number of ways to acquire good time credits and enhanced the value of these credits for current inmates. Another high-profile reform involved the repeal of the Rockefeller Drug Laws in New York and their stringent mandatory minimum sentences.

In all of these instances, declining prison population counts resulted from explicit policy choices to deescalate, just as the ramping up of incarceration rates over the period under study here was driven by new policies aimed at tougher sanctions for those who criminally offend. Hence, reducing incarceration rates in this country requires that we reform the sentencing practices that have caused those high incarceration rates.

As we have noted in several places throughout this book, there is great heterogeneity across states in sentencing policy, and thus suggestions for systematic change must necessarily take on a more general nature. However, we believe that sound reforms could be made in many states and at the federal level that would lead to smarter and much more moderate use of incarceration and would cut across practices that are widespread.

To start, we believe that the laws mandating minimum sentences that have been passed over the last three decades should be revisited, reviewed, and in many cases modified or abandoned. As a general rule, sentencing practices that apply a one-size-fits-all prescription tend toward the punitive, and the resulting sentences often cannot be justified by the severity of the offense or the threat posed by the offender. Key examples of such binding minimum sentences that have undergone recent scrutiny and reform include federal minimum sentences for crack cocaine offenses and California's "three strikes" law. In both instances, deliberate consideration (in the first instance by Congress and the president, and in the latter through the state initiative process) and scrutiny led to the adoption of reforms that generally softened the laws. Although some might argue that these reviews did not go far enough (especially at the federal level, where legislators stopped far short of equalizing punishments for offenses involving different forms of the same drug), both illustrate a maturing of the political process in the United States that has enhanced the polity's ability to rationally reconsider sentencing policies of the past. The high budgetary and social costs associated with mass incarceration, we believe, point to further opportunities to revisit many of our past policy choices regarding mandatory minimum sentences.

Second, we believe that there is much room for reforming policy that governs the discretion available to judges and parole boards in meting out initial sentences and deciding when to release prison inmates. Reviewing and revising mandatory minimum sentencing would in fact restore more judicial discretion to the sentencing process. The discretion of parole boards in release decisions could not be enhanced without softening the truth-in-sentencing time served requirements and deemphasizing the role of administrative formulas in those decisions. Good inmate candidates for early release could probably be identified through modern actuarially based risk assessment methods that incorporate both static factors from an individual's criminal history and dynamic gauges of recent behavior while incarcerated, as well as psychometric measures of criminal thinking and other cognitive markers that are predictive of further offending. Moreover, to the extent that the actions of a parole board credibly connect early release to good behavior and inmates' active attempts to rehabilitate, such policies are likely to create positive incentives for those already incarcerated and result in lower recidivism.

Finally, we believe that U.S. sentencing practices should be reformed with an eye to limiting the use of state and federal prison for first-time offenders. There is ample evidence that former prison inmates face substantial stigma in the workplace and in non-institutionalized society in general. We have shown that the extensive use of prison as punishment is in large part responsible for incarceration growth in the United States over the last three decades and that left in its wake is a large population of former prison inmates, especially among African American males. "Former prisoner" is an identity that basically cannot be fully scrubbed from one's past, and its consequences extend beyond the actual time served. We believe that it is time to exercise greater judiciousness in meting out this label.

SKIN IN THE GAME: THE ROLE OF COUNTIES IN REDUCING INCARCERATION RATES

Short of explicit changes to sentencing policy, however, we believe that states could achieve modest declines in incarceration and improve the efficiency with which prison beds are filled by better aligning the incentives of counties with the interests of the average taxpayer. Currently, there is a fundamental disconnect across the country between the incentives of counties (the main administrative units that generate prison admissions) and the incentives of state governments (the level of government that pays the bill for state prison systems). At the county level, a criminal offender is a nuisance local resident who, when convicted, is sent off to state prison to become someone else's problem. The marginal cost to the county of committing an additional inmate is effectively zero, while the marginal benefit in terms of criminal incapacitation and savings in policing and monitoring resources can only be positive. The prison spell is likely to generate substantial costs for the family and intimates of the convicted offender, but any additional costs to the county would accrue only when the individual is released from prison, and those costs are effectively off the current year's budget. Moreover, these costs are probably given little weight in the decision-making of local elected officials, in particular the local district attorney, who stands to gain politically, as an elected official, from being as tough on convicted offenders as possible.

If counties were made to face some portion of the marginal costs generated by each prison admission, we might expect local officials to be more selective in who they send to prison and for how long. We might also expect counties to look for local strategies for controlling crime that do not involve excessive detentions and that make greater use of community corrections tools. To be sure, the incentives faced by a local district attorney are not perfectly aligned with the budgetary concerns of, say, a county board of supervisors. However, if prison admissions are breaking the local bank and cutting into the county's ability to provide other basic services, we would expect the county to communicate the reality of the local budget constraint to local prosecutors in some direct way.

This discussion intimates that even within a given de jure sentencing regime local actors in the criminal justice system are given sufficient discretion that a change in cost incentives could generate an appreciable change in prison admissions and incarceration rates. Partial yet certainly not definitive evidence of such discretion can be found in large intercounty differences in the use of state prisons within single states. Although we do not have county-specific imprisonment rates for all counties in the nation, we do have data at the county level for California that do indeed suggest that local factors generate large differences in the use of state prisons. Figure 8.2 presents county-specific incarceration rates (the number of a county's residents who were in a California state prison per 100,000 county residents) for counties in or around major metropolitan areas in the state during the three-month period between July and September 2011, just prior to the major corrections reform legislation implemented in October 2011.

The figure reveals enormous heterogeneity in the degree to which counties use the state prisons. Note that all of these counties are operating under the same penal code and the same set of state institutions, yet have drastic differences in incarceration rates. Although some of the differentials observed in figure 8.2 may be attributable to demographic differentials, they are simply too large to be completely explained by underlying crime fundamentals. For example, in 2010 the poverty rates in Santa Cruz and San Diego Counties were fairly close (14.2 and 14.8 percent, respectively), but San Diego's incarceration rate was over 1.8 times the comparable rate for Santa Cruz. Similarly, San Francisco and Orange Counties had very similar poverty rates (12.8 and 12.2 percent, respectively), yet the incarceration rate in Orange County exceeded that of San Francisco by 107 per 100,000. As one final example, the poverty rates for Santa Barbara and San Bernardino Counties in 2010 stood at 17.7 and 18.1 percent, respectively. The difference in incarceration rates between these two counties during the summer of 2011 was 217 per 100,000 (the difference between the two actually exceeding the incarceration rate for San Francisco and several other counties).

Of course, there are many other determinants of crime and regional incarceration rates that may explain these differentials. Moreover, even if idiosyn-

Figure 8.2   State Prison Incarceration Rate for Select California Counties, Averaged over July to September 2011

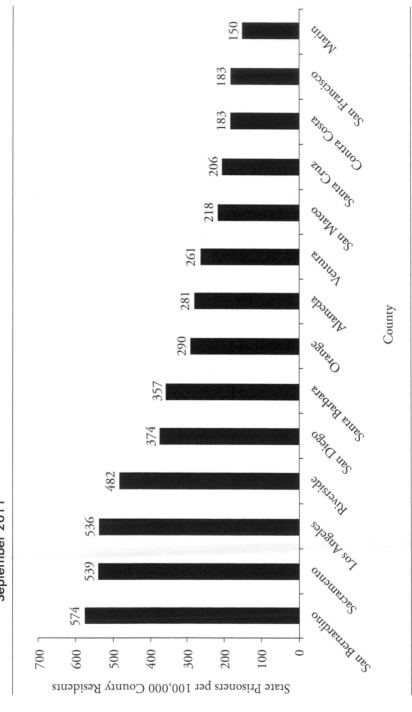

Source: Authors' tabulations from Prison Census Data as of December 31, 2011, California Department of Corrections and Rehabilitation (2011).

cratic local charging and sentencing practices determine intercounty variation in the use of state prisons, there is no guarantee that increasing the costs to counties will change local behavior. There is evidence from a policy reform pertaining to the juvenile justice system in California, however, that suggests that local corrections systems are indeed quite sensitive to cost. In 1996 the state legislature passed a bill that greatly increased the monthly costs for juvenile admissions to the California Youth Authority (CYA), the state agency that at the time ran state juvenile corrections facilities. Prior to this legislation, counties paid $25 per month per CYA ward. Starting in 1997, the monthly payment increased to $150 per month for serious offenders (with severity defined in terms of the commitment offenses). For less serious offenders, counties were required to pay anywhere from 50 to 100 percent of the custody costs to the state. Subsequent legislation passed in 1998 capped the maximum annual per-ward payment from the counties to $31,200. Nonetheless, for all juvenile commitments, and especially for less serious offenders, the increases in costs to counties created by the reform were quite substantial (California Youth Authority 2000).

Figure 8.3 displays annual admissions to CYA institutions between 1980 and 2009. A vertical line is drawn indicating the last year (1996) preceding the increase in county costs for youth commitments. The results of the reform are self-evident. There is an immediate and sustained drop in admissions to CYA beginning in 1997. To be sure, other reforms over the years have further reduced youth admissions and the youth inmate population. Additional legislation passed in 1996 facilitated the transfer to adult prisons of youth inmates convicted in criminal court who would not complete their sentences before the age of twenty-one. In addition, a state ballot initiative passed in 2000 increased the proportion of serious youth offenders tried in adult criminal courts, with those receiving lengthy sentences admitted directly to adult prisons. However, these provisions apply to a small proportion of convicted youth in the state; most of the declining admissions evident in figure 8.3 was driven by the new costs of admissions faced by counties.

This simple example, combined with the great heterogeneity across counties in the use of state prisons, suggests the viability of a reform option for reducing incarceration and fostering efficiency in the use of existing prison capacity. A policy change that ensures that counties have some "skin in the game" is likely to unleash efforts at the local level to be sparing in the use of incarceration and to avoid incarcerating individuals who pose relatively low

Figure 8.3   Annual Admissions to California Youth Authority State
Institutions, 1980 to 2009

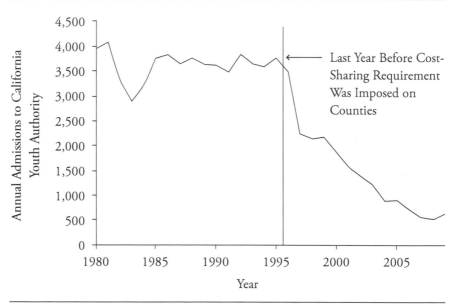

Source: Authors' tabulations from California Department of Corrections and Rehabilitation (2002).

risk. Of course, we would not want to punish poorer counties with an inter-governmental finance structure that charges higher fees to areas with the de-mographics and other local conditions that lead to higher crime rates. How-ever, some creative thinking could certainly generate schemes that better target incentives regarding marginal cases and perhaps combine an implicit tax on counties with a corresponding transfer that leaves county budgets whole while discouraging excessive admissions to state prisons.

For example, the CYA fee structure nominally increases the cost for the most serious offenders—in other words, the state still picks up the tab for those who commit the most serious offenses and whose diversion to an alter-native non-incarceration punishment is simply out of the question. We can imagine a scheme that levies differential tax rates that increase as offense se-verity decreases and that also increase in regard to offenses for which there is the greatest degree of cross-jurisdiction heterogeneity in the proportion of offenders sent to prison.

Alternatively, we can imagine a block grant combined with an incarceration tax. A state could transfer to each county a fixed amount of state funds for the purposes of criminal justice and safety expenditures, to be allocated across potential uses at the county's discretion. The amount of the block grant could be conditioned on local crime rates and demographics. Pairing the block grant with a per-head annual tax for each person admitted from the county to the state prison system would create an incentive to use prison sparingly. Moreover, the additional resources in the block grant and the higher relative price of using prison admissions would create incentives for local officials to create alternative policies that control crime while reducing prison admissions. Another strategy might assign a target incarceration rate to each county based on existing state prison capacity, past crime rates, age structure, and whatever other demographic characteristics are deemed important and legally and ethically appropriate; use of the state prison system could then be permitted free of cost within some narrow band around the target. Counties that come in sufficiently below the target could be rewarded with a grant for criminal justice expenditures that increases in the gap relative to the target, while counties whose county-specific incarceration rates exceed their targets could be symmetrically taxed.

There is much room for policy experimentation here. Currently, incentives are designed to generate too many admissions to prison. Local officials are quite sensitive to cost incentives, however, and that sensitivity should be harnessed to foster a more humane and cost-effective crime control policy.

To close, we could be making greater efforts to be more selective in our use of incarceration, since we certainly have alternatives to a high-incarceration strategy at our disposal. And just as importantly, we could create incentives for actors in the criminal justice system to devise alternative sentences that are certainly onerous but less damaging in the long term to some offenders and their families. Prison would then be reserved for those who pose the greatest danger to society.

CHAPTER 1

1. The figures are based on the population in custody by institution type, not on jurisdiction.

2. David Weiman and Christopher Weiss (2009) demonstrate a pronounced increase in the nation's incarceration rate from the pre- to the post-Prohibition periods from roughly 70 per 100,000 to 110 per 100,000. This earlier episode of high incarceration growth leads the authors to speculate that the nation's correctional systems are subject to episodes of sharp changes, often induced by moral panics surrounding specific categories of crime. Indeed, the authors draw a direct comparison between Prohibition and the contemporary War on Drugs.

3. All references to the overall adult population in the following discussion are based on our tabulations of the 2004 American Community Survey (ACS).

4. National Institute of Mental Health (NIMH), "The Numbers Count: Mental Disorders in America," available at: http://www.nimh.nih.gov/health/publica tions/the-numbers-count-mental-disorders-in-america/index.shtml#Bipolar (accessed November 8, 2009).

5. Unfortunately, there are no nationally representative surveys that record whether an individual is incarcerated and where that individual is incarcerated that would permit such tabulations. Microdata from past U.S. decennial censuses, as well as data from the annual American Community Survey, contain information on whether a respondent is institutionalized, with the overwhelming majority of the institutionalized in these data sets being in prisons and jails. However, we cannot identify the type of institution in these data. To estimate the proportion incarcerated displayed in figures 1.4 and 1.5 and table 1.3, we use the 2004 Survey of

Inmates in State and Federal Corrections Facilities (SISFCF) and the 2002 Survey of Inmates in Local Jails (SILJ) to estimate the distribution of inmates across age, race, gender, and educational attainment groups (with all these dimensions interacted with one another). We apply these distribution estimates to 2007 institutional population totals from the Bureau of Justice Statistics to estimate the number of inmates in each demographic subgroup. We then use microdata from the 2007 American Community Survey (ACS) to estimate the population totals that serve as the denominator in the incarceration ratios presented. Thankfully, the overall incarceration rates combining federal, state, and local jail inmates using the method we describe here match closely the estimates of overall incarceration rates using the ACS institutionalized groups quarters variable.

6. The relationship between education and incarceration risk is even greater than what is implied by the numbers in table 1.3. Many inmates earn GEDs while incarcerated, effectively augmenting the incarceration rate for those with a high school degree while diminishing the incarceration risk for those without one.

7. The California incarceration rate is quite close to the national average in most years. California does differ, however, in the dynamics of its incarcerated population. Given the disproportionate contribution of parole violators to the prison population in California, the typical spell in a prison there is considerably shorter than it is for the nation. The high parole failure rate leads to a much larger prison admissions rate than that for the nation.

8. Note the closer concordance between the lifetime risk measures and the prevalence of prior incarceration experience for 1974, when rates were considerably more stable.

9. Most of the discussion in this subsection relies on data from various years of the *Justice Expenditures and Employment Extracts* produced by the BJS. As of this writing, the most recent year for this data series is 2007.

10. There are numerous intergovernmental grants flowing from the federal government to state governments, from state governments to local governments, and from local governments to state governments. The lion's share of these indirect expenditures flows from the states to counties to help defer local jail expenditures. Figure 1.6 displays direct expenditures only so as not to double-count the value of intergovernmental grants.

11. These data come from the *Data Base on Historical Finances of State Government: Fiscal Year 1942 Through 2008,* compiled by the U.S. Census Bureau (2009).

12. Not all states have readily available estimates of per-inmate costs. Those states

for which we could not find an official per-capita expenditure estimate are indicated in the table.

13. Figures come from the California Legislative Analyst's Office, "Criminal Justice and Judiciary: How Much Does It Cost to Incarcerate an Inmate?," available at: http://www.lao.ca.gov/laoapp/laomenus/sections/crim_justice/6_cj_inmate cost.aspx?catid=3 (accessed August, 11, 2011).

14. This breakdown comes from Joint Legislature Committee on Performance Evaluation and Expenditure Review (2010).

15. Between 1986 and 2009, corrections spending from out-of-state general funds increased by a factor of 4.1, while total state spending out of general fund revenues increased by a factor of 2.3. These figures are based on our tabulations of budget data provided in National Association of State Budget Officers (1987, 2010).

16. The discussion in this paragraph draws on the analysis presented in National Association of State Budget Officers (2010).

CHAPTER 2

1. Of course, our students may beg to differ.

2. Lauren Glaze and Thomas Bonczar (2007) estimate that 75 percent of those on probation are sentenced to probation only and 25 percent receive a split sentence with an incarceration term. Many of those who receive split sentences, however, serve initial short terms in jail rather than prison.

3. The thirty-four states included in the 2004 survey account for 86 percent of those incarcerated in state prisons in the United States in 2004 and 76 percent of all prisoners (state plus federal) for the year. Prison admissions in these thirty-four states amounted to 81 percent of all prison admissions in 2004, while prison releases amounted to 83 percent of the total.

4. The eleven offense categories that we use throughout this and the following chapter are murder and negligent manslaughter (murder, unspecified homicide, voluntary or non-negligent manslaughter, manslaughter vehicular, and manslaughter nonvehicular), rape and sexual assault (rape by force, statutory rape, other sexual assault, and forcible sodomy), robbery (armed robbery and unarmed robbery), aggravated assault (aggravated assault and assaulting a public officer), burglary, larceny and fraud (forgery or fraud, grand larceny, petty larceny, larceny or theft value unknown, embezzlement, and receiving or trafficking in stolen property), motor vehicle theft, drug offenses (trafficking, possession, and unspecified offense involving heroin, crack or powder cocaine,

marijuana or hashish, or other unspecified controlled substance), other violent (kidnapping, simple assault, lewd act with children, blackmail or extortion or intimidation, hit-and-run driving, child abuse, other violent offenses), other property (destruction of property, hit-and-run driving causing property damage, unauthorized use of vehicle, trespassing, and other property offenses), and other crimes (escape from custody, flight to avoid prosecution, weapons offense, arson, rioting, habitual offender, contempt of court, offenses against courts, legislatures, or commissions, driving while intoxicated, driving under the influence, family-related offenses, drunkenness, vagrancy, or disorderly conduct, moral or decency offenses, immigration violation, obstruction—law enforcement, invasion of privacy, commercialized vice, contributing to the delinquency of a minor, liquor law violations, public-order offenses, bribery and conflict of interest, unspecified offenses, and other offenses).

5. We estimate admissions rates using data from the 1984, 2004, and 2009 National Corrections Reporting Program (NCRP) (Bureau of Justice Statistics, 1984, 2004a, 2009). We use the NCRP data to estimate the distribution of admissions across the twelve admission type categories. We then apply these distribution estimates to total state prison admissions for each calendar year reported by the Bureau of Justice Statistics. Although the NCRP data begin in 1983, the number of participating states in the initial year is relatively small. Hence, we chose 1984 as the beginning of our analysis period.

6. Arrests per crime for murder for 1984 actually exceed one. This could be driven by either multiple defendants being arrested for specific incidents or arrests for murders committed during the previous calendar year being made in the current calendar year.

7. Offenders serving subsequent terms for parole violations can only be held as long as their sentence allows. If cumulative time served across commitments on the same offense reaches the original sentence, offenders are released, often without condition.

8. We use 1986 rather than the 1984 base years used in all of the other figures and tables because 1986 is the closest year to 1984 included in a national survey of prison inmates administered by the U.S. Census Bureau.

9. Evelyn Patterson and Samuel Preston (2008) investigate the validity of such indirect estimation techniques for prison populations using simulation methods. They find that calculating time served by using exit rates that assume that the prison population is in steady state usually provides estimates that are quite close to the truth. The authors suggest a corrected version of this steady-state approxi-

mation that adjusts for a growing population. The Bureau of Justice Statistics has adopted this alternative methodology for estimating expected time served in its research bulletins (see, for example, West, Sabol, and Greenman 2010). We have estimated time served using both the simple reciprocal of the exit rate and the exit rate adjusted for population growth and have found very little difference between the two. For simplicity and clarity, here we use the simple exit rate approximation.

10. The low-incarceration states for which we have data are California, Iowa, Maryland, Minnesota, New Jersey, New York, North Carolina, Oregon, Pennsylvania, Washington, and Wisconsin, and the high-incarceration states are Arkansas, Connecticut, Florida, Georgia, Louisiana, Michigan, Missouri, Oklahoma, South Carolina, Tennessee, and Texas. These twenty-two states are those that reported release data, admissions data, and prisoner stock data in the 2005 National Corrections Reporting Program data set.

11. More formally, let i index crime type with $i = (1, \ldots, I)$, s index states where $s = (1, \ldots 22)$, and inc_{si} be the incarceration rate in state s for crime i. For any given state, the state's overall incarceration rate is given by the equation $inc_{s.} = \sum_{i=1}^{I} inc_{si}$. Thus, the variance in incarceration rates across states can be expressed as: $var(inc_{s.}) = \sum_{i=1}^{I} var(inc_{si}) + 2\sum_{i=1}^{I-1} \sum_{j=i+1}^{I} cov(inc_{si}, inc_{sj})$. Dividing each component by the overall cross-state variance gives the proportion of variation in state incarceration rates attributable to either a specific crime-specific incarceration variance or a covariance between any two offense-specific incarceration rates.

CHAPTER 3

1. See, for example, the recent gun control legislation passed by the state of New York in the wake of the Newtown massacre. Although the legislation contains many provisions that directly regulate gun sales and limit access to certain types of firearms and magazine clips, it also includes a requirement that those who treat the mentally ill report to the authorities any individuals who service providers believe pose a threat to others. See Thomas Kaplan and Danny Hakim, "New York Has Gun Deal, with Focus on Mental Ills," *New York Times,* January 14, 2013.

2. Others researchers have reached similar conclusions. Focusing on six major crimes accounting for the vast majority of prison inmates, Alfred Blumstein and Allen Beck (1999) partition the growth in crime-specific incarceration rates into

four variables corresponding to the steps leading from a criminal offense to a completed prison term: changes in crimes, arrests, prison commitment rates, and average prison terms. They find that for all crimes except drug offenses (including the most serious victim crimes of murder, robbery, and assault), nearly 90 percent of the growth in the incarceration rate is "explained" by more prison commitments per arrest and longer prison terms, not by more crimes and more arrests. They conclude that, at least for these crimes, the prison population has grown mainly at the "sanctioning phase" of the process: juries and judges have been handing out new and harsher punishments. Employing similar analyses, Bruce Western (2006, 43–45) reaches the same conclusion.

3. Of course, this crimes-averted imputation strategy overestimates what the crime level would have been in 2004. Surely, some of the additional offenders would have been caught, incarcerated, and incapacitated. Assuming that crime would have been at the level implied by the 1984 incarceration rate fails to take this second-order response into account. Nonetheless, given the general nature of our findings in this chapter, we would rather build assumptions into the simulation that bias us toward finding a role of behavior than otherwise.

4. The remaining unexplained 15 percent increase in steady-state incarceration rates reflects the interaction effect between admissions and time served.

5. This accords with the empirical estimates regarding proportion of time served presented in Sabol and McGready (1999).

6. The March 12, 2012, figure comes from Federal Bureau of Prisons, "Population Report," available at: http://www.bop.gov/locations/weekly_report.jsp (accessed March 23, 2012). The December 31, 2009, figure is reported in Guerino, Harrison, and Sabol (2012).

CHAPTER 4

1. In a hypothetical exchange with colleagues making such propositions, Wilson (1975, xv) writes: "'Crime and drug addiction can only be dealt with by attacking their root causes.' I am sometimes inclined when in a testy mood to rejoin 'Stupidity can only be dealt with by attacking its root cause.' I have yet to see a 'root cause' or to encounter a government program that has successfully attacked it, at least with respect to those social problems that arise out of human volition rather than technological malfunction."

2. In November 2012, California voters passed a ballot initiative that effectively narrowed the definition of a third strike with the aim of limiting the life terms for those who commit serious offenses.

3. Some argue that this sentencing discrepancy in crack versus powder cocaine com-
    pounded racial inequality among those sentenced to prison. For example, in
    2000, 84.2 percent of those arrested for possession of crack were black, compared
    to 30.3 percent arrested for powder cocaine (Mauer and Huling 1996). It is esti-
    mated that over the 1990s black men accounted for 35 percent of arrests, 55
    percent of convictions, and 74 percent of prison sentences for drug-related
    crimes, despite the fact that blacks at the time were estimated to represent about
    13 percent of monthly drug users in the United States. Moreover, the rise in the
    number of drug offenders over the late 1980s and early 1990s accounted for 42
    percent of the total growth among black inmates but only 26 percent of the
    growth among white inmates (Mauer and Huling 1996).

CHAPTER 5

1. This chapter draw heavily from our article forthcoming in the *Journal of Legal
    Studies*, "Assessing the Contribution of the Deinstitutionalization of the Mentally
    Ill to Growth in the U.S. Incarceration Rate."
2. Data on inmates in state and county mental hospitals were drawn from Palermo,
    Smith, and Liska (1991) through 1970 and from Raphael (2000) for later years.
3. Many have questioned the effectiveness of this legislation, however, since the
    number of CMHCs falls far short of projected needs (Foley and Sharfstein
    1983). Moreover, the CMHCs have been criticized as shunning individuals with
    the most severe and chronic mental health problems (Johnson 1990; Jencks
    1994).
4. Torrey (1997, 37) cites a 1992 survey of jails finding that 29 percent of them
    sometimes "incarcerate persons who have no charges against them but are merely
    waiting for psychiatric evaluation, the availability of a psychiatric hospital bed,
    or transportation to a psychiatric hospital."
5. Prior to the mid-1950s, most research found few differences between the men-
    tally ill and the general public, though the methodological soundness of the early
    research is questionable. In her review, Judith Godwin Rabkin (1979) questioned
    the data sources of this early research, noting that it used nonrepresentative
    samples.
6. Henry Steadman and his colleagues (1998) assess the violent behavior of a sample
    of individuals discharged from acute psychiatric facilities. These authors find no
    difference in violent behavior between the mentally ill who do not abuse alcohol
    or drugs and members of the general population who have no symptoms of
    substance abuse. Substance abusers who are mentally ill, however, are relatively

more violent, suggesting some interaction between mental illness and substance abuse. Frank and McGuire (2009) cite several studies that similarly find an interaction effect between mental illness and substance abuse on self-reported violent behavior.

7. These surveys also include a series of questions meant to gauge the presence of symptoms indicative of mania or a psychotic disorder. Prevalence estimates among inmates based on these questions are considerably higher (see James and Glaze 2006). Here we tabulate the data using ever-been-diagnosed to identify the most seriously mentally ill inmates.

8. The national estimates are from the original National Comorbidity Survey (Kessler et al. (1994) and the National Comorbidity Survey Replication (Kessler et al. 2005).

9. Although it could be argued that socioeconomic status based on parental characteristics takes care of this problem, there is strong intergenerational correlation between the mental health of parents and their offspring (Gottesman 1991).

10. In the inmate surveys, the period before arrest to which the question applies pertains to either the period between a previous incarceration and the current incarceration or the year prior to the current arrest. The former is the reference period when there is less than one year between a previous incarceration and the arrest leading to the current incarceration.

11. To be sure, it may be the case that many mentally ill individuals are arrested and held overnight for safekeeping. However, if such arrests are followed by unusually short jail stays (a night or two), in the steady state we may not observe a very large group of inmates held for this reason on any given day.

12. Penrose (1939) makes no attempt to control for other determinants of the institutionalized population or to net out common trends—that is, the panel aspects of the data analyzed are not fully exploited.

13. For each of the census years, we can distinguish those in mental hospitals from those in correctional institutions using the detailed group quarters variable.

14. This theoretical argument is formalized in the appendix to this chapter.

15. The exact model specification that we estimate for each gender is given by

$$\Delta Incarceration_{tsgra} = \alpha_{tsg} + \beta_{sgr} + \delta_{sga} + \gamma_g \Delta hospitalization_{tsgra} + \varepsilon_{tsgra}$$

where t indexes specific ten-year periods, s indexes states, g indexes gender, r indexes race-ethnicity, a indexes age groups, $\Delta Incarceration_{tsgra}$ is the intercensus change in the incarceration rate for a specific ten-year period in state *s* for group *gra*, $\Delta hospitalization_{tsgra}$ is the corresponding change in the mental hospitalization rate, α_{tsg}, β_{sg}, β_{sga}, and ε_g are parameters to be estimated, and ε_{tsgra} is a random error term. Note that the key parameter of interest, γ_g (our measure of transinstitutionalization), is permitted to vary by gender. The specification includes decade-state-gender fixed effects to control for any corrections policy changes that may vary across decades and have differential impacts on gender groups. These fixed effects also control for a possible reverse-causal impact of incarceration growth on hospitalization rates operating through state budgetary displacement, assuming the impact of such budgetary pressures is the same within gender. The state-gender-race fixed effects adjust both series for average differences in ten-year changes in incarceration and hospitalization rates that vary by state, gender, and race, while the state-gender-age fixed effects account for similar differences along groups defined by this triple interaction. We also estimate the equation separately for each of the four racial-ethnic groups, effectively interacting all of the fixed effects with race and permitting the gender-specific transinstitutionalization parameter to vary for each racial-ethnic group. All models are weighted by the number of observations used to compute the incarceration rate in the starting year of the change observation. Finally, in calculating standard errors for our parameters, we cluster on gender-race-state-age cells. In Raphael and Stoll (forthcoming), we present a detailed analysis of the sensitivity of the results to model specification changes.

16.   We also estimated models separately by decade to test for possible heterogeneity along this dimension. We found little evidence of a transinstitutionalization effect.

17.   We also produced similar graphs using specific demographic cohorts for early decades for which we can observe mental hospitalization for both the beginning and ending years—for example, the change from 1970 to 1980 in the Public Use Microdata Samples (PUMS) data. These analyses produced similar results—once again, base-level institutionalization rates are strong predictors of the actual changes within specific demographics groups.

18.   For the period 1980 to 2000, we thus estimate the equation

$$\Delta Incarceration_{gsra} = \alpha_{gsr} + \beta_{gsa} + \gamma_g hospitalization\_1980_{gsra} + \varepsilon_{gsra}$$

where all dimensions and variables are as defined for the early period and where we have substituted the base mental hospitalization rate for the actual change.

There are a few differences between this model and that specified for the earlier period that bear mentioning. First, since we observe only one change per demographic group (following from the fact that we cannot observe hospitalization rates for 1990), we have dropped the time subscript and all interactive fixed effects with time. Second, since we cannot separately identify the incarcerated and mental hospital inpatients in 2000, we effectively assume that all adults within our age range of study who were in institutional group quarters in 2000 were incarcerated in prisons or jails. Hence, the change in incarceration for each subgroup is measured by the overall institutionalization rate in 2000 for that group minus the proportion incarcerated in 1980. Similar to the results for the earlier period, we estimate the equation separately for each racial-ethnic group. The one necessary change when we estimate separate models by race-ethnicity is dropping the gender-state-age interactions, because in these models there is only one observation per age group in each state. Again, all models are estimated by the number of observations used to compute the incarceration rate in the starting year of the change observation.

19. The estimate for white males is statistically significant at the 1 percent level of confidence. For black males, the p-value from a test of the significance of the coefficient is 0.13.

20. Indeed, John Ellwood and Joshua Geutzkow (2009) find that correctional expenditures do displace spending on budget items usually covered by state health services departments.

21. The analysis in the following paragraphs is informed by the formal theoretical model linking the prison incarceration rate and the mental hospital inpatient rate presented in the appendix to this chapter.

22. We estimated several alternative two-stage-least-squares (2SLS) models using a single year of cross-sectional state observations and two alternative characterizations of state involuntary commitment laws. In the first model, we used data from the 1980s and a classification scheme developed by Ruth Ross and her colleagues (1996). Although we did find a weak first-stage relationship, the standard errors from the 2SLS model for our parameter of interest were too large to draw any conclusive inferences. For the second model, we used a classification scheme constructed by the American Bar Foundation (Parry 1994) characterizing state laws as of 1994. Here we find a first-stage relationship. The two classification schemes are sufficiently different to prevent them from combining when forming a two-year panel.

23. Here we are abstracting from any deterrent effects of the increased risk from

incarceration on the prison admissions rate. This necessarily follows from the purely mechanical nature of the model we have laid out, where there is essentially no allowance for systematic behavioral responses to criminal justice or mental hospitalization parameters. So long as the deterrent is relatively small, however, we would still expect an increase in admissions rates in response to increased allocation of resources of police and prosecutorial activity.

24. We could also work through the cross-partial effects of increasing prison sentence lengths (which would cause a decline in T_{PN}) on the marginal effect of further deinstitutionalization on incarceration rates. Naturally, longer sentences enhance the impact reductions in mental hospital admissions and increases in releases.

CHAPTER 6

1. Between 1970 and 2009, the foreign-born proportion of the U.S. resident population increased from 5 to 13 percent (Card and Raphael 2012).

2. See Raphael (2005) for a detailed comparison of the incarceration estimates using these data and estimated correctional populations from the Bureau of Justice Statistics.

3. Jeff Grogger (1998) presents one of the clearest micro-theoretical expositions of these ideas. He offers a model of time allocation between criminal activity, legitimate work, and leisure in which it is assumed that the return to crime diminishes with the amount of effort devoted to crime. With risk-neutral and amoral decision-makers, committing a crime requires that the return to the first hour of criminal activity exceed their potential wages and their reservation wage. The model also predicts that many will find it optimal to both work in the legitimate labor market and engage in criminal activity. This latter result follows from the assumption of decreasing returns to crime.

4. Fagan and Freeman (1999) provide a detailed summary of research conducted through the mid-1990s on the interaction between work and criminal participation.

5. Defining c as the crime rate, p as the incarceration risk, and r as the prison release rate, the steady state incarceration rate will equal $cp/(cp+r)$, where cp gives the prison admissions rate. In practice, cp is a very small number (less than 0.01), while r is a large number (roughly 0.5 in the United States). Hence, we can approximate the steady-state incarceration rate by cp/r. One over the release rate in this simple model equals the effective sentence length served. Hence, the steady-state incarceration rate is approximately equal to *cxpxsentence length*.

6. Specifically, let $i = (1, \ldots, I)$ index I racial groups and $j = (1, \ldots, J)$ index J educational attainment groups. For subgroups of men defined by race and educational attainment, we estimate how much lower the 2000 incarceration rate would have been had the average wages of the group not declined between 1980 and 2000. Specifically, we tabulate the estimates. Differentiation of the steady-state incarceration rate in note 5 with respect to wages, assuming that the crime rate depends directly on wages, gives $\frac{\partial Inc}{\partial wage} = \frac{\partial Inc}{\partial c} \frac{\partial c}{\partial wage} = \frac{r}{(cp+r)^2} \frac{\partial c}{\partial wage}$. Thus, for a given wage change, the change in incarceration is given by $\partial Inc = \frac{\partial Inc}{\partial c} \frac{\partial c}{\partial wage} = \frac{r}{(cp+r)^2} \frac{\partial c}{\partial wage} \partial Wage$. We make several substitutions into this basic framework. First, we specify crime as a function of log wages, since the key citations in this literature provide an empirical estimate of the effect of log wages on crime. Second, we substitute the group-specific change in log wages between 1980 and 2000 to simulate the contribution to incarceration growth associated with the change in earnings potential. Hence, the estimated change in the incarceration rate for the demographic group of race i and educational attainment level j is given by $\partial Inc_{ij} = \frac{\partial Inc}{\partial c} \frac{\partial c}{\partial wage} = \frac{r}{(cp+r)^2} \frac{\partial c}{\partial wage} \partial Wage_{ij}$. The main text discusses the empirical estimates used for the parameters in the equation and the empirical estimates of the wage change.

7. With an annual incarceration risk of 0.02, and making the assumption of no desistance among this population as they age, we can simulate the proportion who will eventually be interviewed in prison or jail over the course of the panel. Specifically, the likelihood of not having been incarcerated after t periods is given by 0.98^t. For any given period, one minus this calculation provides an estimate of the proportion who have ever served time. By 1996 the proportion of men who admitted to engaging in income-generating crimes in 1980 who were interviewed in prison or jail at least once is roughly 0.11 (consistent with the tabulations of presented in Freeman 1996). Assuming no desistance and a 2 percent annual incarceration risk, roughly 30 percent should have been interviewed in prison or jail. Although criminal activity is likely to have declined with age, this overestimate is also likely to indicate that our assumed incarceration risk parameter is too high. Thus, similar to our estimate of wage responsiveness, the assumed risk of incarceration further reinforces our interpretation of the numbers as upper-bound estimates.

8. We explored several alternative strategies for estimating p. One possibility is to estimate the number of crimes reported to the police that would be generated

by the typical prison inmate and then estimate the likelihood of being caught and incarcerated for this number of crimes. Johnson and Raphael (2012) estimate that the average inmate incarcerated between 1979 and 2002 reduced the index crimes reported to the police by approximately 3.5. (The effect on overall crime is closer to 10 given underreporting.) Since reported crimes are likely to generate the police actions leading to an arrest and conviction, one estimate of the likelihood of incarceration is to estimate the likelihood that such an average prisoner would be caught and convicted again should he be released. With an average admissions-to-crime ratio of 0.019, the likelihood of being caught and incarcerated for committing four index crimes in one year is approximately 0.074—calculated as $1 - (1 - 0.019)^4$. Certainly, the marginal offender drawn into crime is not likely to engage in criminal activity with the intensity of the average prison inmate. Thus, our slightly more modest choice of 0.06 seems justified. Another alternative is to make use of the stylized fact presented in Levitt and Venkatesh (2000) that roughly one-third of the sixteen heads of the Chicago drug gang they studied were in prison at any given time. Since all sixteen men can be accurately described as full-time criminals—that is to say, $c = 1$—the incarceration equation for this group can be written as $0.33 = p/(p + \theta)$. With an estimate of the release probability, we can back out the annual risk of incarceration for these full-time criminals. The release probability for all inmates in 2000 was slightly less than 0.50, corresponding to an expected time served of two years. It seems reasonable to assume that the leaders of a violent drug gang are likely to be serving somewhat longer sentences than the average inmate. If we assume a release probability for this group of 0.33 (corresponding to an expected time served of three years), then the annual incarceration risk would be equal to 0.16. Thus, our estimated risk of 0.06 implies that the incarceration risk for a marginal offender is roughly 40 percent of the incarceration risk for a full-time criminal. Although this is clearly a speculation, it seems like a reasonable approximation.

9. Juhn (2003) adjusts the log wage change for the decline in labor force participation among low-skilled male workers by estimating hourly wages from annual data (and is thus able to observe the earnings of a larger proportion of men than he would capture by looking at a monthly survey) and by assigning the wages of comparable part-year workers to individuals with no annual wage and salary income. Juhn's study does not include estimates of adjusted changes in hourly log wages for those with some college education but no degree. However, Juhn provided us with these additional tabulations.

10. Here we focus only on blacks and whites, since other groups were relatively small for the early decades covered by the table.

11. Bruce Western and Becky Pettit (2000) and Pettit (2012) provide extensive analysis of the omission of the institutionalized from many gauges of socioeconomic status and the general biased portrait that it creates with regard to the health of the labor market and the degree of interracial inequality.

12. Jeff Grogger and Michael Willis (2000) use data from the Drug Awareness Warning System (DAWN) on cocaine-related emergency room visits as well as a survey of police chiefs in large cities to date the onset of the crack epidemic for different urban areas. Roland Fryer and his colleagues (2005) use data from the DAWN, data on Drug Enforcement Administration (DEA) cocaine seizures, newspaper citations on crack related stories, cocaine arrests, and cocaine deaths to construct a single index. Both studies date the beginning of the crack epidemic to 1984–1985.

13. Crack cocaine is derived from its powder form by dissolving cocaine in water, mixing it with baking soda, and boiling it (Grogger and Willis 2000). The resulting "rocks" are smoked, which concentrates the cocaine in the bloodstream and brain at a particularly fast rate.

14. A related study on the impact of crystal methamphetamine on crime similarly finds that a large temporary reduction in the availability and purity of the drug caused by a Drug Enforcement Agency (DEA) effort to shut down suppliers of key ingredients caused no measurable decline in crime and a surge in robbery (Dobkin and Nicosia 2009). Note that this lack of an impact on crime coincided with large declines in meth-related emergency room admissions and a large reduction in meth availability.

15. The SHR data provide information on the characteristics of the homicide victim, the characteristics of the offender if the offense is cleared, and the circumstances of the crime. The thirty-two states with complete data for our time period of analysis are Alabama, Arizona, Arkansas, California, Colorado, Connecticut, Delaware, Georgia, Illinois, Indiana, Louisiana, Maryland, Massachusetts, Michigan, Minnesota, Mississippi, Missouri, Nevada, New Jersey, New York, North Carolina, Ohio, Oklahoma, Oregon, Pennsylvania, South Carolina, Tennessee, Texas, Virginia, Washington, West Virginia, and Wisconsin. Data are also available for Washington, D.C.

16. To be specific, for each state we fit a quadratic trend to the black male homicide series and look for periods with sustained homicide rates that exceeded the level of the trend line. If a visual inspection of the trend suggests that the surge oc-

curred at an earlier year, we choose the early year as the start date of the crack epidemic for the state. The earliest year is 1985, observed for California, Washington, D.C., Michigan, and New York. The latest spikes are observed in 1991 and 1992 for Arizona, Delaware, Nevada, and West Virginia.

17. Of course, there are other ways to date the onset and intensity of the crack epidemic. Grogger and Willis (2000) rely on a survey of police chiefs in large cities and surges in cocaine-related emergency room admissions. Evans, Garthwaite, and Moore (2012) date the onset of the epidemic by using vital statistics data to identify the first incidence of two consecutive years of cocaine-related deaths. The correlation across these alternative measures is generally quite weak (under 0.3, according Evans et al. 2012). We believe that black male homicide surges represent a very tangible indicator of the epidemic and the ensuing drug market violence and thus provide a very good indicator of the onset of crime associated with crack cocaine.

18. The averages for the time series depicted in figure 6.8 are weighted by state population.

19. The formal estimation methodology for this exercise is as follows. We begin by estimating the following simple multivariate regression model with our state-level incarceration data: $prison_{it} = \alpha_t + \varepsilon_{it}$, where i is an index for states in our data, t is an index for year, $prison_{it}$ is the incarceration rate in state i in year t, α_t is a year-specific intercept, and ε_{it} is a random error term. Estimating this model involves estimating a multivariate regression with the state incarceration rate as the dependent variable and a complete set of year dummies as the explanatory variables. We omit a common constant term to appropriately scale the estimated time dummy coefficients. The coefficients on the year dummies provide estimates of the average incarceration rate in each year. Since we weight the regression by state population, the year dummy estimates reflect the greater weight placed on more populous states.

Second, we augment this basic model to include our gauge of the onset of crack-related violence. In particular, we estimate the model $prison_{it} = \alpha_t + \beta blackmurder_{it} + \varepsilon_{it}$, where $blackmurder_{it}$ is the black male homicide rate in state i in year t. As an alternative specification, we also estimate the model $prison_{it} = \alpha_t + {}_{j=1}^{5}\beta_j blackmurder_{i,t-j} + \varepsilon_{it}$, where the black male homicide rate is modeled as having a lagged effect on the incarceration rate of up to five periods. For these latter two equations, the coefficients on the time dummies still measure the average state incarceration rate in a given year. However, controlling for our gauge of crack-related violence, the time effect estimates from these two equations show the period shifts in incarceration after controlling for the crime wave associated with crack cocaine. Graphically plotting the time effect estimates from these latter two equations and comparing them to the time effect estimates from the first should reveal the degree to which the crack epidemic explains the rising U.S. incarceration rate.

20. Note that the time path for the model with five lags starts four years later than the other time paths, since we cannot estimate time effects for the earlier year for which there are no lagged black male homicide rates. The four-year difference (rather than five-year) results from the fact that we have data on black male homicide rates beginning in 1976 and data on state incarceration rates beginning in 1977.

21. The underlying models used to estimate the time effects in the lower graph of figure 6.9 include state fixed effects as well as time fixed effects.

22. As we mentioned in our review of the research earlier in the chapter, the index in Fryer et al. (2005) is based on a factor analysis of crack cocaine–related emergency room visits, cocaine-related deaths, arrests, and drug busts, and the relative frequency of newspaper articles that mention crack cocaine. Their index varies by state and city. We employ their state-level index in the empirical work here.

23. We can use this number to provide a rough approximation of the implied ultimate effect on incarceration of this estimate. We estimated earlier that increases in the admissions rates account for at most 75 percent of the increase in incarceration. If crack accounts for 12 percent of the increase in admissions, then roughly 9 percent (0.75 × 0.09) of the increase in incarceration rates can be attributed to this particular shock.

CHAPTER 7

1. These data are complete for about 88 percent of reporting agencies in California. In 2011, where we have complete crime data, the reporting agencies included in this figure accounted for 93 percent of all crime in California.

2. International Centre for Prison Studies, "Country: Netherlands," available at: http://www.prisonstudies.org/info/worldbrief/wpb_country.php?country=157 (accessed June 15, 2012). The comparable incarceration rate for the United States in 2004 was 750 per 100,000. This figure aggregates the U.S. prison and jail populations, as the International Centre for Prison Studies does in its international comparisons. The prison incarceration rate in the United States in 2004 stood at 486 inmates per 100,000 (Guerino, Harrison, and Sabol 2012).

3. By prison-year served, we are referring directly to the benefit of incarcerating someone for an additional year in terms of reduced crime.

4. See the reviews by Michael Gottfredson and Kenneth Adams (1982) and Jessica Mooney and Michael Daffern (2011). A particularly careful empirical analysis for the state of Florida is presented in Cochran et al. (2012).

5. The data come from Steven Raphael's participation on an expert panel that reviewed the security classification process of the California Department of Corrections and Rehabilitation (CDCR 2011).

6. See State of California, *Rules and Regulations of Adult Institutions, Programs, and Parole, Department of Corrections and Rehabilitation,* California Code of Regulations, Title 15 (updated through January 1, 2011).

7. The aggravated assault rate in the United States in 2010 was 252.3 incidents per 100,000 residents. If we assume that for each A1 or A2 violation there was an assault victim (most likely another inmate), a violation rate of 1.86 percent corresponds to an aggravated assault rate of 1,860 per 100,000 inmates per review period. As the average review period is 317 days, or 87 percent of a year, the annual aggravated assault rate in California prisons would be 2,141 per 100,000, fully 8.5 times the national aggravated assault rate. Hence, prisons certainly are violent relative to non-institutionalized society. However, these results clearly demonstrate that the majority of prison inmates are not engaging in violent acts over the course of a year.

8. The figure displays kernel-weighted local polynomial regressions of committing a specific rules violation against age. The gray shaded area shows the 95 percent confidence band around the regression function.

9. Of course, in steady state the incarceration rates of those who commit such crimes will eventually be higher, leading ultimately to more incapacitation.

10. See Raphael (2011) for a detailed discussion of the sampling frame of this survey.

11. The exact wording of the question was: "Next, think about the most recently hired, non-managerial, non-professional position in your establishment. Please tell me if you would have definitely accepted, probably accepted, probably not accepted, or definitely not accepted each type for that position." Employers were then asked about several types of applicants, one of whom was "an applicant who had a criminal record." The survey did not specify whether this meant someone convicted of felony, convicted of misdemeanor, or in possession of an arrest record with no convictions (any of which may turn up in a background check).

12. In what follows we estimate the effects of changes in incarceration on crime rates. As incarceration rates increase, we would expect both greater incapacitation and more general deterrence to the extent that potential offenders observe greater numbers of their peers being sent to prison. The effect of changes in incarceration rates over short time periods (say, one year) on the steady-state population of former inmates is not likely to be fully realized. Hence, we would not expect any effects on long-term offending to influence the estimates using short time intervals. The literature reviews on the long-term effects of incarceration conclude that the net long-term effect is either zero or slightly positive (Nagin et al. 2009), but we believe that our estimates here are biased slightly in the negative direction.

13. A key methodological issue in this literature is the fact that crime rates and incarceration rates may mutually determine each other. For example, a policy change that emphasizes stiff sanctions will reduce crime through incapacitation and deterrence. However, a shock to criminal behavior (for example, the spread of crystal methamphetamine) will increase crime and then the incarceration rates. Researchers have employed a number of strategies to address this problem. Several studies exploit policy-driven prisoner releases (Levitt 1996; Buonanno and Raphael, forthcoming; Barbarino and Mastrobuoni 2012), while others have identified exogenous sentence enhancements (Vollaard 2013). Two studies exploit the variation in incarceration caused by the adjustment between steady-state incarceration rates following a policy change (Johnson and Raphael 2012; Buonanno and Raphael, forthcoming).

14. The data also include observations for Washington, D.C., through 2001, when the District of Columbia stopped operating its own prison system.

15. We do not present results for the final specification because in these shorter time periods our instrumental variable for changes in incarceration is either insignificant or weakly significant in the first-stage regressions controlling for state-specific time trends. See the appendix to this chapter for a more detailed discussion.

16. There are a few missing observations for Alaska and two missing observations at the end of the time series for Washington, D.C., when that city abandoned its prison system.

CHAPTER 8

1. See the discussion on the history of U.S. speed limits at Insurance Institute for Highway Safety, "Q&A: Speed—Speed and Speed Limits," available at: http://www.iihs.org/research/qanda/speed_limits.aspx (accessed January 20, 2013).

2. See Rand Center on Quality Policing, "Cost of Crime Calculator," available at: http://www.rand.org/jie/centers/quality-policing/cost-of-crime.html (accessed January 30, 2013).

3. This is based on a cost per larceny offense of $2,139, a cost per motor vehicle theft of $9,079, and the marginal effects of prison on crime reported for the period 2000 to 2010 in chapter 7.

4. This is based on the assumption that 84 percent of auto thefts and 50 percent of felony larcenies are reported to the police (the 84 percent figure for auto theft comes from Planty and Truman 2012). Theft reporting rates are only 32 percent. For this calculation, however, we employ the higher reporting rate for burglary (57 percent) because the theft reporting rates in the victimization data are dominated by instances of petty larceny.

REFERENCES

Alexander, Michelle. 2010. *The New Jim Crow: Mass Incarceration in the Age of Color-blindness*. New York: New Press.

Anderson, James M., Jeffrey R. Kling, and Kate Stith. 1999. "Measuring Inter-Judge Sentencing Disparity: Before and After the Federal Sentencing Guidelines." *Journal of Law and Economics* 42(1): 271–307.

Apel, Robert, and Gary Sweeten. 2010. "The Impact of Incarceration on Employment During the Transition to Adulthood." *Social Problems* 57(3): 448–79.

Autor, David H., and Lawrence F. Katz. 1999. "Changes in the Wage Structure and Earnings Inequality." In *Handbook of Labor Economics,* edited by Orley Ashenfelter and David Card. Amsterdam: Elsevier.

Autor, David H., Lawrence F. Katz, and Melissa S. Kearney. 2008. "Trends in U.S. Wage Inequality: Reassessing the Revisionists." *Review of Economics and Statistics* 90(2): 300–23.

Barbarino, Alessandro, and Giovanni Mastrobuoni. 2012. "The Incapacitation Effect of Incarceration: Evidence from Several Italian Collective Pardons." Working paper. Torino, Italy: Collegio Carlo Alberto.

Barille, L. 1984. "Television and Attitudes About Crime: Do Heavy Views Distort Criminality and Support Retributive Justice?" In *Justice and the Media: Issues and Research,* edited by Ray Surette. Springfield, Ill.: Charles C Thomas.

Bayer, Patrick, Randi Hjalmarsson, and David Pozen. 2009. "Building Criminal Capital Behind Bars: Peer Effects in Juvenile Corrections." *Quarterly Journal of Economics* 124(1): 105–47.

Becker, Gary S. 1968. "Crime and Punishment: An Economic Approach." *Journal of Political Economy* 76(2): 169–217.

Beckett, Katherine. 1997. *Making Crime Pay: Law and Order in Contemporary American Politics.* New York: Oxford University Press.

Beckett, Katherine, and Theodore Sasson. 2004. *The Politics of Injustice: Crime and Punishment in America,* 2nd ed. Thousand Oaks, Calif.: Sage Publications.

Bjerk, David. 2005. "Making the Crime Fit the Penalty: The Role of Prosecutorial Discretion Under Mandatory Minimum Sentencing." *Journal of Law and Economics* 48(2): 591–625.

Blumstein, Alfred. 1995. "Youth Violence, Guns, and the Illicit-Drug Industry." *Journal of Criminal Law and Criminology* 86(1): 10–36.

Blumstein, Alfred, and Allen J. Beck. 1999. "Population Growth in U.S. Prisons, 1980–1996." *Crime and Justice: A Review of Research* 26: 17–62.

Blumstein, Alfred, and Jacqueline Cohen. 1973. "A Theory of the Stability of Punishment." *Journal of Criminal Law and Criminology* 64(2): 198–206.

Blumstein, Alfred, Jacqueline Cohen, and Daniel Nagin. 1978. *Deterrence and Incapacitation: Estimating the Effects of Criminal Sanctions on Crime Rates.* Washington, D.C.: National Academy of Sciences.

Bonczar, Thomas P. 2003. *Prevalence of Imprisonment in the U.S. Population, 1974–2001.* NCJ 197976. Washington, D.C.: Bureau of Justice Statistics.

Brakel, Samuel J., John Parry, and Barbara A. Weiner. 1985. *The Mentally Disabled and the Law,* 3rd ed. Chicago: American Bar Foundation.

Buonanno, Paolo, and Steven Raphael. Forthcoming. "Incarceration and Incapacitation: Evidence from the 2006 Italian Collective Pardon." *American Economic Review.*

Bureau of Justice Statistics. 1983. *National Corrections Reporting Program.* Washington, D.C.: U.S. Department of Justice.

———. 1984. *National Corrections Reporting Program.* Washington, D.C.: U.S. Department of Justice.

———. 1985. *National Corrections Reporting Program.* Washington, D.C.: U.S. Department of Justice.

———. 1986a. *Probation and Parole, 1984.* NCJ 100181. Washington, D.C.: U.S. Department of Justice, Office of Justice Programs.

———. 1986b. *Survey of Inmates in State Corrections Facilities.* Washington, D.C.: U.S. Department of Justice.

———. 1990. *Compendium of Federal Justice Statistics, 1985.* NCJ-123560. Washington, D.C.: U.S. Department of Justice.

————. 2002a. *Compendium of Federal Justice Statistics, 2000*. NCJ 194067. Washington, D.C.: U.S. Department of Justice.

————. 2002b. *Survey of Inmates in Local Jails*. Washington, D.C.: U.S. Department of Justice.

————. 2003. *National Corrections Reporting Program*. Washington, D.C.: U.S. Department of Justice.

————. 2004a. *National Corrections Reporting Program*. Washington, D.C.: U.S. Department of Justice.

————. 2004b. *Survey of Inmates in State and Federal Corrections Facilities*. Washington, D.C.: U.S. Department of Justice.

————. 2005a. *National Corrections Reporting Program,* Washington, D.C.: U.S. Department of Justice Statistics.

————. 2005b. *Probation and Parole in the United States, 2005*. NCJ 215091. Washington, D.C.: U.S. Department of Justice, Office of Justice Programs.

————. 2009. *National Corrections Reporting Program*. Washington, D.C.: U.S. Department of Justice Statistics.

————. Various years. *Annual Survey of Jails*. Washington, D.C.: U.S. Department of Justice.

————. Various years. *Justice Expenditures and Employment Extracts*. Washington, D.C.: U.S. Department of Justice.

————. Various years. *National Prisoner Statistics*. Washington, D.C.: U.S. Department of Justice.

Bureau of Labor Statistics, U.S. Department of Labor. 2002. *National Longitudinal Survey of Youth 1979 Cohort, 1979–2002* (rounds 1–20) [computer file]. Produced and distributed by the Center for Human Resource Research, The Ohio State University, Columbus, OH.

Bushway, Shawn D., Emily Owens, and Anne Morrison Piehl. 2012. "Sentencing Guidelines and Judicial Discretion: Quasi-Experimental Evidence from Human Calculation Errors." *Journal of Empirical Legal Studies* 9(2): 291–319.

Bushway, Shawn D., and Gary Sweeten. 2007. "Abolish Lifetime Bans for Ex-Felons." *Criminology and Public Policy* 6(4): 697–706.

Butcher, Kirsten F., and Anne Morrison Piehl. 1998. "Recent Immigrants: Unexpected Implications for Crime and Incarceration." *Industrial and Labor Relations Review* 51(4): 654–79.

————. 2006. "Why Are Immigrant Incarceration Rates So Low? Evidence on Selective Immigration, Deterrence, and Deportation." Working paper. New Brunswick, N.J.: Rutgers University.

California Department of Corrections and Rehabilitation. 2002. *Characteristics of First Admissions: 1959–2001.* Division of Juvenile Justice, California Department of Corrections and Rehabilitation. Available at: http://www.cdcr.ca.gov/reports_research/docs/research/charfa_59-01.pdf (accessed September 30, 2012).

———. 2011. *Expert Panel Study of the Inmate Classification Score System.* Sacramento: CDCR, Office of Research (December). Available at: http://www.cdcr.ca.gov/Reports/docs/2010-2011-Classification-Study-Final-Report-01-10-12.pdf (accessed August 15, 2012).

———. 2011/2012. Weekly Population Reports from January 2011 through October 2012, Sacramento, CA.

———. 2012. *Prison Census Data As of December 31, 2011.* Offender Information Services Branch Estimates and Statistical Analysis Section Data Analysis Unit, CDCR, Sacramento, CA.

California Youth Authority. 2000. *Population and Facilities Management Master Plan, 2001–2006.* Available at: http://www.cdcr.ca.gov/Reports_Research/docs/research/five_year.pdf (accessed September 10, 2012).

Card, David, and Steven Raphael. 2012. "Immigration, Poverty, and Socioeconomic Inequality." Working paper. University of California at Berkeley.

Carson, Anne E., and William J. Sabol. 2012. *Prisoners in 2011.* Washington, D.C.: U.S. Department of Justice, Bureau of Justice Statistics.

Chalfin, Aaron. 2012. "What Is the Contribution of Mexican Immigration to U.S. Crime Rates? Evidence from Rainfall Shocks in Mexico." Working paper. University of California at Berkeley.

Chalfin, Aaron, Amelia Haviland, and Steven Raphael. 2012. "What Do Panel Studies Tell Us About a Deterrent Effect of Capital Punishment? A Critique of the Literature." *Journal of Quantitative Criminology* 25(1): 1–39.

Chalfin, Aaron, and Justin McCrary. 2012. "The Effect of Policy on Crime: New Evidence from U.S. Cities, 1960–2010." Working paper. University of California at Berkeley.

Charles, Kerwin Kofi, and Steven N. Durlauf. 2012. "Pitfalls in the Use of Time Series Methods To Study Deterrence and Capital Punishment." *Journal of Quantitative Criminology* 29(1): 45–66.

Chen, M. Keith, and Jesse M. Shapiro. 2007. "Do Harsher Prison Conditions Reduce Recidivism? A Discontinuity-Based Approach." *American Law and Economic Review* 9(1): 1–29.

Cochran, Joshua C., Daniel P. Mears, William D. Bales, and Eric A. Stewart. 2012. "Does Inmate Behavior Affect Post-Release Offending? Investigating the

Misconduct-Recidivism Relationship Among Youth and Adults." *Justice Quarterly* 2012: 1–40.

Cohn, Steven F., Steven E. Barkan, and William A. Halteman. 1991. "Punitive Attitudes Toward Criminals: Racial Consensus or Racial Conflict?" *Social Problems* 38(2): 287–96.

Corman, Hope, and H. Naci Mocan. 2000. "A Time-Series Analysis of Crime, Deterrence, and Drug Abuse in New York City." *American Economic Review* 90(3): 584–604.

Cullen, Francis, and Paul Gendreau. 2000. "Assessing Correctional Rehabilitation: Policy, Practice, and Prospects." In *Criminal Justice 2000: Policies, Processes, and Decisions of the Criminal Justice System*, edited by Julie Horney. Washington, D.C.: National Institute of Justice.

Daly, Rich. 2008. "People with Mental Illness Target of New Gun Law." *Psychiatric News* 43(3): 1.

Deschenes, Elizabeth Piper, Susan Turner, and Peter W. Greenwood. 1996. *Experimental Evaluation of Drug Testing and Treatment Interventions for Probationers in Maricopa County, Arizona, 1992–1994*. Santa Monica, Calif.: RAND Corporation.

Dezhbakhsh, Hashem, and Joanna M. Shepherd. 2006. "The Deterrent Effect of Capital Punishment: Evidence from a 'Judicial Experiment.'" *Economic Inquiry* 44(3): 512–35.

Di Tella, Rafael, and Ernesto Schargrodsky. 2004. "Do Police Reduce Crime? Estimates Using the Allocation of Police Forces After a Terrorist Attack." *American Economic Review* 94(1): 115–33.

Ditton, Paula M., and Doris J. Wilson. 1999. "Truth in Sentencing in State Prisons." NCJ 170032. Washington, D.C.: Bureau of Justice Statistics.

Dobkin, Carlos, and Nicole Nicosia. 2009. "The War on Drugs: Methamphetamine, Public Health, and Crime." *American Economic Review* 99(1): 324–49.

Donohue, John J., and Justin Wolfers. 2005. "Uses and Abuses of Empirical Evidence in the Death Penalty Debate." *Stanford Law Review* 58(3): 791–845.

———. 2009. "Estimating the Impact of the Death Penalty on Murder." *American Law and Economics Review* 11(2): 249–309.

Drago, Francesco, Roberto Galbiati, and Pietro Vertova. 2009. "The Deterrent Effects of Prison: Evidence from a Natural Experiment." *Journal of Political Economy* 117(2): 257–80.

Ehrlich, Isaac. 1975. "Capital Punishment and Deterrence: A Question of Life or Death." *American Economic Review* 65(3): 397–417.

Ellwood, John W., and Joshua Guetzkow. 2009. "Footing the Bill: Causes and Budgetary Consequences of State Spending on Corrections." In *Do Prisons Make Us Safer? The Benefits and Costs of the Prison Boom,* edited by Steven Raphael and Michael Stoll. New York: Russell Sage Foundation.

Evans, William N., Craig Garthwaite, and Timothy J. Moore. 2012. "The White-Black Educational Gap, Stalled Progress, and the Long-Term Consequences of the Crack Epidemic." Cambridge, Mass.: National Bureau of Economic Research Working Paper #18437.

Evans, William N., and Emily G. Owens. 2007. "COPS and Crime." *Journal of Public Economics* 91(2): 181–201.

Fagan, Jeffrey, and Richard B. Freeman. 1999. "Crime and Work." *Crime and Justice: A Review of Research* 25: 225–90.

Federal Bureau of Investigation. 1984. *Annual Uniform Crime Reports: Crime in the United States.* Washington, D.C.: Federal Bureau of Investigation.

———. 2004. *Annual Uniform Crime Reports: Crime in the United States.* Washington, D.C.: Federal Bureau of Investigation.

———. 2009. *Annual Uniform Crime Reports: Crime in the United States.* Washington, D.C.: Federal Bureau of Investigation.

Foley, Henry A., and Steven S. Sharfstein. 1983. *Madness and Government: Who Cares for the Mentally Ill?* Washington, D.C.: American Psychiatric Press.

Fox, James A., and Marc L. Swatt. 2009. *Uniform Crime Reports [United States]: Supplementary Homicide Reports with Multiple Imputation, Cumulative Files with Multiple Imputations, 1976–2007.* Northwestern University College of Criminal Justice.

Frank, Richard G., and Shelly Glied. 2006. *Better but Not Well: Mental Health Policy in the United States Since 1950.* Baltimore: Johns Hopkins University Press.

Frank, Richard G. and Thomas G. McGuire. 2009. "Mental Health Treatment and Criminal Justice Outcomes." Working paper no. 15858. Cambridge, Mass.: National Bureau of Economic Research.

———. 2011. "Mental Health Treatment and Criminal Justice Outcomes." In *Controlling Crime: Strategies and Tradeoffs,* edited by Philip J. Cook, Jens Ludwig, and Justin McCrory. Chicago: University of Chicago Press.

Freeman, Richard B. 1987. "The Relationship of Criminal Activity to Black Youth Employment." *Review of Black Political Economy* 16(Summer-Fall): 99–107.

———. 1996. "Why Do So Many Young Americans Commit Crimes and What Might We Do About It?" *Journal of Economic Perspectives* 10(1): 25–42.

Friedman, Lee S., Donald Hedeker, and Elihu D. Richter. 2009. "Long-Term Effects of Repealing the National Speed Limit in the United States." *American Journal of Public Health* 99(9): 1626–31.

Fryer, Roland G., Paul S. Heaton, Steven D. Levitt, and Kevin M. Murphy. 2005. "Measuring the Impact of Crack Cocaine." Working Paper 11318. Cambridge, Mass.: National Bureau of Economic Research.

Gilens, Martin. 1999. Why Americans Hate Walfare: Race, Media, and the Politics of Anti-Poverty Policy. Chicago: University of Chicago Press.

Gilliam, Franklin D., Jr., and Shanto Iyengar. 2005. "Prime Suspects: The Influence of Local Television News on the Viewing Public." *American Journal of Political Science* 44(3): 560–73.

Glaze, Lauren E., and Thomas P. Bonczar. 2007. "Probation and Parole in the United States, 2006." NCJ 220218. Washington, D.C.: Bureau of Justice Statistics.

Glaze, Lauren E., and Laura M. Maruschak. 2009. *Parents in Prison and Their Minor Children.* NCJ 222984. Washington, D.C.: Bureau of Justice Statistics (originally published August 2008; revised January 8, 2009).

Godwin Rabkin, Judith. 1979. "Criminal Behavior of Discharged Mental Patients: A Critical Appraisal of the Research." *Psychological Bulletin* 86(1): 1–27.

Gottesman, Irving I. 1991. *Schizophrenia Genesis: The Origins of Madness.* New York: W. H. Freeman and Co.

Gottfredson, Denise C., and M. Lyn Exum. 2002. "The Baltimore City Drug Treatment Court: One-Year Results from a Randomized Study." *Journal of Research on Crime and Delinquency* 39(3): 337–56.

Gottfredson, Michael R., and Kenneth Adams. 1982. "Prison Behavior and Release Performance." *Law and Policy Quarterly* 4(3): 373–91.

Gould, Eric D., Bruce A. Weinberg, and David B. Mustard. 2002. "Crime Rates and Local Labor Market Opportunities in the United States: 1979–1997." *Review of Economics and Statistics* 84(1): 45–61.

Grogger, Jeff. 1998. "Market Wages and Youth Crime." *Journal of Labor Economics* 16(4): 756–91.

———. 2000. "An Economic Model of Recent Trends in Violence." In *The Crime Drop in America,* edited by Alfred Blumstein and Joel Wallman. Cambridge: Cambridge University Press.

Grogger, Jeff, and Michael Willis. 2000. "The Emergence of Crack Cocaine and the Rise of Urban Crime Rates." *Review of Economics and Statistics* 82(4): 519–29.

Guerino, Paul, Paige M. Harrison, and William J. Sabol. 2011. *Prisoners in 2010.* NCJ 236096. Washington, D.C.: U.S. Department of Justice.

———. 2012. *Prisoners in 2012.* NCJ 236096. Washington, D.C.: Bureau of Justice Statistics.

Gunter, David L., Peter R. Orszag, and Thomas J. Kane. 2002. "State Support for

Higher Education, Medicaid, and the Business Cycle." Working paper. Washington, D.C.: Brookings Institution.

Hamilton, Candace, Chris Meyer, and Steven Raphael. Forthcoming. "The Evolution of Gender Employment Differentials Within Racial Groups in the United States." *Journal of Legal Studies.*

Harcourt, Bernard. 2006. "Should We Aggregate Mental Hospitalization and Prison Population Rates in Empirical Research on the Relationship Between Incarceration and Crime, Unemployment, Poverty, and Other Social Indicators?" Public Law and Legal Theory Working Paper 114. Chicago: University of Chicago Law School.

Hatsukami, Dorothy K., and Marian W. Fischman. 1996. "Crack Cocaine and Cocaine Hydrochloride: Are the Differences Myth or Reality?" *Journal of the American Medical Association* 276(19): 1580–88.

Heaton, Paul. 2010. *Hidden in Plain Sight: What Cost-of-Crime Research Can Tell Us About Investing in Police.* Occasional paper. Santa Monica, Calif.: RAND Corporation, Center on Quality Policing.

Hedwig, Lee, and Christopher Wildeman. 2011. "Things Fall Apart: Health Consequences of Mass Imprisonment for African American Women." *Review of Black Political Economy* (November, published online). Available at: http://link.springer.com/article/10.1007%2Fs12114-011-9112-4 (accessed August 15, 2012).

Helland, Eric, and Alexander Tabarrok. 2007. "Does Three-Strikes Deter? A Non-Parametric Estimation." *Journal of Human Resources* 42(2): 309–30.

Hjalmarsson, Randi. 2009. "Crime and Expected Punishment: Changes in Perceptions at the Age of Criminal Majority." *American Law and Economics Review* 11(1): 209–48.

Hjalmarsson, Randi, Helena Holmlund, and Matthew J. Lindquist. 2011. "The Effect of Education on Criminal Convictions and Incarceration: Causal Evidence from Microdata." Working paper. Queen Mary, University of London.

Holzer, Harry J., Paul Offner, and Elaine Sorensen. 2005. "Declining Employment Among Young Black Less-Educated Men: The Role of Incarceration and Child Support." *Journal of Policy Analysis and Management* 24(2): 329–50.

Holzer, Harry J., Steven Raphael, and Michael A. Stoll. 2006. "Perceived Criminality, Criminal Background Checks, and the Racial Hiring Practices of Employers." *Journal of Law and Economics* 49(2): 451–80.

———. 2007. "The Effect of an Applicant's Criminal History on Employer Hiring Decisions and Screening Practices: Evidence from Los Angeles." In *Barriers to Reentry? The Labor Market for Released Prisoners in Post-Industrial America,* edited by Shawn Bushway, Michael Stoll, and David Weiman. New York: Russell Sage Foundation.

Hurwitz, Jon, and Mark Peffley. 2005. "Playing the Race Card in the Post–Willie Horton Era: The Impact of Racialized Code Words on Support for Punitive Crime Policy." *Public Opinion Quarterly* 69(1): 99–112.

Institute for Research on Labor and Employment. 2003. *2003 Survey of California Establishments.* Berkekey: University of California.

International Centre for Prison Studies. World Prison Brief. Available at: http://www .prisonstudies.org/info/worldbrief/wpb_stats.php (accessed July 26, 2011).

Italian Ministry of Interior. 2009a. Criminal Statistics, 2004–2008. "Number of crimes reported to the police." Italian Ministry of Interior, Ministero dell'Interno, Dipartimento della Pubblica Sicurezza, Direzione Centrale della Polizia Criminale, Servizio Analisi Criminale.

Italian Ministry of Interior. 2009b. Prison Population Data, 2004–2008. "Number of inmates in Italian prison." Italian Ministry of Justice, Ministero della Giustizia, Dipartimento Amministrazione Penitenziaria, Ufficio per lo Sviluppo e la Gestione del SIA, Sezione Statistica.

James, Doris J., and Lauren E. Glaze. 2006. *Mental Health Problems of Prison and Jail Inmates.* NCJ 213600. Washington, D.C.: Bureau of Justice Statistics, Office of Justice Programs.

Jencks, Christopher. 1994. *The Homeless.* Cambridge, Mass.: Harvard University Press.

Johnson, Braden Ann. 1990. *Out of Bedlam: The Truth About Deinstitutionalization.* New York: Basic Books.

Johnson, Bruce, Andrew Golub, and Eloise Dunlap. 2000. "The Rise and Decline of Hard Drugs, Drug Markets, and Violence in Inner-City New York." In *The Crime Drop in America,* edited by Alfred Blumstein and Joel Wallman. Cambridge: Cambridge University Press.

Johnson, Rucker. 2009. "Ever-Increasing Levels of Parental Incarceration and the Consequences for Children." In *Do Prisons Make Us Safer? The Benefits and Costs of the Prison Boom,* edited by Steven Raphael and Michael Stoll. New York: Russell Sage Foundation.

Johnson, Rucker, and Steven Raphael. 2009. "The Effect of Male Incarceration Dynamics on AIDS Infection Rates Among African-American Women and Men." *Journal of Law and Economics* 52(2): 251–93.

———. 2012. "How Much Crime Reduction Does the Marginal Prisoner Buy?" *Journal of Law and Economics* 55(2): 275–310.

Johnston, Lloyd D., Patrick M. O'Malley, Jerald G. Bachman, and John E. Schulenberg. 2012. *Monitoring the Future National Survey Results on Drug Use, 1975–2011:* vol. 2, *College Students and Adults Ages 19–50.* Ann Arbor: University of Michigan, Institute of Social Research.

Joint Legislature Committee on Performance Evaluation and Expenditure Review (PEER). 2010. *Mississippi Department of Corrections' FY 2010 Cost per Inmate Day.* Report 550 to the Mississippi Legislature (December 14). Available at: http://www.peer.state.ms.us/reports/rpt550.pdf (accessed August 10, 2011).

Juhn, Chinhui. 2003. "Labor Market Dropouts and Trends in the Wages of Black and White Men." *Industrial and Labor Relations Review* 56(4): 643–62.

Juhn, Chinhui, and Simon Potter. 2006. "Changes in Labor Force Participation in the United States." *Journal of Economic Perspectives* 20(3): 27–46.

Kessler, Ronald C., Patricia Berglund, Olga Demler, Robert Jin, Kathleen R. Merikangas, and Ellen E. Walters. 2005. "Lifetime Prevalence and Age of Onset Distributions of *DSM-IV* Disorders in the National Comorbidity Survey Replication." *Archives of General Psychiatry* 62(June): 593–602.

Kessler, Daniel, and Steven D. Levitt. 1999. "Using Sentence Enhancements to Distinguish Between Deterrence and Incapacitation." *Journal of Law and Economics* 42(1): 343–63.

Kessler, Ronald C., Katherine A. McGonagle, Shanyang Zhao, Christopher B. Nelson, Michael Hughes, Suzann Eshleman, Hans-Ulrich Wittchen, and Kenneth S. Kendler. 1994. "Lifetime and 12-Month Prevalence of *DSM-III-R* Psychiatric Disorders in the United States." *Archives of General Psychiatry* 51(January): 8–19.

Kessler, Daniel P., and Anne Morrison Piehl. 1998. "The Role of Discretion in the Criminal Justice System." *Journal of Law, Economics, and Organization* 14(2): 256–76.

Kleiman, Mark. 2009. *When Brute Force Fails: How to Have Less Crime and Punishment.* Princeton, N.J.: Princeton University Press.

Kneebone, Elizabeth, and Steven Raphael. 2011. *City and Suburban Crime Trends in Metropolitan America.* Washington, D.C.: Brookings Institution Press.

Kuziemko, Ilyana. 2013. "How Should Prison Inmates Be Released from Prison? An Assessment of Parole Versus Fixed-Sentence Regimes." *Quarterly Journal of Economics* 128(1): 371–424.

La Fond, John Q., and Mary L. Durham. 1992. *Back to the Asylum: The Future of Mental Health Law and Policy in the United States.* New York: Oxford University Press.

Langan, Patrick A. 1991. "America's Soaring Prison Population." *Science* 251(5001): 1568–73.

Lang-Golub, Andrew, and Bruce D. Johnson. 1997. *Crack's Decline: Some Surprises Across U.S. Cities.* Research brief. Washington, D.C.: National Institute of Justice.

Lee, David S., and Justin McCrary. 2009. "The Deterrent Effect of Prison: Dynamic

Theory and Evidence." Working paper. Princeton University, Industrial Relations Section.

Levitt, Steven D. 1996. "The Effect of Prison Population Size on Crime Rates: Evidence from Prison Overcrowding Legislation." *Quarterly Journal of Economics* 111(2): 319–51.

———. 1997. "Using Electoral Cycles in Police Hiring to Estimate the Effects of Police on Crime." *American Economic Review* 87(3): 270–90.

———. 1998. "Juvenile Crime and Punishment." *Journal of Political Economy* 106(6): 1156–85.

———. 2002. "Using Electoral Cycles in Police Hiring to Estimate the Effects of Police on Crime: Reply." *American Economic Review* 92(4): 1244–50.

Levitt, Steven, and Sudhir Alladi Venkatesh. 2000. "An Economic Analysis of a Drug Selling Gang's Finances." *Quarterly Journal of Economics* 115(3): 755–89.

Liedke, Raymond, Anne Morrison Piehl, and Bert Useem. 2006. "The Crime Control Effect of Incarceration: Does Scale Matter?" *Criminology and Public Policy* 5(2): 245–75.

Lipton, Douglas, Robert Martinson, and Judith Wilks. 1975. *The Effectiveness of Correctional Treatment: A Survey of Treatment Evaluation Studies.* New York: Praeger.

Lochner, Lance. 2011. "Education Policy and Crime." In *Controlling Crime: Strategies and Tradeoffs,* edited by Philip J. Cook, Jens Ludwig, and Justin McCrary. Chicago: University of Chicago Press.

Lochner, Lance, and Enrico Moretti. 2004. "The Effect of Education on Criminal Activity: Evidence from Prison Inmates, Arrests, and Self-Reports." *American Economic Review* 94(1): 155–89.

Loeffler, Charles E. 2010. "Pre-Imprisonment Employment Drops: Another Instance of the Ashenfelter Dip?" Unpublished paper, University of Pennsylvania.

Loury, Glenn C. 2002. *The Anatomy of Racial Inequality.* Cambridge, Mass.: Harvard University Press.

———. 2008. *Race, Incarceration, and American Values.* Cambridge, Mass.: MIT Press.

MacCoun, Robert, and Peter Reuter. 2001. *Drug War Heresies: Learning from Other Vices, Times, and Places.* Cambridge: Cambridge University Press.

Machin, Stephen, Olivier Marie, and Sunčica Vujić. 2010. "The Crime-Reducing Effect of Education." Working paper. University College London.

Marcotte, David E., and Sarah Markowitz. 2009. "A Cure for Crime? Psycho-Pharmaceuticals and Crime Trends." Working Paper 15354. Cambridge, Mass.: National Bureau of Economic Research.

Marlowe, Douglas B., David S. DeMatteo, and David S. Festinger. 2003. "A Sober Assessment of Drug Courts." *Federal Sentencing Reporter* 16(2): 153–57.

Martinson, Robert. 1974. "What Works? Questions and Answers About Prison Reform." *The Public Interest* 35(Spring): 22–54.

Marvell, Thomas B. 1995. "Sentencing Guidelines and Prison Population Growth." *Journal of Criminal Law and Criminology* 85(3): 696–709.

Marvell, Thomas B., and Carlisle Moody. 1996. "Determinate Sentencing and Abolishing Parole: The Long-Term Impacts on Prison and Crime." *Criminology* 34(1): 107–28.

Mauer, Marc, and Tracy Huling. 1996. *Young Black Men and the Criminal Justice System: A Growing National Problem.* Washington, D.C.: The Sentencing Project.

Mechanic, David, and David A. Rochefort. 1990. "Deinstitutionalization: An Appraisal of Reform." *Annual Review of Sociology* 16: 301–27.

Monahan, John. 1992. "Mental Disorder and Violent Behavior." *American Psychologist* 47(4): 511–21.

Mooney, Jessica L., and Michael Daffern. 2011. "Institutional Aggression as a Predictor of Violent Recidivism." *International Journal of Forensic Mental Health* 10(1): 52–63.

Motivans, Mark. 2012. *Federal Justice Statistics, 2009—Statistical Tables.* NCJ 233464. Washington, D.C.: U.S. Department of Justice.

Murakawa, Naomi. 2005. "Electing to Punish: Congress, Race, and the American Criminal Justice State." PhD diss., Yale University.

Mustard, David. 2001. "Racial, Ethnic, and Gender Disparities in Sentencing: Evidence from U.S. Federal Courts." *Journal of Law and Economics* 44(1): 285–314.

Nagin, Daniel S. 2013. "Deterrence: A Review of the Evidence by a Criminologist for Economists." *Annual Review of Economics* 5.

Nagin, Daniel S., Francis T. Cullen, and Cheryl Lero-Jonson. 2009. "Imprisonment and Reoffending." *Crime and Justice* 38(1): 115–200.

Nagin, Daniel S., and John V. Pepper. 2012. *Deterrence and the Death Penalty.* Washington, D.C.: National Academy of Sciences.

National Association of State Budget Officers (NASBO). 1987. *1987 State Expenditure Report.* Washington, D.C.: NASBO.

———. 2010. *2009 State Expenditures Report.* Washington, D.C.: NASBO.

Nicholson-Crotty, Sean. 2004. "The Impact of Sentencing Guidelines on State-Level Sanctions: An Analysis over Time." *Crime and Delinquency* 50(3): 395–411.

Owens, Emily. 2009. "More Time, Less Crime? Estimating the Incapacitative Effects of Sentence Enhancements." *Journal of Law and Economics* 52(3): 551–79.

———. 2011. "Truthiness-in-Punishment: The Far Reach of Truth in Sentencing Laws." *Journal of Empirical Legal Studies: Judgment by the Numbers—Converting Qualitative to Quantitative Judgments in Law* 8(S1): 239–61.

Pager, Devah. 2003. "The Mark of a Criminal Record." *American Journal of Sociology* 108(5): 937–75.

———. 2007. *Marked: Race, Crime, and Finding Work in an Era of Mass Incarceration.* Chicago: University of Chicago Press.

Pager, Devah, Bruce Western, and Bart Bonikowski. 2009. "Discrimination in a Low-Wage Labor Market: A Field Experiment." *American Sociological Review* 74(5): 777–99.

Palermo, George B., Maurice B. Smith, and Frank J. Liska. 1991. "Jails Versus Mental Hospitals: A Social Dilemma." *International Journal of Offender Therapy and Comparative Criminology* 35(2): 97–106.

Parry, John. 1994. "Survey of Standards for Extended Involuntary Commitment." *Mental and Physical Disability Law Reporter* 18(3): 329–36.

Patterson, Evelyn J., and Samuel H. Preston. 2008. "Estimating Mean Length of Stay in Prison: Methods and Applications." *Journal of Quantitative Criminology* 24(1): 33–39.

Penrose, Lionel. 1939. "Mental Disease and Crime: Outline of a Comparative Study of European Statistics." *British Journal of Medical Psychology* 18(1): 1–15.

Pettit, Becky. 2012. *Invisible Men: Mass Incarceration and the Myth of Black Progress.* New York: Russell Sage Foundation.

Pettit, Becky, and Bruce Western. 2004. "Mass Imprisonment and the Life Course: Race and Class Inequality in U.S. Incarceration." *American Sociological Review* 69(2): 151–69.

Peffley, Mark, Jon Hurwitz, and Paul M. Sniderman. 1997. "Racial Stereotypes and Whites' Political Views of Blacks in the Context of Welfare and Crime." *American Journal of Political Science* 41(1): 30–60.

Pew Center on the States. 2010. *Prison Count 2010: State Population Declines for the First Time in 28 Years.* Washington, D.C.: Pew Center on the States.

Planty, Michael, and Jennifer Truman. 2012. *Criminal Victimization, 2011.* Washington, D.C.: Bureau of Justice Statistics.

Raphael, Steven. 2000. "The Deinstitutionalization of the Mentally Ill and Growth in the U.S. Prison Population: 1971 to 1996." Working paper. University of California, Berkeley.

———. 2005. "The Socioeconomic Status of Black Males: The Increasing Importance of Incarceration." In *Poverty, the Distribution of Income, and Public Policy,* edited by Alan Auerbach, David Card, and John Quigley. New York: Russell Sage Foundation.

———. 2011. "Improving Employment Prospects for Former Prison Inmates: Challenges and Policy." In *Controlling Crime: Strategies and Tradeoffs*, edited by Phillip J. Cook, Jens Ludwig, and Justin McCrary. Chicago: University of Chicago Press.

———. 2013. "The Effects of California's Correctional Realignment on the State's Prison Population, Jail Population, and Crime Rate Through December 2011." Working paper. University of California at Berkeley.

Raphael, Steven, and Jens Ludwig. 2003. "Prison Sentence Enhancements: The Case of Project Exile." In *Evaluating Gun Policy: Effects on Crime and Violence*, edited by Jens Ludwig and Philip J. Cook. Washington, D.C.: Brookings Institution Press.

Raphael, Steven, and Michael A. Stoll. 2004. "The Effect of Prison Releases on Regional Crime Rates." In *The Brookings-Wharton Papers on Urban Economic Affairs*, vol. 5, edited by William G. Gale and Janet Rothenberg Pack. Washington, D.C.: Brookings Institution.

———. 2009. "Why Are So Many Americans in Prison?" In *Do Prisons Make Us Safer? The Benefits and Costs of the Prison Boom*, edited by Steven Raphael and Michael Stoll. New York: Russell Sage Foundation.

———. Forthcoming. "Assessing the Contribution of the Deinstitutionalization of the Mentally Ill to Growth in the U.S. Incarceration Rate." *Journal of Legal Studies*.

Raphael, Steven, and Sarah Tahamont. 2012. "Summary of Findings from the Regression-Discontinuity Analysis of Inmate Behavioral Outcomes." In California Department of Corrections and Rehabilitation, *Expert Panel Study of the Inmate Classification Score System*, appendix I. Sacramento: CDCR.

Raphael, Steven, and Rudolf Winter-Ebmer. 2001. "Identifying the Effect of Unemployment on Crime." *Journal of Law and Economics* 44(1): 259–84.

Ross, Ruth E., Aileen B. Rothbard, and Arie P. Schinnar. 1996. "A Framework for Classifying State Involuntary Commitment Statutes." *Administration and Policy in Mental Health* 23(4): 341–56.

Rossman, Shelli B., John K. Roman, Janine M. Zweig, Michael Rempel, and Christine H. Lindquist. 2011. *The Multi-Site Adult Drug Court Evaluation*. Washington, D.C.: Urban Institute Justice Policy Center.

Sabol, William J., and John McGready. 1999. *Time Served in Prison by Federal Offenders, 1986–1997*. NCJ 171682. Washington, D.C.: U.S. Department of Justice.

Sabol, William J., Katherine Rosich, Kamala Mallik Kane, David Kirk, and Glenn Dubin. 2002. *Influences of Truth-in-Sentencing Reforms on Changes in States' Sentencing Practices and Prison Populations*. Washington, D.C.: National Institute of Justice.

Sampson, Robert J., and John H. Laub. 2003. "Life-Course Desisters? Trajectories of Crime Among Delinquent Boys Followed to Age 70." *Criminology* 41(3): 301–39.

Schnittker, Jason, Michael Massoglia, and Christopher Uggen. 2011. "Incarceration and the Health of the African-American Community." *Du Bois Review* 8(1): 133–41.

Sentencing Project, The. 2012. *Felony Disenfranchisement Laws in the United States.* Washington, D.C.: The Sentencing Project.

Snell, Tracy L. 1993. *Correctional Populations in the United States, 1993.* NCJ 156241. Washington, D.C.: U.S. Department of Justice.

Sorensen, Jon, and Don Stemen. 2002. "The Effect of State Sentencing Policies on Incarceration Rates." *Crime and Delinquency* 48(3): 456–75.

Steadman, Henry J., Edward P. Mulvey, John Monahan, Pamela Clark Robbins, Paul S. Applebaum, Thomas Grisso, Loren H. Roth, and Eric Silver. 1998. "Violence by People Discharged from Acute Psychiatric Inpatient Facilities and by Others in the Same Neighborhoods." *Archives of General Psychiatry* 55(5): 393–401.

Stemen, Don, Andres Rengifo, and James Wilson. 2006. *Of Fragmentation and Ferment: The Impact of State Sentencing Policies on Incarceration Rates, 1975–2002.* Washington, D.C.: National Institute of Justice.

Surette, Ray. 1998. *Media, Crime, and Criminal Justice: Images and Realities,* 2nd ed. New York: Wadsworth.

Taggert, William A., and Russell G. Winn. 1993. "Imprisonment in the American States." *Social Science Quarterly* 74(4): 736–49.

Tahamont, Sarah. 2012. "The Effect of Visitation on Prison Misconduct." Working paper. University of California, Berkeley.

Tonry, Michael. 1996. *Sentencing Matters.* Oxford: Oxford University Press.

Torrey, E. Fuller. 1997. *Out of the Shadows: Confronting America's Mental Illness Crisis.* New York: John Wiley & Sons.

Travis, Jeremy. 2005. *But They All Come Back: Facing the Challenges of Prisoner Reentry.* Washington, D.C.: Urban Institute Press.

Uggen, Christopher, and Jeff Manza. 2002. "Democratic Contraction? The Political Consequences of Felon Disenfranchisement in the United States." *American Sociological Review* 67(6): 777–803.

Uggen, Christopher, Jeff Manza, and Melissa Thompson. 2006. "Citizenship, Democracy, and the Civic Reintegration of Criminal Offenders." *Annals of the American Academy of Political and Social Science* 605(1): 281–310.

U.S. Census Bureau. 1950. "One Percent Public Use Microdata Sample of the 1950 U.S. Census of Population and Housing," Washington, D.C.

———. 1960. "One Percent Public Use Microdata Sample of the 1960 U.S. Census of Population and Housing," Washington, D.C.

———. 1970. "One Percent Public Use Microdata Sample of the 1970 U.S. Census of Population and Housing," Washington, D.C.

———. 1980a. "One Percent Public Use Microdata Sample of the 1980 U.S. Census of Population and Housing," Washington, D.C.

———. 1980b. "Five Percent Public Use Microdata Sample of the 1980 U.S. Census of Population and Housing," Washington, D.C.

———. 1990. "One Percent Public Use Microdata Sample of the 1990 U.S. Census of Population and Housing," Washington, D.C.

———. 2000. "One Percent Public Use Microdata Sample of the 2000 U.S. Census of Population and Housing," Washington, D.C.

———. 2007a. *American Community Survey 2007 Public Use Microdata Sample,* Washington, D.C.

———. 2007b. *American Community Survey 2008 Public Use Microdata Sample,* Washington, D.C.

———. 2009. *Data Base on Historical Finances of State Government: Fiscal Year 1942 through 2008,* Washington, D.C.

———. 2010. *American Community Survey 2010 Public Use Microdata Sample,* Washington, D.C.

U.S. Sentencing Commission. 2011. *Report to Congress: Mandatory Minimum Sentences in the Federal Justice System.* Washington, D.C.: U.S. Sentencing Commission.

Vagins, Deborah J., and Jesselyn McCurdy. 2006. *Crack in the System: Twenty Years of the Unjust Federal Crack Cocaine Law.* Washington, D.C.: American Civil Liberties Union.

Vincent, Barbara S., and Paul J. Hofer. 1994. *The Consequences of Mandatory Minimum Prison Terms: A Summary of Recent Findings.* Washington, D.C.: Federal Judicial Center.

Vollaard, Ben. 2013. "Preventing Crime Through Selective Incapacitation." *The Economic Journal* 123(March): 262–84.

Wacquant, Loïc. 2000. "The New 'Peculiar Institution': On the Prison as Surrogate Ghetto." *Theoretical Criminology* 4(3): 377–89.

Wadsworth, Tim. 2010. "Is Immigration Responsible for the Crime Drop in the United States? An Assessment of Immigration on Changes in Violent Crime Between 1990 and 2000." *Social Sciences Quarterly* 91(2): 531–33.

Wakefield, Sara, and Christopher Wildeman. 2012. "Children of the Prison Boom:

Mass Incarceration and the Future of American Inequality." Unpublished manuscript. New Haven, Conn.: Yale University.

Wassley, Annemarie, Scott Grytdal, and Kathleen Gallagher. 2008. "Surveillance for Acute Viral Hepatitis: United States, 2006." Atlanta: Centers for Disease Control and Prevention (March 21). Available at: http://www.cdc.gov/mmwr/preview/mmwrhtml/ss5702a1.htm (accessed November 8, 2009).

Weaver, Vesla M. 2007. "Frontlash: Race and Development of Punitive Crime Policy." *Studies in American Political Development* 21(2): 230–65.

Webster, Cheryl M., Anthony N. Doob, and Franklin E. Zimring. 2006. "Proposition 8 and Crime Rates in California: The Case of the Disappearing Deterrent." *Criminology and Public Policy* 5(3): 417–48.

Weiman, David F., and Christopher Weiss. 2009. "The Origins of Mass Incarceration in New York: The Rockefeller Drug Laws and the Local War on Drugs." In *Do Prisons Make Us Safer? The Benefits and Costs of the Prison Boom,* edited by Steven Raphael and Michael A. Stoll. New York: Russell Sage Foundation.

Werner Cahalan, Margaret. 1986. *Historical Corrections Statistics in the United States, 1850–1984.* NCJ 102529. Washington, D.C.: U.S. Department of Justice.

Werth, James L. 2001. "U.S. Involuntary Mental Health Commitment Statutes: Requirements for Persons Perceived to Be a Potential Harm to Self." *Suicide and Life-Threatening Behavior* 31(3): 348–57.

West, Heather C., William J. Sabol, and Sarah J. Greenman. 2010. *Prisoners in 2009.* NCJ 231675. Washington, D.C.: U.S. Department of Justice.

Western, Bruce. 2002. "The Impact of Incarceration on Wage Mobility and Inequality." *American Journal of Sociology* 67(4): 526–46.

———. 2006. *Punishment and Inequality in America.* New York: Russell Sage Foundation.

Western, Bruce, and Becky Pettit. 2000. "Incarceration and Racial Inequality in Men's Employment." *Industrial and Labor Relations Review* 54(1): 3–16.

Wildeman, Christopher. 2009. "Parental Imprisonment, the Prison Boom, and the Concentration of Childhood Disadvantage." *Demography* 46(2): 265–80.

———. 2010. "Paternal Incarceration and Children's Physically Aggressive Behaviors: Evidence from the Fragile Families and Child Well-being Study." *Social Forces* 89(1): 285–310.

———. 2012. "Imprisonment and Infant Mortality." *Social Problems* 59(2): 228–57.

Wilson, James Q. 1975. *Thinking About Crime.* New York: Basic Books.

INDEX

Boldface numbers refer to figures and tables.